OUR
GRAND
FINALE

A Daughter's Memoir

LARAINE DENNY BURRELL

SHE WRITES PRESS

Published 2017
Printed in the United States of America
Print ISBN: 978-1-63152-238-3
E-ISBN: 978-1-63152-239-0
Library of Congress Control Number: 2017945184

For information, address:
She Writes Press
1563 Solano Ave #546
Berkeley, CA 94707

Cover design © Julie Metz, Ltd./metzdesign.com
Interior design by Tabitha Lahr

She Writes Press is a division of SparkPoint Studio, LLC.

Names and identifying characteristics have been changed to protect the privacy of certain individuals.

For:

Mum, Dad,
Loretta & Mark
Love you always x

CHAPTER

ONE

I t is late afternoon in April, and only hours after landing in England, I find myself standing in the ward corridor in the Queen Alexandra Hospital in Portsmouth. My mother points through the open door of a hospital room toward a man reclining in a bed. I look past my mother and through the doorway at the man I have traveled thousands of miles to visit, and the smile I carried with the anticipation and eagerness in seeing him again dissipates at the sight of him. My nervous excitement instantaneously vanishes, to be replaced by an invisible barrier of distress preventing me from taking the final steps forward in my journey toward him. My brow furrows, my head tilts to one side. My mouth opens and then shuts, unable to find the right words, while my mind tries its best to make sense of the scenario. This isn't him. I don't recognize this person. Mum has made a mistake and shown me the wrong room. I am aware of my mother walking away toward the waiting area, unaware of her mistake, leaving me alone to spend the remainder of the visiting hour with this stranger. I desperately want to call my mother back, to demand an explanation, but the words—shouting at me, creating an uproar in my head—find no voice.

As is expected of me, I walk slowly toward the bed, each foot feeling unnaturally heavy, hindering my progress as if in tune with my mind's refusal to accept the circumstances, joining in my hesitancy to approach the man. I grip the handles of my handbag tight, feeling comfort in something tangible and known versus this intangible surrealism I find myself surrounded by. My eyes remain fixed on my destination, relying on the overbroad smile fixed to my face to belie the disorder in my mind. Above all and regardless of the situation, I must not exhibit my distress.

With each step I take, I mentally interrogate myself. This cannot be him. Surely not! This is not what I had expected. I had planned for something other than this. I had rehearsed this meeting over and over. It was supposed to be exuberant, signs of happiness to see each other again. There were things I was supposed to say. This is all wrong.

‑‑Sensing my presence, he slowly turns to watch me approach. His blue eyes gaze intently into my own as if drawing me closer. Standing beside the bed, I stare into the blue eyes. I know those eyes. Their familiarity saddens me, and my spirit deflates. There is no mistake.

This is my father.

My gaze scans the bed, looking down at my father's frame, diminished and hidden under the bedding innocuously covering the disease that is winning its battle against him. My father's arms, once muscular and strong from years of labor, now lie above the bedding, bloated and useless from the illness. I reach down and gently take his hand in my own, wanting to feel something human in this sterile environment. I look at his hand and compare his yellowed, discolored, swollen skin to the paleness of my own. I am afraid to hurt him, yet need to touch him. I look at his face, his eyes, not daring to breathe, hoping if I can just hold my breath, I can also hold back my tears. His mouth is drawn tight, silently speaking his pain. His eyes explain his understanding of the inevitable.

"Ah wuvoo."

I barely understand what he is saying to me. His false teeth have been removed, and he has difficulty speaking without them. Without his teeth, his jaw droops awkwardly, distorting his face and making him barely recognizable. His hair is brushed all wrong.

"Ah wuvoo."

Carefully I sit down on the edge of the bed, clasping his hand a little tighter and smiling at him, tears falling from my own blue eyes.

"I love you too, Dad."

It is late afternoon. I am exhausted and overwhelmed. The already long journey from the States had been lengthened with delays both before my departure from Las Vegas and through an emergency landing for a sick passenger in Canada. Now finally here in England, my confused mind cannot take in the circumstances. My father is far worse than I expected, and somewhere in the back of my mind I am angry. My mother and sister had not prepared me for this. I had known my father was in the hospital, but the telephone calls in recent weeks were optimistic. Mum had told me that Dad was talking; he was his ever-feisty self, wanting to leave the hospital and go home. My mother and sister had seen his decline but chose not to share that information with me, and now I can't help feeling resentful, cheated. Seeing my father's poor condition today is an unexpected and unfair surprise.

It was only three days ago that Mum had called to say that Dad probably would not leave the hospital any time soon, and perhaps I might want to come over to England and see him sometime. That call was the first time I sensed the urgency in my mother's voice, and it alarmed me. For the first time, I understood that Dad's time was limited. I immediately made arrangements for myself and my son, Mark, to fly to England, not wanting to miss a moment with Dad. Still, I thought there would be more time than this. I thought we would have a couple of weeks or longer together. I thought we would have time to talk; time for me to say those things I had always wanted to say to my father; time for us to have those conversations people always plan on having sometime; time for me to tell my dad how much I love him and respect him, how much I appreciate everything he has done for me; time for Dad to tell me he is proud of all I have achieved. I desperately need to hear that, to know I have earned his approval, his respect.

I see now, and all too late, that I have got it wrong. I had been given fifty years with my father. Fifty years to talk to him, to spend time with him, to share moments and achievements with him, to tell him I love him. I see now that I have spent my life doing what I want to do, traveling the world, rarely visiting with my family, thinking there would always be time at some later date; but now the time we had been given together has passed. The time for those most important of conversations is gone. My heart breaks as I now recognize all I have regrettably lost.

There is a movement behind me as Mark enters the room. Without looking away from my father's face, I sense Mark's presence as he stands on the other side of the bed. I study my father's face intently, trying to read his expression, to get some sense of how he is doing, how he is feeling. His surprise and delight at seeing me and then Mark is expressed by a toothless grin, an incongruous ray of sunshine piercing through the shadow of the moment. He hadn't been told that we were coming. The sheer joy in his eyes as he looks at Mark, then at me, and then back at Mark again is moving. Tears well up in his blue eyes. My heart breaks at the sight of this man who had been so strong and reassuring as a father, but who is now physically diminished, lying weak and helpless in this hospital cot like a needy child.

Mark and I behave nonchalantly, talking cheerfully about how happy we are to see him, and how we hope he is feeling fine, as though we just happened to have time to pop over from the States to visit. It is a charade, and not a good one. Everyone knows we are here because we have been given the final summons. Our presence, unannounced and unexpected, completes the family circle, and the family is together again for only one reason.

Dad wiggles his fingers, and his mouth opens as he struggles to talk, but his guttural sounds make no sense. He is looking at me, wanting me to understand him, but I don't. I retain my smile like some grotesque grinning mask, but inside I am panicking. What is he trying to tell me? I stand rigid, unable to comprehend and respond to his words, feeling like some inanimate object devoid of intelligence or feeling. I don't want to do or say the wrong thing, but I am clueless as to what is the right thing. This situation is foreign to me, and I don't have the language skills to interpret my father's wishes. When Dad turns to speak to Mark, I take the opportunity to escape from the room, shouting, "I'll be right back, Dad."

After finding Mum in the waiting room, I lose my composure. The stress of the long journey and its unanticipated conclusion wreak havoc with my vulnerable state. My emotions, barely held at bay in front of my father, now take control, causing me to stand in the doorway of the waiting room sobbing, tears streaming down my face, my head and shoulders shaking. I run my hand through my short blonde hair, unable to contain my frustration at my incomprehensible ineptitude.

"I don't know what he's saying, Mum. I don't know what he wants. I can't understand him." Ignoring the sympathetic glances from other visitors and not caring that I'm making a spectacle of myself, I hold my hands out toward my mother as if begging for an answer. "I can't help him, Mum. I don't know if he wants a drink, or what he wants to say. I don't know what to do for him." I, the well-educated, professional woman, am standing like a petulant weeping child. It isn't supposed to be like this.

Mum walks back with me to the hospital room. With her soothing voice, Mum tends to her husband, using years of nursing experience to plump up his pillows and tuck in his blanket. She then holds a plastic beaker up to his mouth so he can take a sip of water through the straw, his slurping sounding childlike. I watch with sadness as Mum cares for Dad, as she makes sure he is comfortable and has what he needs. She speaks to him softly, answering his awkward mumblings. She knows what he is saying. Cathy and Ian—childhood friends and then sweethearts, they had been together more than sixty years. Mum understands him.

A bell rings throughout the ward, its shrill sound impatiently announcing that visiting time is over. Its annoying ring continues for many minutes, impervious to the disappointment of visitors and patients alike at the command to say goodbye. The hour and a half I spend with my father has passed quickly, and I was useless. All I was able to say over and over again was "I love you, Dad," as I stood awkwardly by the side of the bed with a silly smile plastered on my face.

I am thankful that Mark was able to speak to his grandfather with a charming ease, his banter making up for my own ineffectiveness. I resolve to go home now, regroup my thoughts, and come back tomorrow. Tomorrow I will be better prepared. Tomorrow I will say all the things I need to tell my father. Even though I might not understand what he says to me, even though I might never hear or understand him say how proud he is of me, I will tell him how proud I am of him. That is more important. I will tell him that all of my achievements were motivated by him. He is my shining example of the best in people. He is my mentor. He is my hero.

We leave the room with promises to return the next morning. I turn one last time to wave goodbye to my father.

"I love you, Dad."

"Ah wuvoo."

In the middle of the night, the telephone rings, its shrill tone rudely disturbing the silence of the sleeping house. The abrupt sound startles me, dragging me instantly from dream state to black reality. The bedroom is still dark, evidence of the early hour, but then a sliver of light slips under the door, cutting across the dark floor of the room as the hall light goes on. I hear my mother's footsteps descending the stairs to answer the phone. Despite the time difference and the weight of my jet-lagged body, my mind is alert. Instinctively I know what the call is, and I wait for a knock on the bedroom door. It comes soon and Mum's head peers round the door. "That was the hospital. Dad's not doing too well. They think we should come." Mum had left instructions with the nurses that if they thought Dad was coming to the end, they were to call her. This is the call.

My sister, Loretta, had been called, and now she, Mum, Mark, and I walk along the deserted hospital corridors, our footsteps amplified by the stone floors and walls. It feels as though we are trespassing. We are here outside of business hours, outside of visiting hours. But it is one of those occasions when the rules are waived, when you don't have to stand in line or take your turn to get assistance. I don't want it to be one of those occasions. I silently acknowledge to myself that sometimes we don't get to choose. The one person we do pass in the hallway looks at us knowingly, smiles sympathetically, and then turns away. Only one reason brings people to a hospital in the early hours of the morning.

We follow the signs and find the elevator to the ward. My senses tune into the environment. The hospital epitomizes the British institution. Built around 1904 as a military hospital, its painted stone walls do nothing to disguise the sparse and somber character of a National Health facility. Serviceable, with no frills, this is a typical part of British life as I remember it. It is the life I escaped from many years ago. Yet as I walk along the hallways with my family, it is as though I have never left. I feel myself slipping back into my British persona. Life is simpler, more no-nonsense here.

Dad's room has taken on a different character from yesterday. It has become a theater set, lit to reflect the somber mood and with Dad as the focal point of the scene. A track light angled from the ceiling spotlights Dad's face. The tiny lights and beeps from machines add to the effect. Dad lies sleeping, his breathing labored. The nurse says he had taken a bad turn after we had left yesterday, and he has been given morphine to ease his last few hours.

His last few hours. This is it. I follow my mother and sister as we take our places of vigil around the bed. Mark chooses to lie down on the floor in the corner of the room, falling asleep immediately, still exhausted from his journey from the States. I look down at my son, his six-foot-four frame curled in a fetal position, his mind oblivious to the world. I think, *You silly boy. These are*

the final moments for your grandfather, and you do not have the
strength or stamina to remain alert. I wasted fifty years with him. I
am not wasting these last few hours.

I sit down on a chair next to my sister, committing myself
to remaining to the end, however long that might be. I look at my
father and wordlessly share my thoughts with him: *I'm not going*
anywhere Dad. I am here for you. I look down at Dad, asleep, his
blue eyes no longer visible. I know I will never see those blue eyes
again, and I am again overcome by a crushing sadness and heartache. I ask myself, *Do people dream when they are on morphine?*
Oh Dad! I hope you are having the sweetest dreams.

With nothing to do but wait in witness of my father's final
hours, I sit and listen as the gentle flow of each breath my father
takes slowly extinguishes his life. The dimness, the silence, the
reverent atmosphere of the room lends itself to reflection, and I
begin to philosophically ponder those questions we all have but
never want to ask: How is it going to end, not only for ourselves,
but also for those close to us? I chastise myself and tell myself not
to be morbid. Of course, I knew this time would come; it is a natural part of living. The life given to us, the experiences, the accomplishments, the challenges, the relationships, the good times and
bad—all come with a price, mortality. We are allowed to experience that most wonderful of human emotions, of loving someone,
but only if that experience is accompanied by its antithesis, the
pain of death, of losing that same loved one.

Every life consists of a unique tableau of connected scenes
ending with its own finale, an unknown mysterious conclusion
keeping us in suspense until the very end. The practical lawyer in
me reminds me that at least my father's finale is not a completely
unexpected event. I did get a chance to say goodbye, sort of. I
think back to yesterday's brief visit and I am again overcome by
remorse. I mentally chastise myself. I am stupid! Stupid! Stupid! I
thought I would have today to tell Dad all the things that I wanted
to tell him. Again I see how I have got it all wrong. Fifty years, and
I have run out of chances to get it right.

But I did tell him I love him. Was that enough for him? I have read or heard of those times when the dying hold on to life just long enough to allow loved ones to come and share a final moment. I wonder, *Was that what had happened here?* Had Dad held on long enough to allow me and Mark to come from the States to share a final moment? Was that all he had needed? To see that we had come to pay our last respects? Had he then allowed himself to let go? So many questions that I know will never, can never, be answered.

Hours pass without conversation, without interruption. Each second counted by the rhythmic beeps of a machine. Somewhere outside it is now daylight. People are getting on with their day, life continues on. But inside the hospital room, life is momentarily suspended as we three women sit quietly, not wanting to leave our vigil around the dying man. Each of us with hands touching the man in the hope that somehow he knows we are there for him. On the floor, my son sleeps in some other world, oblivious to the dying man's labored breath counting down to the end.

The vigil begins taking its toll. My body is becoming stiff, and my back aches. I lean forward, then back, stretching a little from side to side and rolling my head and shoulders, encouraging my muscles to find some relief from the hard plastic chair that is unforgiving in its rigid support. My body and mind are exhausted. But I am not moving. I am resolved to be by my father's side every last moment that he has on this earth.

I look across at my mother, taking a moment to observe the older woman in this rare, unguarded state. I am taken aback at the love and softness in my mother's expression as she looks down at her husband. I don't believe I have ever before seen my mother look that way at Dad. The Scottish termagant has a soft side.

Mum and Dad had been childhood friends since the Second World War, when my paternal grandmother rented a room in the house owned by my maternal grandmother for herself and her three sons, Dad and his two brothers. Their friendship blossomed over the years, and on Christmas Eve 1954, they were married and

author's mum and dad

became Mr. and Mrs. Denny. Mum was a strong woman and had been the boss in their marriage, often joking at Dad's expense. More often than not, he was referred to as "Eejit!" Not Ian. Typical man, he never did anything right! And Mum didn't care who she told. In contrast, my father was a quiet man. I never heard him say a bad thing about anyone. He rarely complained about anything. He met his wife's comments and bossiness with a resigned but good-natured silence.

As I now study my mother, I think that the woman's soft expression makes her look much younger. For a moment, I see a glimpse of the young woman I knew as a child. I can't help but smile to myself. Despite her routine castigation of Dad, my mother really does love him. Poor Mum, sixty-two years with this man. He has always been there for her, with her. What will she do now? Is she thinking about life alone? Is she reliving their moments together from the past? Is she silently talking to him, sharing the private thoughts of a woman to her man in the last moments of his life? I don't know, and I am not going to ask. It is not for me to intrude on Mum's private thoughts.

My sister, Loretta, is sitting on my right side, and I turn to look at her. Her head rests on her arm, which lies atop the metal side rail of the bed. Loretta, sensing my gaze, turns toward me and smiles sadly. *Poor baby*, I think. Diabetes has plagued Loretta since she was twelve years old, forcing her to battle so many episodes of illness, numerous blood transfusions, diabetic comas, and eventually leaving her an amputee. She walks with a prosthetic limb and a cane. She relies on Dad to help her with odd jobs, to help drive her to the shops, or to doctors' appointments. Life will be more complicated for her without him. But Loretta is resilient. She has spent much of her adult life in hospitals, battling one illness and setback after another, and all the doctors, nurses, and staff know her on sight. People love her. Everyone admires her spirit. If the roles had been reversed and I had been the diabetic, losing a leg and always ill, I am certain I would not have been as strong as Loretta, or as gracious in accepting the circumstances of my difficult life.

Diabetes has been mean to Loretta. Fortunately, countless family members and friends are there for her, but I'm not one of them. Being honest with myself, it is only these circumstances, this time of vigil for Dad, that has brought me home. I guiltily acknowledge that I would not have come otherwise. I would not have made the time or effort to come and see my family, were it not for my father's imminent passing.

I look to my left at my adult son. Some time ago, a nurse came into the room to check on Dad and, seeing Mark asleep on the floor, she found a large, comfy chaise for him. He has somehow contracted his tall frame to allow himself to curl up on the chaise asleep with his dreams, still oblivious to the moment. I wonder if I should wake him. Will he resent sleeping through his grandfather's final hours? Does he want to be awake? I honestly don't know, so I let him sleep on.

The minute hand of the wall clock clicks past the number twelve, and a new day begins. Dad's breathing has been more labored over the past couple of hours. The rattling sound of mucus in his throat as he struggles to breathe is harsh and painful to listen to. Shamefully I admit to myself that part of me wants my father to die now, to get his suffering over with, to be at peace. Part of me never wants to let go. A couple of times his breathing halts, and I look at his face expectantly, but they are false alarms. His breathing continues on.

At five minutes after one on Saturday morning, my father takes his final breath, a soft, peaceful sigh of farewell to us all. I wait for his breathing to continue, but it doesn't. I realize then that he is gone. I whisper, "Mum, he's stopped breathing!" I hear a whimper, but I don't know if it is mine. My mother says nothing, but the pain in her eyes and cheerless expression acknowledges her husband's death. Beside me, Loretta weeps.

I go over to my sleeping son and gently prod him. "Mark. Mark, wake up, son." Startled he jumps up. "Mark, your grandfather is gone."

Mark uncurls his frame, stretches his arms out above him, and gets up out of the chaise, wiping the blur from his eyes. He stands at the end of his grandfather's bed, completing the family circle. We all look down at the shell of our loved one. My father's face is calm, serene. He is finally at peace. In the briefest of instances, he had been alive, here with us in this room, a survivor of a long and challenging life, full of contributions, love, and memories shared with these members of his intimate family, but then less than a moment later he is forever gone. His life's finale concluded. No one moves to get the nurse. No one speaks. This is our moment.

Standing at my father's bedside, looking down at what remained of my father's tangible presence on earth, I feel a stark emptiness. A part of my existence, something that had always been with me, has been taken, leaving an ethereal void. My father is gone. Forever. Twenty-one hours I had sat by his bedside, holding his hand, keeping vigil. Twenty-one hours for a life extending seventy-six years. One by one, we kiss him goodbye.

It is three o'clock in the morning by the time the rest of the family and I return home from the hospital. Saying nothing, oblivious to the people around her, my mother retires to her own bedroom to lie alone in the bed next to the void in her life. Loretta goes to the spare bedroom, choosing to spend the night at our mother's house rather than start the grieving process alone in her flat. Mark goes to his own room, no doubt to resume the sleep interrupted by his grandfather's death. I hear the doors closing around me, wooden requests respectfully seeking solitude for the rooms' occupants.

Going to my own room, I close the door behind me, securing my own solitude. Too tired to undress, I flop onto the bed and close my eyes, yearning, hoping to escape from this unwanted reality; but even with the jet lag and the fatigue from the long vigil at my father's side, I can't sleep. My mind won't stop thinking, remembering.

CHAPTER

TWO

The wallpaper is about six inches from the end of my nose, so close that it is making my eyes cross and giving me a headache. I close my eyes to alleviate the discomfort that these seemingly innocuous blue-and-silver flowers decorating the wall can create. But by closing my eyes and shutting down one sense, I heighten another, and my nostrils are attacked by the close chemical odor of the dyed and pasted wallpaper. I cannot move away. I am not allowed to move. My confinement in this corner is mandatory. My punishment—to stand and face the corner for an hour—is the result of my egregious crime of playing records on my parents' record player.

My head falls forward until my brow rests on the cool surface of the wall. I sigh deeply, unconsciously exhaling the disagreeable artificial particles which try so hard to invade my senses and make me dizzy. I crave fresh air and turn to my imagination for help.

I visualize the ocean, as blue as the flowers on the wallpaper. I see a shimmer of silver as the sun shines her beams on the tips of the waves. The blue water cheekily runs up to the sand at the edge of a beach, taps it with watery fingers, and then turns and runs away, as if taunting the pristine, peachy-beige sand to come play.

The sand ignores the invitation, preferring instead to lie basking in the tropical warmth beneath the umbrellas of the palm trees standing guard along the beach. The palms ignore the childish antics of the ocean below them, instead embracing the wind, which acts as puppet master as it artfully moves their fronds in unison, creating a ballet against the blue sky. I imagine I can smell the fresh, salty sea air, and I inhale deeply, welcoming my vision.

"Laraine! Stand up straight!"

Quicker than an instant, my eyes open wide, my head snaps up, and my back stiffens as I instinctively respond to the terse admonition shouted from the space behind me. Pulled back into reality, I stand to attention, arms straight down at my sides, facing the angle of the blue-and-silver flowers. I have been well conditioned by my career-navy father to assume the stance and not move or speak. I dread my father's next words, praying he doesn't extend my punishment.

"You're not there to fall asleep! You are being punished, so stand up straight. You have another thirty minutes to think about what you did."

I hear my dad's footsteps walking away from me, his purposeful gait muffled by the carpet as he moves out of the room and down the hallway. Thankful to be alone again, I allow a rush of air to escape from my mouth, and my shoulders relax with relief. Only another thirty minutes. Thirty minutes to think about what I did, about why I am being punished.

It's the school holidays. As an only child, I face day after day of being left alone in the house, responsible for finding ways to alleviate the hours and hours and more hours of boredom. Mum and Dad go to work during the day. Dad leaves early, cycling to work on his ship at the navy dockyard while it is still dark. Mum leaves at about eight thirty in the morning. She'll be home a little after five o'clock this evening. I am only seven years old and not allowed out of the house. My friends all live a distance away, and I am not allowed to use the telephone, because even local calls cost money. There are no television programs until later in the day.

My days are a routine of sheer boredom, usually beginning with me sitting on the couch in the living room staring out the window, up at the sky as endless as my day. I wonder what to do. My dolls are somewhere at the back of my wardrobe, having been tossed there with disinterest after being dressed, undressed, and redressed ad nauseam. My books, read and reread, have nothing new to offer. I have pencils and crayons but no interest in drawing something that will never be seen by anyone else and has no purpose outside the cover of my sketchbook. Inevitably I get up from the couch, go over to a drawer in the side cabinet, and pull out a pack of playing cards. I sit down cross-legged on the floor and begin laying out the cards in an organized formation on the carpet. Most mornings, I play solitaire.

Life suddenly becomes more interesting when my parents buy a radiogram with a record player. The new technology heralds a fresh era into the family home, with music now competing with the television to provide our entertainment. I am fascinated by the transformation, particularly in my mother, as I catch her singing and even dancing in the living room to her favorite records. Her eyes are closed and she smiles mysteriously. She is somewhere in a different world. I find myself itching to get my hands on this wondrous machine and to control the music for myself. I want to dance and sing and give my mind a new array of wonderful, imaginative moments.

The next Monday morning, I wait a full five minutes after Mum leaves the house for work before I commandeer the record player. My new favorite thing to do is listen to music. I don't have my own records, so I play my favorites from Mum and Dad's collection. They have songs and music performed by Dean Martin, Buddy Holly, and Roger Miller; the Jimmy Shand Band and the Glasgow Police Pipe Band. I like to sing and dance around the living room to such classics as "King of the Road" and "The Muckin' o' Geordie's Byre." Two evenings a week and on Saturday mornings, I have dance classes, and now I use my dance education to choreograph dances to each song.

author in tutu, photo © Ian Denny

I move the living room furniture to the side of the room, move my chair next to the record player, and get ready to fantasize about being a famous performer. I know how to turn on the record player, put records on the changer, select the right speed for the size of the record, and make sure the needle gently traces the grooves to read the music as the record rotates on the turntable. This morning I have selected a variety of Glenn Miller and Andy Stewart songs to sing and dance to. I know the words to "King of the Road" and "A Scottish Soldier" and "Tunes of Glory." Sometimes there is a program on the telly called *The White Heather Club* with a band that plays Scottish music while Scottish dancers perform reels and the Gay Gordons. This morning, I am a Scottish dancer performing before an appreciative audience. I jump on one foot, placing the other foot with pointed toes behind and then in front of my supporting leg. One hand is raised above my head and the other on my hip.

I dance for about an hour until I am hot and sweaty. I go into the kitchen and get a glass of tap water and chug it down.

The kitchen clock tells me it isn't even ten o'clock yet. I have hours before Mum and Dad come home.

To give myself a rest, I turn to singing. I really want to be a singer. I think I can be a better singer than a dancer. I know how to express the words of a song. I have deep down feelings that I can use to perform the song well. I have been told by adjudicators at dance competitions that I have "stage presence," which makes people pay attention to me when I am on stage. If I could have singing lessons, I could use my emotions and be a brilliant singer. Mum says there isn't enough money for singing lessons, and besides there are no singing teachers in Portsmouth. I looked through the phone book and couldn't find a single singing teacher. I shall just have to teach myself and practice a lot.

I put a Shirley Bassey record on the turntable, gently placing the stylus on the groove for the song "As Long As He Needs Me." I close my eyes, listen to the musical introduction, and see myself standing alone on the unlit stage. The spotlight gently emerges, and I take a deep breath, drawing in every ounce of emotion I can muster. I look out at the blackness of the auditorium as I sing the first words of the song, slowly, stretching them out, "As . . . long . . . as . . . he . . . needs . . . me . . ." My voice is perfect and haunting. My chest muscles tighten as I push out word by word, note by note, the pure passion I feel as I lure the audience into my performance, wanting them to feel the love I feel for this lyrical man. My choreographed movements take me around the stage to each section of the audience, ensuring that everyone is captivated by my words. I pause center stage, close my eyes, and clench my fists as I dramatically push my top note into the heavens and then slowly sing the final notes as my voice softens, tears running down my cheeks as I make my final plea to the audience to understand my story and to feel the emotion I feel. Finally, my head bows as the last note is played. The brief moment of silence after the final note is replaced by the thunderous applause of the audience hidden from my view. I remain motionless, bathed in the aura of the moment.

With the performance over, I return to reality and take the stylus off the record. I wipe the tears from my eyes and sit alone in the silence, my mind lingering in the imaginary auditorium. I feel mentally and physically drained from my performance, but at the same time, I feel oddly fulfilled. Today, just for a moment, and even though only in my imagination, I was a true performer, the person I believe I can be, the person full of passion and emotion I know lives within me, but who has yet to be released out into the world.

I take a deep breath and ready my emotions for another performance. I place the stylus on the record for the song "I (Who Have Nothing)," another favorite of mine and my imaginary audience.

I am able to amuse myself for over two hours by combining music and my theatrical imagination. Deciding to take a break, I make myself beans on toast for lunch and pour some orange squash. After lunch I decide I have had enough of the melodramatic music and it is time for something more rousing to get me through the afternoon.

I put a Scots favorite, "Campbeltown Loch," on the turntable and set the record in motion. I move to the center of the room, ready to sing my heart out.

"Ohhhh . . .
Campbeltown Loch, I wish you were whiskey
Campbeltown Loch, och-aye
Oh Campbeltown Loch, I wish you were whiskey
Then I would drink you dry."

I have played Mum and Dad's records so often that they are scratched, and some songs have become unplayable. Dean Martin's voice sounds rough and hoarse like a ten-pack-a-day smoker. The bagpipes from the Scottish Pipe Band are accompanied by a rhythmic "thump" as again and again the needle travels across the gouges scratched into the vinyl. I tell myself that scratches are normal for vinyl records. Scratches are not my fault. Everybody scratches records.

The weekend comes, and Mum decides she is going to play her favorite Dean Martin records on the new radiogram. She is a huge fan of Dean Martin and often asks Dad the question that cannot be answered: "Why are you not Dean Martin? How come I didn't marry Dean Martin?" Dad simply shakes his head, unable to answer the unanswerable, and gets on with whatever it is he is doing.

I watch Mum put a record on the turntable and decide to disappear upstairs out of the way. From the distance of my bedroom I hear "That's Amore" playing, but the needle skips the occasional beat, making it sound as though Mr. Martin has hiccups. Then I hear a definitive complaint from my mum projecting its way upstairs, "Laraine! Have you been playing my records?"

I am not sure how to answer. Of course I have been playing Mum's records. I cannot lie about that. I go downstairs to face Mum. I say nothing. No admission. No denial. Mum's finger pointedly jabs toward my face. "You are not to play my records! You have scratched them and I cannae play them! You are ruining my lovely Dean Martin records!"

"Yes, Mum. Sorry, Mum." I disappear back upstairs to my bedroom, thinking I have got off easy.

Later, however, after Mum has finished playing her records, Dad comes up to my room and points his own finger at me. "You are not to play your mother's records! You are scratching them and ruining them!"

I say nothing, wondering if I will be visiting the corner.

"I have taken the plug off the radiogram so you cannae play it anymore." With that, Dad leaves my room.

I feel deflated. As an only child, I spend a lot of time on my own, and my self-entertainment now revolves almost entirely around playing music. Music helps me endure the long hours, and the even longer days spent alone, in some semblance of sanity. Without music, what can I do to pass the time?

Monday morning comes. Mum and Dad are away at work. I know where the plug to the radiogram is, in the cupboard in the living room, and I have seen Dad put plugs on things, so I think

I can put the plug back on the radiogram. I take the plug, find a screwdriver, and fix the plug back onto the radiogram. It is easy. The plug works fine. I spend the day playing records and enjoying the music even more, now that it is illicit. I reason that adding scratches to the already scratched records will not be noticed. Just before Mum and Dad get home, I shut the record player down, take the plug off the electric cord, and put the plug back where it had been left. I am pleased with my resourcefulness.

This routine goes on for several days. Mum and Dad go to work, and I attach the plug to the radiogram and play records. When I'm done, I take the plug off and put it back in the cupboard. But within time, my parents, specifically Mum, realize that the records are still getting scratched. After another admonishment about not playing her records, Mum takes the plug from the record player, puts it in the wardrobe in her and Dad's bedroom, and locks the bedroom door, taking the key away with her to work. Hmm. What can I do about that?

After Mum and Dad have gone to work in the morning, I go upstairs to investigate the lock on their bedroom door. I know the lock is unusual because it has an unusual key. I visualize the key and its long shank with almost star-shaped cogs sticking out, which would catch the bits in the lock and make it turn. It looks a bit like a screwdriver. I peek through the hole in the lock and can see the cupboard on the other side of the door. I go get a screwdriver.

After several attempts at turning the screwdriver counterclockwise in the lock, and feeling the screwdriver catch against something inside the lock, the door unlocks, and I open it. I am pleased with my cleverness. I get the plug, attach it to the radiogram, play music, and take the plug off when done. The big question now is whether I can relock the bedroom door. I turn the screwdriver clockwise in the lock. I feel the screwdriver catch against something in the lock and I keep turning. I try the door handle: success! I have locked the bedroom door again.

Within time, my parents realize the records are still getting scratched. They don't know how I am getting the radiogram plug from the locked bedroom and interrogate me about a spare key that they thought had been lost. I deny having the spare key. They search me and the things in my room but do not find one. As a resolution, my father takes the plug and puts it up in the attic. The attic's only access is through a ceiling panel many feet above my head, which I cannot reach.

After my parents go to work in the morning, I get the step-ladder from the back garden, where it is kept behind the garage. I drag its cumbersome, wooden frame through the garden, into the house, and up the stairs and place it under the ceiling entryway to the attic. I climb up the ladder, push open the attic hatch, and after gingerly balancing on the top and very narrow rail of the ladder, hoist myself up into the attic space. Luckily the plug is left right next to the entrance. I grab the plug and carefully lower myself onto the top rail of the ladder. Then after descending the ladder and going back downstairs, I put the plug on the record player and listen to music all day. Just before my parents get home, I reverse the whole process.

The scratched record episode comes to an abrupt halt after Mum buys Dad a brand-new record of American band favorites for his birthday, and even though it was tucked away in Mum's wardrobe until it was time to give it to Dad, I find it, and play it. Unfortunately, the record becomes scratched before she gives it to Dad.

Dad's birthday arrives. We are all standing in the living room. Mum hands Dad the now wrapped present. I cringe as I watch Dad's delight at unwrapping the gift and finding a brand-new record. I have a horrible sick feeling inside me as I watch Dad carefully remove the record from its sleeve, lay it on the turntable, and then carefully lift the stylus and place it at the edge of the record. The music starts, a rousing rendition of the "Star-Spangled Banner." The first few seconds sound great, but then the needle hits the first of the scratches in the vinyl and starts to jump across notes, playing what sounds more and more like a Star-Mangled Banner. I listen to the awful scraping and abrasive sound of the music and see the look of disappointment on Dad's face. I feel terrible. He turns and looks at me.

"I'm so sorry, Dad."

Dad shakes his head.

The wallpaper is about six inches from the end of my nose. I am going cross-eyed staring at it because it is so close. The blue-and-silver flowery design repeated again and again over the walls of the living room is well known to me. As is this corner. I have to stand here staring at the corner for an hour. It is my punishment. I don't mind standing here right now. It is what I deserve.

CHAPTER

THREE

itting on the kitchen stool with my hands clasped tensely in my lap, I stare intently at the wall clock as its large hand ticks past each second. At exactly nine o'clock, I will begin my carefully planned, big adventure. First I have to make sure Mum is well on her way to work before I leave the house. But I cannot leave too late or I will miss the bus. It is two minutes before nine. My Mackintosh is hanging on a hook in the hall. My cloth shoulder bag is packed with necessities for the day and waiting under my bed. My Wellington boots are clean and sitting at the bottom of my wardrobe. The large hand ticks against the number twelve. It is nine o'clock. Time to go!

I move with preplanned choreography, running upstairs, putting on my wellies, grabbing my bag, and then running downstairs, throwing on my Mackintosh, and checking the electrics are all turned off. Taking my "Horse Finding Preparation Checklist" out of its hiding place in my pocket, I run down the items on my list: bus, check; money, check; outfit, check. Everything is in order. I make my way to the back door of the house.

I am only eight years old, and I'm not allowed out of the house by myself. I don't have a key. So my plan is to exit by the back door so I can leave it unlocked and get back into the house later. I make sure the door is shut behind me, and I go through the back garden, shutting the garden gate and making sure the latch is secure.

It is raining, which allows me the excuse of pulling my hood down over my face to help disguise my identity as I begin my clandestine walk down the road and around the corner to the bus stop. I am catching the number thirty-two bus to the village of Clanfield. I don't have to wait long. The bus is uncharacteristically on time. I get on the bus, pay my fare, and move to a seat at the back, praying that I will not meet anyone I know. My parents would kill me if they knew what I was doing. I settle into my seat next to the window and stare out at the brick buildings rushing past at the same speed as the bus, my view of the drab day obscured by raindrops racing each other to the bottom of the glass. The journey will be about an hour, plenty of time to sit and think about my day.

After the incident with the record player, my options for self-amusement during the school holidays are reduced even more. My main source of entertainment has become the meager selection of television programs offered during the day. *Play School*, a young children's program, airs every morning at eleven. The main programming starts around four o'clock. In the meantime, the only offering is afternoon horse racing. I start watching the racing through a lack of anything else to do. Within time, it becomes an afternoon ritual, and as usual, I am not happy to be a mere observer. If I am going to spend time watching the races, I must learn all I can about them, and the horses.

Some evenings Mum gets the newspaper that has the list of the next day's horse races. I turn to the back of the paper and educate myself about the anticipated weather and racing conditions. I review the horses' form. I know the going can make a difference for the horses. Some horses do better when the going is soft, others when it is firm. Some horses do better over a shorter distance, others over a longer one. I review the numbers for each horse:

the wins, the places, the shows. The horses have names, and I see if any names appeal to me. I circle my favorite with a pencil and cross my fingers that my choice will win the race.

The more I watch and learn about the horses, the more I come to appreciate their unique qualities. Through this sport of kings, I recognize how special these animals are. I admire how elegant the thoroughbreds are compared to ordinary horses. I like the way they prance, almost dancing on delicate legs, and the graceful arc of the neck holding a regal head. I am drawn to these magnificent creatures when they gallop flat out, and muscle and equine physique work together with perfect efficiency to create speed with grace. I see the link between the athleticism and grace of the horses and my dance studies, and I understand the hard work it takes to become the best. I want to ride horses. I want to learn to control their grace and speed, and to partner my dancer's body with that of my equine counterpart.

I wish I had a horse. I wish I could live in the country and ride horses along country lanes. I read everything I can about horses. I borrow library books and learn about grooming and taking care of horses. I learn how to ride horses properly. In my mind, I know how to hold the reins, how your foot should sit in the stirrup and the angle of your leg against the horse's side. I know the different paces a horse has. I know the names of the fences: the oxer, the upright, and the parallel bars. I cut out all the pictures I can find of horses and match them to my knowledge. I even have a book on the different breeds of horses and know Arabians are bred from the Byerly Turk, the Darley Arabian, and the Godolphin Barb. I can recognize different breeds from different countries. I know the colors of horses, and that grays can be any shade from white to steel gray.

Every night I read the back of the evening newspaper where people advertise horses for sale. I can tell how tall a horse is by the number of hands listed. I look at where the horses are kept in the countryside; I look at the phone book to see where riding stables are located, and I know the best horsey areas. Horses cost a lot to buy, and I know from my reading that they cost a lot to feed and look after. I still want a horse. Maybe I can't have one today, but someday I will have a horse of my own.

Even if I can't own a horse, I wish I could see real horses. I live in the middle of the city. The only horse I see is the rag-and-bone man's old nag dragging the cart behind it as it lumbers along the streets. My cousins are lucky. They live farther north in the city, and if you stand on the bed in one of their upstairs bedrooms, you can just see the top of Portsdown Hill peeking out over the rooftops. My cousins think I am daft.

"Laraine, what are you doing? Why are you standing on the bed?" The cousins—Malcolm, Stephen, Ronald, and Andrew—stand behind me with that puzzled *Why are girls so daft?* look on their faces.

"I'm trying to see Portsdown Hill. I can just make out the forts along the top of the hill." It is hard keeping my balance as I stand on tiptoe on the soft mattress and raise my head as high as I can to see as far as I can over the rooftops.

"Why?" asks Malcolm, the oldest and closest in age to me.

I turn to the boys and explain with simple logic, "Because horses live on the other side of the hill!"

"You can't see horses from here."

"I know, but I can see the hill, and I know horses are on the other side of the hill." *Honestly. Boys!*

The cousins look at each other with that confused look boys get when they're trying to understand girls, and after a final shrug of his shoulders, Malcolm leads the others out of the room and downstairs.

I take one last look out the window. In my mind, Portsdown Hill is where the country begins. People with horses live in the country. I wish I lived in the county.

I have a brilliant idea! One day I will go to the country to find real horses. I know the buses go to the country, and the bus schedule is at the back of the phone book. I know where the main horsey areas are in the country. So I will get a bus to a horsey area and find real horses. I need to save my pocket money for the fare.

author winning a dance competition, family photo

I am currently getting pocket money, a shilling a week. When I am bad, the pocket money stops for a while, but right now I get my weekly shilling. I make the sacrifice of not buying sweets for the Saturday film, and each week put my shilling inside one of the dance trophies in my bedroom. My shillings are adding up. When I have almost a pound, I decide I will go to the village of Clanfield. I will call the bus station to check on the return fare.

Finally, after weeks of planning, here I am, on the bus, on my big adventure.

The bus conductor wakes me from my daydreaming by announcing, "Clanfield." immediately grab my bag and jump up from my seat. Making my way toward the door, I ask the conductor where I get the bus back to Portsmouth, and he points through the bus window at the stop across the street.

I step out of the bus and into the street. The bus drives away, leaving me standing conspicuously alone. Feeling out of place, I look around at the village. Thankfully it is quiet, so I don't have to face inquisitive stares. The only other person is a woman walking a dog some distance away. Looking around me, I see stone buildings, some with thatched roofs, and a church. I am not interested in buildings. I want to get away from the buildings, away from people. I look along both sides of the street and make a decision which way to go. Where can I find horses? I decide to go to my right.

I am prepared for my walk. I am wearing my Mac, a woolen hat, and my wellies. I carry a flowery cloth shoulder bag, and inside I have my cloth purse with my change. I stride along the road purposefully. I want people to think I know where I am going and that there is nothing odd about an eight-year-old wandering alone along country lanes.

I walk for what seems like hours, looking for telltale signs of horses. I walk up and down lanes, taking note of where I am so I can find my way back to the village. I am surrounded by greenery. The air is fresh and a little damp. It is quiet except for the occasional birdsong. The lanes are lined with trees, bracken, and bushes. The hedgerows are high, and I have difficulty looking over them to see if there is a horse in the field. In some places the greenery is thinner, and I trek through the bracken and bushes to see what is on the other side. No horses. The earth is damp and the ground is muddy in places. That is why I am wearing my wellies. I smile, pleased with myself. I did a good job at getting ready for this walk. Now where are the horses?

I push back the sleeve of my Mac and look at my Cinderella watch. I have been walking for over an hour. I remind myself of the time the bus leaves the village to go back home and calculate that I have forty-five minutes left.

I am getting tired and a little frustrated. My wellies are a bit big for me and are beginning to hurt my feet. I should have worn thicker socks. The damp is finding its way between the layers of my clothes and making me cold. I sigh heavily, watching a puff of steam escape from my mouth. This is a wasted trip. I stop walking and wonder whether to go farther up this lane or to give up and go back toward the village. Standing in the middle of the lane, I look behind me and see the narrow tarmac road lined with greenery. I look at the road ahead of me and see only more of the same. I know there are no horses behind me. The only possible positive outcome lies up the lane.

As I push my tired legs forward, my wellies go *clomp-clomp* on the road as the rubber soles hit the tarmac with irritation. I adjust my bag to make it more comfortable on my shoulder and wipe sweat from my brow with my woolen glove. I look along the road, hoping to see anything other than bushes and trees, and then I see it—something exciting on the lane, a few yards ahead. I run quickly toward it to investigate. Is it? Yes it is! Horse poop! I am thrilled. This is a critical sign and worthy of investigation. I examine the poop and walk past it. I see more poop farther up the lane, and as I walk up to it, I hear a distinctive neigh on my right. Impatiently I push my way through the greenery. I don't see a horse, but I know I am getting close.

I walk up the lane a little farther with my senses on full alert. Then I hear it, the distinctive *clip-clop* of shod horses' hooves on the road. I stop and listen. The sound is coming from behind me, down the lane. I look back and coming into view are not one, not two, but five real horses and riders. I stand with my mouth open and stare as the horses come closer, knowing enough not to abruptly move and spook them. I know I look strange standing in my Mac and wellies in the mud at the side of the lane. I know I look like a "townie." I know I look out of place, but right now I don't care what people think. My life is complete. I am looking at real horses.

The horses are all brown and of a similar size. Two have brown manes and tails while the others have black manes and tails. I watch the horses and riders as they get closer. I am fascinated by the saddles and bridles, the swishing of the horses' tails. I look at the riders in proper riding helmets and jodhpurs. They are wearing jumpers or quilted jackets, and they have crops in their hands. They are holding the reins just as I learned from my books. I smile as they come level with me. I take a deep breath. I can smell a distinctive sweaty, horsey smell. I smell leather. Then the third horse lifts up its tail and poops on the road. I smell the fresh horse poop. I am thrilled at this real-life experience. What a fantastic day!

"Good afternoon," the first rider says to me politely as she rides by.

"Good afternoon," I reply, thrilled to be on speaking terms with a real equestrian.

One by one, the horses and their riders pass. The riders are all ladies. I watch them intently, taking in as much as I can. The way the horses nod their heads as they walk. The riders' positions in the general-purpose saddles. The bridles with a variety of single and double bits. Too soon I am looking at the horses' rears as they walk up the lane. Now what do I do?

I decide to let the horses go up the lane and out of sight, and then I follow them. I want to know where they are going. At the end of the lane is a dirt path leading off to the right which goes alongside a field. I see a wooden signpost at the side of the path which says CLANFIELD RIDING STABLES. I am excited to find a riding stable, but I won't go up the path. I don't have the money for a ride, and they probably won't like strangers intruding. I decide I will save my pocket money and come back to this stable to ride horses. With that future plan of action in place, I turn back and head toward the village. I look at my Cinderella watch. I have about thirty minutes until the next bus back to Portsmouth.

My return journey is uneventful. I have planned my trip well. I arrive home and go into the house the way I left, through the back garden, shutting the garden gate and the back door of the house. I put away my things and turn the telly on. I sit innocently on the couch watching television as though my great adventure had never happened. It is four thirty. Mum will be home soon.

"How was your day, love?" Mum is home. "What did you do?"

"Day was okay. I just played with my toys and watched some telly." I can't tell her about my adventure. It is my secret, and I am pleased with it. I went to the country and saw real horses. I didn't get caught, and I didn't end up in the corner.

That night as I lie in bed, I cannot sleep. I feel I am walking, not lying down. My mind sees images of horses and riders and country lanes. I close my eyes and take in deep breaths. I smile. I smell sweaty horses, leather, and horse poop.

I continue to save my pocket money. I know it will cost about a pound for an hour's ride, and I am diligent in trying to be good and earn my shillings. I also know I will have to convince my dad to drive me out to the stable in his car. I lie in bed at night and think of a good way to convince him. I get money from my grannies for my birthday, and with my saved pocket money, I soon have more than enough for a ride.

Dad has just picked me up from dance class in his car, and we are driving home, when I make my move.

"Dad?"

"What, love?"

"I have been saving my pocket money really hard because there is something special that I have always wanted to do."

"What's that, love?"

"Well, I want to go horse riding. I love horses, and I think it would be good for me to learn something new, and not only that, but being in the fresh country air would be good and healthy for me."

Dad says nothing.

I want Dad to understand that I have thought it through. "There is a stable in Clanfield, and I can get a bus there and back. I have enough money. I am old enough I can go on my own."

"You can't get a bus to Clanfield by yourself! You're not old enough!" Dad's tone is firm.

I sigh deeply. Dad doesn't understand. He doesn't know—and I cannot tell him—that I have already taken the bus to Clanfield and back. I am disappointed by his response and don't know how else to convince him to let me go riding.

"You said you've already saved money for a ride?"

"Yes, Dad."

"I will drive you to the stable. Make it Sunday afternoon, and I can drive you. I will wait for you to have your ride and then bring you back."

"Really, Dad?" I smile. My ploy has worked. Dad doesn't want me taking the bus alone, so he thinks he should drive me up there.

"Yes." I hear the soft sigh of resignation in my dad's voice.

"Thank you, thank you, thank you!"

I call and book a ride. I learn I have to wear sensible shoes with a small heel, and the stable has hard hats I can borrow. Dad keeps his word, and early Sunday afternoon he drives me to the stable in Clanfield. Now, for the first time in my life, I am astride a real horse. Sally, the stable owner, will lead the ride. She adjusts my stirrups, shows me how to hold the reins, and gives me some tips on using my legs to encourage the horse to move and how to use the reins to steer him.

I learn my horse's name is Oppo, which is navy slang for buddy or mate. He is a brown gelding fifteen hands high, and I feel as if I am on top of the world. I look around the stable yard, seeing the world from my new perspective way above the ground. It is a perfect sunny day, and I inhale the smell of grass and horse. I feel giddily happy as I wave goodbye to my dad, who sits patiently in his car as the ride moves out.

I am in the middle of the pack of a dozen horses and riders as we make our way out of the stable yard, down the lane I have already visited on my solo journey to Clanfield, through the village, and into the countryside. I ride along country lanes, up a dirt trail, and across a field. Everywhere is the fragrant scent of foliage. I duck under low-hanging tree branches and guide Oppo along, making sure we keep up with the other riders. I put my hours of reading horse books into practice as I check the saddle, the connection of the bridle and reins with Oppo's mouth, the horse's gait, and my own position in the saddle. I enjoy the feel of Oppo's steady gait beneath me, the way horse and rider move together, the rhythm of my body in the saddle making it easier for him to walk, which in turn makes my position in the saddle more comfortable. I feel at home on horseback, as I knew I would. My whole being is smiling, enjoying this wonderful experience.

From time to time Sally pulls her horse back to check on me, to see how my ride is going. "You have a nice position in the saddle and seem to know what you are doing," she says to me. "Have you been riding long?"

"This is my first time on a horse."

"Your first time?" Sally's surprise is evident by her raised eyebrows and open mouth. "You look good on horseback. You are a natural. Good job." Sally smiles at me and pushes her mount back to the front of the ride.

She says I am a natural! A huge grin commandeers my face. I cannot stop smiling. My posture straightens, and I sit taller in the saddle. I look around me at the other riders, the countryside, and feel a new affinity with the horsey set. I am going to be an equestrian. My life is going in a new direction. I can't wait to tell my dad.

After an hour of bliss, the ride ends back at the stable yard, and I dismount just as Sally shows me. I suddenly feel very small with two feet back on the ground. I pull the reins over Oppo's head as directed and lead him to a groom. I say *goodbye* and *thank you* to Sally and make my way back to Dad's car.

On the drive home, I can't stop talking as I excitedly share my ride with Dad. I tell him about the horse, his name, the lanes we rode along, the new things about horses and riding I have learned.

"Guess what Sally said?" I didn't wait for Dad to answer. "She said I am a good rider. I am a natural." I ignore the lack of response from Dad. I keep talking about the ride, about horses, and how it was the best time I have ever had, barely taking a breath before continuing on with my excited narration. I want to go back and ride again and again.

"Dad. Can I go again next week? I have the money. Please?"

"No. You've done it once. That's enough. There's better things to spend money on than horses. Your mum and I spend a fortune on your dancing. You get enough."

"But, Dad!"

"No!"

I glance sideways at my dad and see his stoic face focusing on the road ahead. I say nothing. The finality in my dad's voice shocks me into silence. He said no! I can't believe it. He said no! The exuberance I felt from the ride is suddenly dampened by the cold splash of my father's unfair conclusion that once is enough.

I turn to look to my other side, out the passenger window. The view of the passing trees and fields is blurred by my tears. I know better than to argue with my dad. He has given me my moment with horses, and I must accept it and be thankful for what I have been given. But I don't feel very thankful. I feel that life can be so unfair, especially when I have parents who just don't understand, and if something gives me such pleasure, why wouldn't my parents want me to enjoy it more?

I think of the hours of entertainment I have enjoyed watching the horse races, the passion I felt when reading and thinking about horses. I relive the exhilaration of riding Oppo on a beautiful Sunday afternoon in the pretty English countryside. I know Mum and Dad grew up very poor during the World War; they tell me about it often enough, and about how I am lucky to have more than they ever dreamed of. I am astute enough to realize that this is not an argument to be won today, and I have to let it go. For the rest of the drive home, I silently stare out of the window, reluctantly allowing melancholy instead of exuberance to come home with me.

Slowly and with a dejected spirit, as if saying a final farewell to an integral part of my hopes and dreams, I put all my pictures of horses and my horse books in a box and put the box into the toy graveyard at the back of my wardrobe. They all seem pointless now. I no longer turn on the television for the afternoon races. I have to find something else to amuse myself. Inside my chest, my internal clock takes a prominent step forward and starts counting; counting the years, the months, the days until I am old enough to take control of my own life, leave home, and do what I want to do. I want to ride horses. I want to dance, visit tropical beaches, and ride horses.

CHAPTER

FOUR

"Hey, Mum," I call from the kitchen. "We should go soon. It's nine thirty, and you can use your bus pass now." I have finished drying the breakfast dishes and now lay out the dishtowel to dry. Not hearing a response from my mother, I walk into the living room and find Mum sitting as expected in her favorite chair, nursing an empty teacup, staring out the window at some imaginary scene. I pause at the doorway, sad at what has become a familiar sight in recent days—my mum worlds away in her thoughts, a shimmer of moisture in her eyes. I don't move. I hate to interrupt my mother's thoughts, thinking that wherever her mind has taken her is better than this grueling reality.

The days following my father's passing seem interminably slow, the overlong hours unkindly prolonging the healing process, cruelly forcing the family to endure long days of heartbreak, sorrow, and sad reflection of happier times. Solemnity pervades the family house, taking charge of the grave duty of banishing cheer, optimism, and levity from the premises and ensuring instead that a shroud of somber reflection resides within. The wooden furniture, dressed in its darker mourning polish, pulls sentry duty around the perimeter of the rooms. The brighter colors in

author's mother in reflection, photo © Laraine Denny Burrell

the carpet and wallpaper respectfully blend back into the darker shades, becoming properly subdued in deference to the occasion. The cloud-gray daylight is permitted to provide illumination but cannot reach some corners and the more secluded areas of the house. Noise is censored, leaving a cathedral-like atmosphere in which the house's occupants can meditate. This environment is unknown to me. Never before have I experienced this sadness in the family home.

As expected, my mother is morose. Her words and calm expression as she exists through each day—conversing with visitors in a subdued Scots brogue, engaging in the mundane—cannot conceal the sadness in her eyes or the dejection in her body language, which diminishes her already tiny frame even more.

Loretta, too, is unusually quiet, sitting in the leather chair in the living room, sometimes with her leg on, sometimes with it lying on the floor beside her. Her walking cane is always by her side, ready to offer support when needed. Sometimes she reads her paperbacks, staring at the pages for hours on end, and sometimes she vacantly watches television, offering no reaction to the words on the page or on the screen. Her conversation is monosyllabic; her tone is abrupt, disinterested, and sometimes mean. She offers no help. Her only routine is to take care of her insulin needs and eat when necessary, and then sit in the center of her own secluded world.

I don't know what to do with or say to my sister; I am unused to Loretta's disability and do not want to offend her, but I could use some help, particularly as Loretta has constantly been with Mum and Dad over the years and will know best what needs to be done and where everything is. Then I have second thoughts. Perhaps it is easier for me to take on the work that needs to be done, and just let my sister be.

The family's happy days appear to have gone, at least for a while. The only person immune to the loss is Mark. He spends most of his time away from the house, out and about with his cousins, familiarizing himself with this town of his birth, enjoying things that young people like to do, even taking himself off to the local pub in the evenings. Youth's natural exuberance simply refuses to be extinguished.

For the rest of us, we are all marking time in our lives, knowing that this healing process cannot be rushed, that there is no shortcut to one's reconciliation with the loss of a loved one. For me, the time spent in contemplation of the twists and turns in my own life, and life in general, forces me to reach one definitive conclusion. Even though death is inevitable, the one event in life that can be guaranteed to happen, we are never really ready for it when it comes.

It is one thing for me not to have my father around because he is in the hospital; it is another thing not to have him around because he has passed away. The thought of never seeing Dad sitting in his leather chair again, never having him there to greet me when I come in the front door, and never seeing him pottering around the garden or in the shed in his overalls is difficult to accept. But the simple fact is that we have no choice in the matter. Life must go on for the living. I deal with my grief by pushing it aside, making it secondary to my daily responsibilities.

My father's affairs have to be organized, but where do we begin? My mother is lost, not knowing what needs to be done for her husband, not knowing the extent of his affairs or the order in which they have to be conducted. By default, I take charge, putting aside my own array of indeterminate feelings—my anger, my grief, my shock—to take care of Mum and Loretta.

Instinctively, I know certain basic things have to be taken care of immediately, and whether we want to do them or not, the law dictates they must be done. Only Mum has the authority to take care of most of them, including recording Dad's death and signing the documents to take over his bank accounts. But a malaise has consumed my mother, sapping her person and her personality. I will find my mother as I do now, sitting in her chair in the living room, just staring out the window, her thoughts elsewhere, oblivious to what is going on around her. Her mind is suspended somewhere in the past. Is she seeing images in her mind, the scenes of happier times and memories of life with her best friend and partner?

I focus on my mother and attempt to keep her busy, to make sure that someone is always with her, engaging her in conversation, keeping her mind occupied, keeping her from dwelling on the sadness she must feel. Family and friends dutifully call throughout the day, respectfully leaving prayers and condolences with the new widow, and this helps. I am heartened by the number of people who come to pay their respects and pledge to do whatever my mother needs and to take care of her once I go home. Cards and flowers are delivered, compelling my mother to set aside her reflection as each card is carefully read, as it should be, and then placed in deference on the mantel or sideboard. The flowers are put into vases and positioned at various intervals around the living room. The beauty of the flowers and their fragrant scent permeate the house, sweetening the somber mood.

I am chagrined by the written notes in the cards, messages to my mother and sister. I am not mentioned by name, and part of me silently cries out, *But what about me? He was my father too! I am grieving too. It is just as much my loss.* But it is natural that people don't think of me. I rarely visit England. Many have never met me. When visitors come to see Mum, I politely remove myself from the room, preferring solitude elsewhere to sitting on the sidelines listening to the unfamiliar memories of other people, knowing they shared moments with my father that I did not. It would have been a good way for me to learn more about my father, about what others thought of him and how they remember him, but that doesn't enter my mind. I prefer to be alone to sulk.

The attention to my mother is all well and good during the day, but I know that I cannot prevent the loneliness that must inevitably come to her as she lies alone in her bed at night. I can't help but wonder if Mum cries when she is alone in her room, finally allowing the tears that are stoically kept in check during the day to surface. Does she talk to her husband as if he were still there with her in the dark shadows of her bedroom? Does she tell him that she misses him? Is the love of a seventy-three-year-old woman for her mate still alive in her heart? Poor Mum. I pay extra attention to her, giving her more hugs and kisses and telling her she is loved, hoping the love of a daughter can compensate for the missing love of a husband.

Leaning down, I put an arm around my mother's shoulder. I gently bring her back to the present, urging her to get ready to face the day. "Can I get you anything? Do anything for you?"

"No, love. I'm fine."

"Let me take that for you." I reach out to take the empty teacup from my mother's hand, smiling cheerily at her, feigning bravado, but Mum doesn't notice. She isn't looking at me, isn't looking at anything in particular.

"I'll go get my shoes and coat."

Mum stands up, sighs after the effort, and then shuffles her way toward the door, her pink fluffy slippers laboriously stroking along the carpet. My gaze follows my mother. I see the rounded shoulders and the downward tilt of my mum's head. Mum is on automatic, knowing what needs to be done without having to think it through. Doing what she is told to do as I usher her through what will be another long day. I can't wait for the healing to begin, for the time when the hurt is a little less stabbing, when there are moments when we actually forget my father has died, when we remember to laugh. In the meantime, we can only go through the processes.

There cannot be a funeral for my father until some of the necessary paperwork and processes have been completed. Bureaucratic red tape, forms expressing the intimate details of the death in cold black type, making sure there is no doubt that a loved one is gone, uncaring that they are enforcing the grief and prolonging the healing process. I take Mum back to the hospital to talk to the grievance counselor, then to the doctor to get the death certificate and to discuss releasing the body for burial. I am adamant that Mark and Loretta go with us. I insist they be part of the process. They need to understand and learn about responsibilities; rather than evade the disagreeable, they must learn to accept it as part of life and do their part for the family when needed.

It is strange, all of us sitting in the little consulting room at the hospital with its bright, cheery, painted walls and yellow plastic flower arrangement on the small table in the middle of the room, as though this will help to mitigate our grief. It doesn't. On a side table are pamphlets on the grieving process. Four pages devoted to all you need to know, including bullet points, as if it were a simple five-step program: follow the steps and your grief will be gone, like some television infomercial. "For nineteen ninety-five, you too can get over the death of a loved one!" Likely written by someone who has never lost anyone close, who has no idea that it takes more than four cheery pages of cheerleading rhetoric to come to terms with the loss, the regrets, the self-recrimination.

In time, both the doctor and the grief counselor stop by the room to speak with us, giving the speeches that are no doubt well rehearsed by now, with the appropriate words of condolences and with facial expressions suitable for the circumstances. We sit and listen, reading forms, taking in information, all the while knowing that somewhere in the hospital, Dad is still there too, lying cold, without visitors, and that we arrive and leave without even acknowledging that he is still in the building.

Mum sits through the processes like an anxious, confused child, uncomprehending. When the doctor mentions an autopsy, she begins to cry and shouts vehemently at the doctor, "I don't want you to do an autopsy! I am no' going tae allow them tae do one tae him. They cannae do that tae my husband. I won't allow it! No one is going tae cut open Ian. He doesn't deserve that. He doesn't need that. Leave him alone!" Mum is weeping, tears running down her face, her head shaking, crying, "No! No!"

I put my arms around my mum. Loretta hands her a tissue. Mark sits stoically, the typical male reaction to emotional women. The doctor stands awkwardly, her mouth opening and closing but not having the right words for this unexpected outburst.

But as a lawyer, I understand that sometimes the law unilaterally takes over our lives, even when we don't want it to, such as now when an autopsy might be required by law. When my father was in the navy, he worked in the ship's engine room in the days when asbestos was routinely used on ships. I know if there is any sign of asbestosis, an autopsy might be required, and Mum has no say in the matter. The moment is tense. Tears stream down my mother's face, guided by the wrinkles made more pronounced by her furrowed brow and pursed lips. The doctor excuses herself to check my father's medical records, and I pray that she will find no need for the intrusive investigation. We are fortunate. The doctor returns with good news. She has determined an autopsy is not needed. I sigh, thankful that particular unpleasantness has been averted and that Mum does not have to face that indignity to the body of her husband.

Once the body can be released, the funeral arrangements have to be made. It becomes apparent that Mum and Dad had not discussed this matter. Mum knew Dad wanted to be cremated, that much was written into his will, but no one had thought about what to do with his ashes. I mention that there must be some nice memorial garden or similar place where those who are cremated are laid to rest, somewhere they can be visited by family and friends rather than spending eternity in an urn and, knowing Mum, stored in a box at the bottom of a cupboard somewhere. She isn't the type to have her dead husband in an urn on display on her mantel, being a nuisance and gathering dust, creating more housework for her. I am surprised that Mum and Dad hadn't thought more about what to do with each other's remains and that they hadn't considered a memorial garden. Perhaps they had simply chosen to ignore that unwelcome specter, preferring instead to focus on being alive.

I recognize a connection between this selective ignorance of death and Mum's failure to acknowledge Dad's illness to anyone. I have heard from other family members that they did not know how ill Dad really was, and that they would have visited him more often in the hospital, only Mum had said that was not necessary. They had been told that Dad would be home soon. I understood that Mum would have her reasons. Perhaps like me now, she was pushing away the fear, the uncertainty, the insecurity that the death of a loved one can bring. It is easier to stay focused on the moment than to worry about what will come. By not telling people how ill her husband was, Mum did not have to face their questions or concerns. Until she acknowledged out loud that his illness was terminal, it could not happen.

I go through the phone book to see if there are any local memorial gardens and find that the local crematorium has a chapel and memorial garden and is in Portchester, not too far away. This small town, now more a suburb of Portsmouth, is named for Portchester Castle, which was originally an old Roman fortification dating back to the late third century. The castle

view from atop Portchester Castle looking across Portsmouth Harbor toward Portsmouth,
photo © Laraine Denny Burrell

stands at the northern edge of Portsmouth Harbor, looking across the water to the city on the other side. The nearby crematorium and memorial park have a series of beautiful gardens where loved ones can be laid to rest. Dad had sailed in and out of the harbor during his naval career, and he had been an avid gardener who loved his flowers. The location and setting is perfect. Mum doesn't like grass and flowers. She would have been happy with concrete slabs out in the back garden. But placing Dad in a beautiful garden with a peaceful environment where family and friends can visit is ideal. Thankfully, Mum agrees, and we make arrangements. The garden has just opened a new section on the side of a hill. Nearby is a wooden shed. Mum thinks it will be nice to place Dad near the shed, as it represents so many aspects of his life. She also buys a plot there next to Dad for herself.

Mum wants the local coop to do the funeral arrangements. At least that much has been decided, but sitting in the too-warm and cloying atmosphere of the visitor's room with the funeral home's representative and going through the books of caskets, flowers, and other arrangements, perspiration begins forming on my brow, and my clothes are now sticking uncomfortably to my skin. I feel nauseous and unfocused and reluctantly take a back seat in the arrangements. Mum knows Dad's favorite flowers. Mum knows precisely what kind of floral arrangements she wants for him. She hates lilies; they are death flowers. She wants something bright and cheerful: thistles, Scottish flowers from the homeland. She also wants a piper in a kilt to play the bagpipes as Dad's coffin makes its way to the chapel.

Loretta knows Dad's favorite songs and from memory gives the funeral representative a list of Scottish songs to be played by the piper. I sit mute, feeling dazed by the decisiveness of the arrangements. I know none of this. He was my father, he loved his garden, and yet I did not know what his favorite flowers were. My father loved his Scots music, but I do not recognize the songs my sister names. I feel like an interloper, watching Mum and Loretta make decisions as to what my father would want for his tribute. And I have nothing to offer. I sink back into the chair and look down at the floor, away from the photographs of caskets and flowers, pretty ornate things intended to mitigate the unbearable, but nonetheless reminding me that my father is gone, and I know so little about him. Overriding my sadness is the consistent reminder that I had spent so little time with Dad in the past years. I become determined to find something to offer; I must make up for my neglect in some way. But how?

CHAPTER

FIVE

$\mathcal{D}$ad and I walk along the floating jetty, a series of metal platforms linked together which allow us to walk out over the water from the naval base at Whale Island to where my dad's ship is anchored in the harbor. The jetty is uneven, and each platform has a life of its own as it moves up and down or sways from side to side, pushed by the movement of the surrounding water. I am not scared. I am a navy brat. I have walked this and other jetties many times. I have been on my dad's ship many times, even sailing onboard her one time when the navy had maneuvers out in the Solent and English Channel, and families were allowed to join in and experience the exercise firsthand.

Almost at the ship, I pause in my tracks and take a moment to look up at the vessel. Navy ships are typically painted the same gray color. But my dad's ship is different. She has a stunning navy blue hull, with a bright red band running along the bottom of the hull at the waterline. Along and around the top of the hull is painted an elegant gold ribbon, and on the point of the bow is a round, colorful heraldic crest. The gold ribbon and crest look like a dainty pendant on the ship's décolletage. The bulkheads and superstructure above the rail running along the main deck are painted white, while the one funnel and three masts are a cream color. To me, she is the most beautiful ship in the Royal Navy.

Of course, I am not being completely honest. This isn't really my dad's ship. It is just the ship he works on. The ship is called the Royal Yacht *Britannia* and actually belongs to Her Majesty, the Queen. Her crew are referred to as royal yachtsmen or "Yotties." I don't think the Queen will mind me referring to it as "my dad's ship."

"Come on, love," Dad calls for me to catch up.

"Coming," I call back as I jump from platform to platform until I am standing beside Dad at the gangplank. We climb up to the main deck of the yacht where we are greeted by the duty seaman. Immediately I hear the low but familiar hum I associate with the ship—the air conditioning, the electronics, and the metal hull housing its own community. The vessel is never asleep.

Mum isn't with us today. She stayed at home. Apparently Dad only wanted me to come onboard with him today. I don't know why. I don't really care why. I love visiting the ship. I feel at home on the ship. Being in the navy and sailing the seven seas is on my "To Do" list for when I grow up.

Sometimes when we bring visitors onboard on Sundays, the other kids and I are allowed to play outside on the decks, and we play chase and hide-and-seek, provided we are not too rambunctious or noisy. Sometimes, just to be silly, we watch the ferryboat sail around the harbor with tourists. When the ferry sails near the yacht, the other children and I wave regally to the tourists, who take photographs of us, thinking perhaps we are important when really we are not. I know my way around the ship inside and out. I like to visit the galley, which always has lots of lovely hot, smooshy chips, and sometimes the cook gives me a large plate of them.

Today Dad and I are going straight down to the mess. I follow my dad along the passageways with their riveted metal bulkheads, through rounded hatches or doors, and down steep narrow ladders or stairs. I don't have to follow Dad. I know the way to the mess by myself.

As we enter the mess, some of Dad's shipmate friends are there having a drink and a good laugh. I like sitting in the mess with my dad and his friends; it is a warm, cozy place. The sailors like to make jokes, and I get to drink Coca-Cola. The mess bar is called The Verge Inn. People laugh at the name. I don't understand why.

I sit on a stool at the bar, and Frank, my dad's friend who is pulling duty behind the bar, pours me a glass of Coca-Cola. People in the mess are laughing and having a good time. I like being on the ship; I enjoy the atmosphere. I wish the Royal Navy let girls sail on ships, because I want to be a sailor on a ship like my dad. He travels the world going to lots of interesting places and meeting fascinating people. One day I want to live on a big ship and travel around the world to foreign places. I look around at the naval décor, the pictures of royal family members, the plaques and pennants of naval insignia, and some photographs of the yotties themselves.

I turn back to take a sip of my drink when I notice my dad has gone. Frank sees me looking around and says, "Your dad has just stepped out to get something for you. He'll be right back."

"Okay."

What has Dad gone to get for me? I wonder. *Why did I have to come onboard the yacht to get whatever it is?* Hmmm. My brow furrows. I am curious.

A few minutes later, Dad returns with a square, brown cardboard box. He puts it on the bar in front of me. I look at the cardboard box, which has a round hole cut in the top. It doesn't look like anything much. Suddenly a little head pops up from the hole in the box. It is a stripy kitten. The kitten head looks around and then pops back down into the box.

"Oh!" I am surprised. The kitten peeks out again. "Aww, he's so cute!"

Frank nods toward the box. "You get to take him home with you."

I look behind me at my dad. I frown. "Dad?"

"That's right," Dad says. "This is Schickrys. He was given to Her Majesty, the Queen Mother, and he's the yacht's mascot. We get to take him home and look after him."

"Gosh!" At first I am shocked that this is a royal cat, the yacht's mascot, and he is sitting on the bar in front of me. Once I get over the shock, I smile with delight at the thought that I have a kitten, and I get to take him home with me. I have to share him with the Queen Mum, but he gets to live at my house. Carefully I put my hand into the hole until I can feel the warm, soft fur.

"He's a special cat," my dad tells me. "He's Manx. He doesn't have a tail."

I don't understand until my dad takes the lid off the box, lifts out the kitten, and places him gently on my lap. I hold the kitten carefully and peer round at his bum. I am surprised. Dad is right. The kitten doesn't have a tail!

"He's from a place called the Isle of Man, and the cats there are special because they don't have tails," my dad explains to alleviate my confusion.

"What's his name, Dad?" I didn't understand the first time Dad told me. The name sounded funny.

"His full name is Mannanagh Schickrys, but we'll call him Schickrys."

"Shick-riss," I repeat. "Shick-riss. Shick-riss. Mancks."

"M-a-n-x," my dad spells out to me. "Anything from the Isle of Man is Manx."

"M-a-n-x, Manx," I say to paste it into my brain.

Dad educates me on the history of Schickrys. I learn that earlier this year, 1963, Queen Elizabeth, the Queen Mother went on a royal visit to the Isle of Man where she was presented with this Manx kitten. The kitten is a pedigree cat, which makes it important, and it has its own hand-painted pedigree certificate. The Queen Mum presented the kitten to the royal yacht as its mascot. Because the ship sails abroad, for quarantine reasons, the kitten cannot be kept on board the ship. So an investigation was conducted to find a suitable family to take care of the cat; a family with not too many children to annoy the cat, but a responsible family who can take good care of him. As fate has it, my family was chosen. I feel very important. I like the idea that someone thinks I am a responsible person. This is Mannanagh Schickrys, a pedigree Manx kitten, a present to the Queen Mum, the yacht's mascot, and he is coming home with me. What a glorious thing!

Dad and I take the bus home. I sit with the cardboard box on my lap, holding it like the precious treasure it is, loving every time the little tiger-striped head pops up to see what is going on with the world. I stroke his little head, softly wanting him to get to know me and get used to me. I know that I will now be in love with cats forever.

Dad hasn't told Mum we are bringing the cat home. Mum is not much of an animal lover, or at least not since our budgie, Chris, flew into her cup of tea and scalded himself and died. That was when I was two years old. But here we are with a kitten, and a royal one at that. Mum can't say no. She can't turn down the Queen Mum's cat. "Schickrys," I remind myself.

Dad enters the house first. "Cath, we're home!"

I cautiously enter through the doorway behind my dad, clutching the box to my chest with one hand, my other hand over the hole in the top, keeping the furry resident from popping up and scaring Mum before Dad has a chance to explain.

"Cath, we have a wee surprise."

Along the passageway, Mum's head peers round from the kitchen door. "What surprise?"

"It's fer the wean."

"Just what did you get her now?" Mum's head disappears back into the kitchen. "I'm putting the kettle on."

My dad pushes me by my shoulder toward the kitchen door. "Best show yer mum what we have." He sounds uncertain, making me hesitate.

Pushed by my dad, I lurch toward the kitchen and pause at the door. I grin broadly at Mum. "Look what we have." I extend the box toward Mum, just as a little stripy head pops up and stares at her.

"Aaaargh! What is that? Is that a rat?" A metal clatter follows as Mum drops the kettle she is holding, and it bounces off the tiled kitchen floor. Mum takes two steps away from the box, her screech causing the furry head to disappear back into the box.

"Ian! What is that? Is that a rat?"

"Haud yer weescht woman! It's a wee cat. A kitten for the wean. It's time Laraine had a pet."

"A cat? A cat!" Mum's posture changes from frightened victim in a horror movie, holding her hands up to her face to ward off the terrible beast, to standing with hands on hip, scowl on face, ready to do battle with Dad for bringing an animal into her house. "What did ye bring that home fer?"

I stand between Mum and Dad, my arms around the box, trying to shield the kitten from this less than welcoming introduction into the family home. "He's really little, and so cute," I offer, feeling a need to defend the little guy.

"We were chosen, Cath. It's the yacht's mascot that was presented to the Queen Mum, and we were asked to look after it, to keep it here in our home." Dad's tone appears to placate Mum, but she still has questions.

"How long have you known about this? Why didn't you tell me you were bringing a cat home?"

"Because I know you don't like animals, but this will be a lovely pet for Laraine."

"Well you"—Mum points her finger right at my nose—"had better take good care of it, and keep it away from me."

"I will, Mum. I promise." With that, Schickrys becomes a part of our family.

Schickrys is my personal responsibility and gets all my attention. I feed him, brush him, and play with him. Dad gives me some string to play chase. I run around the house upstairs and downstairs, dragging the string behind me, and followed by the quick attacking paws of the kitten. When Schickrys catches the string, he grabs it with his front paws, chews it, and kicks at it with his hind paws. Silly kitten!

When Schickrys settles down to rest, I check to see where he is to make sure he is okay. He might be sleeping in the corner

*author with Schickrys, photo courtesy of The News,
Portsmouth, England.*

of the living room or under my bed. If he is in reach, I tenderly stroke the fur along his back, letting him know he is loved.

Our taking care of the kitten is apparently a newsworthy event, because the *Evening News* comes to our house to interview Mum and Dad for an article, and the man takes a picture of me with the cat to put in the paper. I become a minor celebrity at school, having appeared in the local newspaper with the Queen Mother's cat and the royal yacht's mascot. All sorts of people stop at the house to see and take pictures of the royal cat. Mum tolerates the fuss. She kindly lets people take photographs of the kitten while Schickrys ignores it all.

Mum makes sure Schickrys goes outside into the garden a lot because she doesn't want him pooping in the house. Schickrys doesn't stay in the garden; he jumps onto the fence and wanders off, but the clever fellow knows where his home is and always comes back, sometimes meowing and pawing at the back door, sometimes at the front. Mum makes me laugh, though. She makes a big show of ceremoniously opening the front door so the neighbors can see her letting the royal cat into the house, all the while smiling and calling, "Here puss, puss." But then she herds him through the house and shoos him out the back door again while grumbling something about, "Hairy moggy." Royal cat or not, he is allowed to roam the neighborhood, just like the domestics.

At bedtime, Schickrys sleeps with me. He cuddles against my chest as I tenderly stroke his fur. "Who's a handsome boy then?" I whisper to him as he closes his eyes and relaxes, mesmerized by my soft touch and gentle voice. I study him, the striped blacks and browns of his fur, the lighter shades of his underbelly, the petite size of his paws, and the innocence on his face. *Life is strange,* I think to myself. Things I want I don't get, and things I cannot even imagine come true. I must be the luckiest girl in England, snuggling with a royal cat every night. What a unique experience, and why me? I fall asleep cuddling Schickrys to my chest, stroking his fur and hypnotized by his throaty purr.

I am snuggled under my bedcovers deep in my dream world when I hear an awful caterwauling. I feel movement on my bed as a terrified feline briskly leaves me to find safety in some corner of the dark room. As I become semiconscious, I grasp that this spine-chilling racket is not some demon in my dreams but something happening in reality. Now awake, I realize the noise emanating from some lower extremity of the house is Dad singing, and despite it being the middle of the night, he is going to entertain Mum, the cat, the walls of the house, and whomever and whatever is within earshot with his lousy singing.

This is not an unusual phenomenon. Dad often goes out to social and navy events with his naval buddies from the Royal Yacht *Britannia*, and it is a guarantee that they will all have a considerable amount to drink and a buoyant good time.

Dad starts singing a rousing rendition of "Scotland the Brave":

"Land o' the high endeavour
Land o' the shining river
Land o' my heart forever
Scotland the brave."

I feel the off-key tones hit and reverberate around the walls of the small house. I bury my head under my pillow, under the bedcovers, trying to dampen the sound made worse by the loud Scots accent and the probability that Dad has lost his false teeth. Again. Poor Schickrys, he must be cowering somewhere under the bed. Poor neighbors, they have to be hearing this too. The neighbors are Irish. I am not sure they will appreciate being wakened in the middle of the night by "Scotland the Brave." Fully awake now, I lie in my bed wondering how long this disturbance will continue.

Dad stops singing as he thumps his way up the stairs; perhaps his ability to do two things at once is impaired by an inebriated lack of coordination. He can do feet or mouth but not both. I then hear Dad playing peek-a-boo with Mum as he stumbles at the top of the stairs and into their bedroom. I hear, "Shush Ian. Get in tae bed, ye daft eejit!"

I hear some stumbling and thumps from my parents' room, but eventually the house quiets down and returns to its nighttime tranquility.

"Schickrys, Schickrys," I call out softly to the kitten, wanting him to leave his hiding place and cuddle with me on the bed. He obliges, and I feel a gentle movement on my bedspread as he lightly steps along my bed until he is next to my pillow. I feel him settle and give him a gentle hug before closing my eyes and drifting back to sleep thinking about my parents. They do make me laugh.

The next morning, I slowly lumber down the stairs, one arduous step at a time, not fully recovered from the previous night's rude interruption of my sleep. I pull my dressing gown tighter around me and stop at the bottom step to get my bearings. Schickrys's absence from my bed this morning, together with an odd clattering sound, has brought me downstairs. The noise is coming from the kitchen, a *tap-tap, clatter-clatter-clatter* sound. I slowly open the kitchen door and see the naughty puss playing with the upper set of my dad's false teeth. He is chasing them between the chair legs under the kitchen table. The *tap-tap* of his little paws against the pink-and-white teeth, followed by an attacking dive onto the choppers, causes them in turn to career across the tiled floor, creating a clatter as they hit the wooden table leg. I bend forward to pick up the teeth but change my mind. Schickrys is having such fun with them that I don't have the heart to take them away. I look around but don't see the bottom set of teeth. Oh well. That is Dad's problem once he wakes up.

I get myself a drink of water and go into the living room, where I flop on the couch to give my body a chance to fully wake up. I relive last night's entertainment, courtesy of Dad, and find myself laughing. My parents are funny people. Dad is the main instigator, and his jokes are often at Mum's expense. "Do you know why they cannae find the Loch Ness Monster up in Scotland? Because it's living in England married to me!"

I happily follow my dad's lead. We are coconspirators in the plots to get a rise out of Mum with fake bugs, cat poop, and many other corny attempts to score points on her. But Mum is easy prey and invites the teasing with such gems as "Well, we are all out of bread, so we'll have to have toast for supper." I find myself shaking my head and smiling to myself. I can definitely say that my parents' strictness is balanced with congeniality.

I jump off the couch and go upstairs to get dressed. There is a lot to do today. Tonight is an important event for Mum and Dad, and I want to help as much as I can. Because of Dad's assignment on the yacht, he and Mum get invited to many special events every year hosted by members of the royal family. Dad likes his annual trips to Windsor Castle with the other yotties. Prince Philip, the Duke of Edinburgh or Prince Charles generally host these events.

Tonight, Mum and Dad are going to a ball at Buckingham Palace. Fancy my mum and dad getting invited by the Queen to a ball. Who would think, looking at Dad pottering around his garden in shabby overalls, or Mum sitting with her feet up having a cuppa in front of the telly watching her westerns, that they would be invited by royalty to balls and teas at palaces and castles? It sounds like something in a fairy tale and is definitely a long way outside our simple, working-class lifestyle.

I help my mum get into the new dress bought especially for this occasion, and help her do her hair. I am extra helpful when she is getting ready, because I really want her and Dad to have a wonderful time at the ball. Dad is going to drive them up to the palace in London. They leave early so they have plenty of time to get there. Ordinarily, parking in London is very difficult to find. Dad says with a wink that the palace should have plenty of spaces available. I think he is being cheeky with me.

With Mum and Dad out for the night, I am left alone in the house to take care of myself. I have the television, and I have Schickrys, and Mum bought me some sweets as a treat while I watch the Saturday night comedy shows. Not a bad night. Still my mind wanders to what Mum and Dad might be doing: mingling with members of the royal family, drinking champagne, eating little fancy bites, all while the twinkling lights of the chandeliers dance around the ballroom leaving sparkling flashes on the gowns, tuxedos, and uniforms of the prestigious guests, and across the velvet curtains, gold sconces, and historic oil paintings decorating the walls. I wonder if my mum and dad are dancing to the orchestra, some elegant waltz perhaps. I smile. I bet they make a sweet couple among the elite.

The morning after the ball, I am eager to hear all about it, ready to sketch images in my mind of handsome princes and beautiful ladies in ball gowns and the Queen holding court. My mum and dad got back from London in the early hours of the morning, and are sleeping in late. I sit in the living room reading my book, with Schickrys resting on the couch next to me. I am impatient for them to get up and tell me about the ball at Buckingham Palace. Eventually I hear noises from upstairs. Dad is awake first. I hear him come downstairs and go into the kitchen, and then I hear the metallic *plonk* of the kettle being placed on the stove. Not long after, Mum comes down. With cups of tea in hand, Mum and Dad join me in the living room and tell me about the ball. I soon learn that the night before, my dad earned a unique distinction.

Mum tells the story. "We're driving to London to attend the ball at Buckingham Palace when the fan belt in your father's car broke. Again! It's always breaking . . . remember that time in Scotland?"

"Mum! Forget about Scotland. Tell me about last night!"

"Well, we didn't think we would make it to the palace."

Oh no! I think to myself.

"We knocked on the door of a nearby house and ask to use the phone to call a garage, explaining the circumstances, and the homeowners kindly let us use their phone. The RAC came and brought us a new fan belt. We had a long wait."

"Mum!"

"Well, as Dad was fixing the fan belt, he got oil on his hands and the cuffs of his white uniform shirt. Later that evening at Buckingham Palace, after the Queen had been introduced to her guests, Her Majesty selected someone to have the first dance. As fate would have it, she chose your father. Can you imagine? Out of all the people she could have chosen, she chose him! When the equerry came over to Dad to say that he had been chosen to dance with the Queen, Dad had to say no and explain that he could not dance with the Queen with oil on his hands and cuffs. The honor went to someone else."

Dad adds his personal touch to the story. "I couldn't possibly hold the Queen's white-gloved hand with oil ground into the lines of my hands. Heaven forbid if I got oil on the white royal gloves, and I would have been ashamed for Her Majesty to see the dark stains on my shirt cuffs and for her to think that I don't maintain my uniform properly." Dad shakes his head. "I must be the only man who has ever refused to dance with the Queen of England."

Mum and Dad laugh at the story, but above my father's smile I can see the disappointment in his eyes. Despite his strictness and harsh rules, and his tendency to give me the belt when I am bad, he is human after all, prone to the same emotions of hurt, disappointment, and sadness we all feel. I empathize with my dad. My heart mirrors his sadness. I know what it is like to want something so much, only to be disappointed when it doesn't happen. Sometimes laughing about it is good. But sometimes laughing is just a simplistic coping mechanism used to deal with innate sadness. Poor Dad. I wish he could have danced with the Queen.

I remain sitting on the couch in my own world of contemplation, trying to conjure up the picture of Mum and Dad at the ball and Dad declining to dance with the Queen. Schickrys lies beside me, purring as I absently stroke the fur along his back. I find my gaze drawn across the room to a display cabinet and a photograph of the Queen Mum holding Schickrys in a little basket, taken the day she was presented with the kitten. I wonder if the Queen Mum ever thinks of him or wonders how he is doing. I conclude, probably not. She is too busy with her own amazing life.

Next to the photograph is a keepsake china plate with the image of Her Majesty, looking gracious with her crown and jewels. My gaze moves left toward the painting of the Royal Yacht on the wall above the fireplace. The royals had infused a touch of extraordinary into our lives. I think of how exceptional it is to have parents who get invited to Buckingham Palace, and to be sitting here petting a royal cat. I wonder if my future will be extraordinary, if I will ever have exciting tales to tell. *Probably not*, I tell myself. *Probably not.*

CHAPTER

SIX

A s everyone expects, I pass the national eleven plus exam. I now attend the all-girls grammar school just over the other side of Fratton Bridge. It is the Portsmouth Southern Grammar School for Girls or "PSGSG" as it is known. My education now takes a more serious turn. During the next few years I must decide what subjects to focus my studies on, and what career path I want to take. I am considering becoming a vet because I love animals, so I know I must do well in my science classes—biology, chemistry, and physics. I also want to travel, so my French classes are important. In the background my dance training still hovers as an alternative career path. I secretly want to go to Bush Davies, a theater arts school. I want to dance and sing, and act. I don't mention it to anyone because I am not sure I am good enough. I don't want to be laughed at, or to disappoint myself. As I said, it is an alternative option.

I am at the grammar school. It is early afternoon, and I am sitting in school assembly on a bench, up on the balcony with my classmates and teacher. It is the end of the term when awards are presented. As a lower fourth, I am now eligible for a particular award, and I wait nervously wondering if my name will be called. I haven't said anything to my friends, thinking they will tease me if I say I am hoping for this award. They might even call me a "creep," the name reserved for teacher's pets, and others who try and worm their way into people's good graces. My time at the grammar school has been uneventful. I am quiet in class. I don't speak up. I don't stand out. I admit I am shy. Perhaps it would be best if I don't get any attention after all. Perhaps I won't win the award.

I look at Mrs. Dudgeon, the headmistress, standing on the stage at the front of the hall. She is standing in her black robe at the lectern, reading from pages of notes she has in front of her. There are hundreds of girls sitting on the lower floor of the hall. They are sitting cross-legged, in rows according to year, from third years up to the sixth formers. Their teachers are sitting on chairs around the perimeter of the hall. From my vantage point on the balcony, I look down and I can see them all.

Mrs. Dudgeon announces that she will now name the girls who have won Deportment Belts. As the lower fourths are the youngest and lowest-ranking students eligible, I know that if my name is not mentioned within the first one or two on the list, I will not get the award.

"From the lower fourth, Laraine Denny."

What? Mrs. Dudgeon has read my name! Before I can react, there is a burst of movement and applause from around me on the balcony as my classmates cheer and clap. I feel pats on the back. Oh my goodness! I need to get downstairs to the stage. I am on automatic pilot. I have imagined this moment many times. I have rehearsed it in my mind. I know just what to do, where to go. Getting up from the bench, I rush out of the door behind me, down the stairwell, and reenter the lower floor of the hallway through a back door. I have to walk the entire length of the hall, past the hundreds of girls and teachers with every pair of eyes on me, and me knowing I am blushing bright red at the attention. I walk to the steps at the front of the stage, climb up them to the stage, and approach the headmistress. I shyly receive my deportment belt to the continuing clapping of the entire school and the cheers from my classmates. I thank the headmistress and shake her hand. I make my way back up to my seat on the balcony.

A deportment belt is a special blue cotton-weaved belt to wear around my waist with ribbons dropping down the left side of my uniform skirt to show I am neat and tidy, carry myself well, and am a good example of ideal behavior for the other girls. I was hoping for the honor because as a dancer I have good deportment, I carry myself well, I walk and sit with a straight back, I am attentive to my schoolwork, and I am well mannered. I am the first girl in my year to be awarded such a belt, and when I get back to my classroom, my classmates cheer for me. I am delighted to have accomplished something, put my name on the record for some achievement.

I proudly take the belt home and show it to my mother, who is in a bad mood. I stand in the kitchen listening to the cruel words.

"Och, yer a clatty bitch. Yer rooms never tidy. Yer a mess. Yer no a guid example of anything. Only an eejit would give ye that belt."

She promptly tells me that I won't have it long, and that the school will probably take it away from me once they realize I don't deserve it. Mum says she doesn't understand why anyone would give it to me.

I am horrified by my mother's unfathomable meanness. What is wrong with her? My mother's words tear my self-esteem to the quick and contribute to the gulf developing between us. I go up to my room, where I sit on my bed and inspect the deportment belt. I feel its weave with my fingers. The light blue color will stand out against the navy blue of my school uniform skirt. I am pleased with myself. I am angry with my mum.

The issue of the deportment belt is simply another in a long line of grievances I have with my mother. Mum and I don't get on well these days. We are always arguing. I can't do anything right. I am growing up. I have my own opinion on many things, but Mum doesn't want to know, or care, about what I think.

I think back on a prime example from a couple of weeks ago. I was given my first dance solo on pointe and asked to perform it at a gala concert. I was Anne Boleyn and dressed head to toe in black as I danced around the stage interpreting Anne Boleyn's last days in the Tower of London. I wore a suitably woeful expression on my face as I held a bible and prayed while I danced. The performance concluded with me on my knees front and center on the stage with the bible clutched to my chest. As the last note of the music played, I abruptly let my head fall forward, symbolizing Anne Boleyn's ultimate beheading. My performance garnered appreciative applause from the audience, and I left the stage thinking that I had interpreted the role well, and that I had captured the drama of that last moment of Anne Boleyn's life. My self-satisfaction was short-lived as my mother came to me in the dressing room and chastised me.

"You didnae smile once!"

I knew then that there are things I will do in life that my parents will never understand, things that their less-educated minds can never comprehend. One thing I do comprehend is that the older I become, the greater the rift between us grows, and the more the rift widens, the greater my desire to leave home.

I go down for my tea. An awful smell hits me as I enter the kitchen and on seeing Brussels sprouts on the dinner plate left for me, I automatically say, "Yuck!" I announce to Mum, "I'm not eating the Brussels sprouts."

"Don't talk to me in that tone of voice!"

Tone of voice? I simply stated a fact; I didn't raise my voice or anything. She is making a fuss over nothing.

"If you don't like my cooking, you can get out of here. Miss high and mighty now you have a bloomin' blue belt."

Mum's words make me mad and I dramatically respond, "Fine! I am leaving this house and never coming back!" I support my statement by getting my coat and shoulder bag from the hall, opening the front door, and stepping outside. To accent my leaving, I slam the door behind me, making its glass tremble at the shock. I shall run away. Again. We'll see how sorry Mum is when I don't come back and she starts worrying about me.

This isn't the first time I have run away after arguing with Mum. I do it every now and then: not for too long of course, and always when my dad is away as he is the one person I fear will punish me for being bad.

It is just after six o' clock in the evening. It is still daylight out so I walk down Penhale Road, which takes me to the main street of Fratton Road, where I wander aimlessly up and down the street, even though the shops close at five o'clock and there is not much to do or see at this time. I purposefully stride along the cement-slabbed pavement, pretending to anyone who sees me that I am going somewhere, even though I am simply walking up and down the streets, biding my time, making a point. Once I think I have been away from home long enough so that my point is made, and that Mum will be suitably contrite after her mean behavior and worried if I am all right, I go back home, my way of showing my forgiveness of my mother.

However, tonight, unknown to me, Dad comes home while I am "running away." I return to the house ready for my mother's apology and contrite expression. I close the front door, step into the hallway, and immediately hear voices in the living room. I hear my father talking to my mother. Instantly I recognize my misstep. My father's anger always results in hurt; more often these days it's a beating with his belt or hand rather than being sent to the corner. There is a momentary glint of hope that he will understand my side, have some compassion for me having to deal with my mother's berating comments. But as soon as he appears in the hallway, the momentary glint of hope runs away, leaving me to deal with my father's anger alone.

To say Dad is angry is an understatement. He yells at me because how dare I be so disrespectful to my mother. How dare I talk back! How dare I stand up for myself, try to explain my position, believe I have any rights in this house! My father is ready for me. I get the belt. Even though I am now the same height as my father, I cannot escape the punishment as he is so much stronger than I am and his iron hand holds me tight at the wrist as the leather whacks against my behind, each painful blow causing me to cry out so I can barely hear my father's words above my own crying. Between each slap of the belt he shouts.

"If you don't want tae live in this hoose, you don't need to."

Whack!

"You don't disrespect yer mother, and you don't talk back tae her."

Whack!

"This is not your hoose. You have nae rights here." Whack! "You're nothing. Get oot!"

He drags me by the hand, through the hallway, then through the living room, where he opens the back door and shoves me out into the garden, locking the back door behind me. The curtains are then drawn. I can't see into the house. I am locked out for the night, left to sleep in the garden.

I look around me but see little. The day has gone and taken every pixel of color and light with it over the horizon. The grass is damp, as always. There is no place to sit or lie down. Not that I want to as my behind is sore and each movement I make accents the pain. I turn and slowly walk toward the back of the garden, finding my way among the familiar silhouettes, along the small path behind the garage, avoiding the walls because I think there will be spiders and other life forms crawling around. I make my way to the other side of the garage where I know there is a pile of wood. I feel for and find the wood, carefully climb onto the pile, and sit down, finding my balance and as much comfort as I can on the logs. I sit upright. There is nowhere to lie down to sleep. Not that I want to sleep. I am too scared of the scuttering noises uncomfortably close, and the blackness obscuring every-thing around me. *At least it isn't raining,* I think, searching for anything positive during this miserable moment. But it is cold. I pull up my knees and I wrap my arms around them, curling into a ball, hoping I can keep myself warm. My stomach rumbles angrily. I didn't have any dinner. Perhaps I should have eaten the Brussels sprouts.

I momentarily despise my parents. They don't treat me like a person. They don't even try to see things from my point of view; they treat me like I'm an idiot, like I don't have a brain. I am growing up, evolving as a person just like anyone else at my age. Just as they once did. I cannot wait to leave home, to become my own person, to live by my own rules. I don't need my parents. I don't need anyone!

I sit on the logs for what seems like several hours, occasionally adjusting my position to try and give different portions of my behind relief from the painful contact with the hard wood. The only light is far above me. I see the moon rise and pass across the sky. I watch the stars circulate above me. I try to think good thoughts, uncertain of how this event is going to play out.

In the early hours of the morning, I hear the back door of the house open. Dad comes out to the garden and quietly calls me back into the house. Apparently remorse has replaced his anger, and he now feels bad that he had left me outside in the dark. Dad apologizes to me with a big hug, making everything better. Everything is now okay. We have made our peace. Dad loves me in his own way. His punishments are harsh, no doubt a product of his own strict upbringing, but designed to teach me to be good, and to keep me on track in life. I hold nothing against my dad, or mum. I know they only want what is best for me.

CHAPTER

SEVEN

I stand in the middle of my parents' bedroom, surrounded by the hush that I always associate with this room. The bay windows on my left side invite light into the room to enhance the pink, white, and wood-accented décor, while the double glazing holds back the noise from the passing traffic outside. The only sound permitted is the "tick" of the small gold alarm clock on one of the bedside tables. I look at my mother's dressing table standing in the bay window, at the pink and white porcelain dishes holding my mother's jewelry and other knickknacks, sitting on white doilies, all mirrored in the glass behind. These dishes are familiar Mother's Day presents from forty-plus years ago. I look toward the double bed and then generally around the room. This is my parents' private province. Cloistered away in drawers and behind the closet doors are items my parents kept away from the prying eyes of others, but now, as the dutiful daughter I am required to encroach on my father's privacy.

Mum has asked me to go into Dad's wardrobe and sort through his belongings. It is something Mum doesn't want to do herself. When she speaks about getting rid of Dad's things, her tone is one of disengagement. She doesn't want to know what he had. She doesn't care. Mum wants none of it.

"Get rid of the lot," she instructs me. "No reason tae keep anything."

I am unsettled by my mother's disengagement from the process; that she doesn't even want to look at my father's personal belongings and see what is there. I don't question my mother's directive, but I want to. It doesn't seem right that she can just throw everything away as if it has lost its value. I pause for a moment and realize that perhaps without my father everything has lost its value. But doesn't Mum want any mementos? Is there nothing of his that she wants to hold on to, to remember him by? But Mum was always of a certain mindset, and if she doesn't want any of Dad's things and they are to go out, then out they go.

I move to stand in front of my father's wardrobe, staring at the wooden sliding doors hiding my father's personal effects, his clothing, things he kept away from the inquisitive, even Mum. I reach out and slowly push one of the doors to the side, its movement rumbling across the metal track, and like a theater curtain revealing a scene, the door makes way for the display of male belongings, dutifully hanging or lying where they were last placed. I run my hand through the garments hanging along the rail, and then crouch down to see what lies on the wardrobe floor. This access to my father's privacy feels odd, intrusive. I have the strange, awkward feeling we all feel when going through someone else's property, even when we are given permission to do so.

Mum's instructions are that Dad's clothes are to be piled into plastic bags to be taken to the charity shop. I find large black plastic bags and do as directed, not liking the offhanded way Dad's clothes are to be discarded. I sort through my dad's sweaters, his ties, other items. They are—were—personifications of him. His gray plaid sweater was worn so often it was an integral part of my father's wardrobe, and his light gray raincoat was worn most times my father left the house. His ties with navy insignia were worn for special events with his shipmates. As one by one I take items off the hangers and hooks in the wardrobe, I picture Dad wearing each of them, but they all have to go.

There are shelves on the one side of my dad's wardrobe that house a carefully arranged assortment of objects. I see some of my father's many books, mostly car mechanic books and maps of Britain. The roadmaps are familiar to me. When I was old enough, I became the family navigator on long trips to and around Scotland. Mum didn't have the patience for that sort of thing and was happy to pass the job off to me. I came to know the route to take on the motorways and main roads from Portsmouth to Glasgow, the roads from Glasgow to such cities as Edinburgh and Ayr, and how to get to tourist areas in the Highlands such as Loch Lomond and Loch Ness.

Dad's car books are named by car model and year. They are grimy from being handled by oily fingers, no doubt Dad's as he followed the manuals' instructions for repairing a car. One thing Dad had known well was how to take care of a car. It was rare that his own car had to have work done for it to pass its MOT each year. Many times he was a life and money saver for family and friends whose cars would come to a halt, followed by a call to Dad asking if he could please fix it. I make a mental note to see what makes of car my family members have and if anyone can use these books.

I find several bottles of good whiskey standing on the wardrobe floor. No doubt gathered for the next *Hogmanay* party bringing in a New Year that Dad will not see. On a shelf of the wardrobe are coin collections in blue presentation boxes and plastic sleeves, some minted for special events, including the wedding of Prince Charles and Lady Diana, and some collected from his travels abroad. And there are his medals from his navy days, including the Royal Victorian Medal and citation he had received from the Queen. I know the whiskey will be given away to family and friends, and Mark will get the coins and his grandfather's medals.

At the back of the wardrobe is a cardboard box, its weight challenging my heaving and pulling as I drag it out into the daylight. I kneel on the floor next to the box and pull back its cardboard flaps to see what is inside that is so heavy and immovable.

I feel a cold hard sphere, my dad's bowling ball. I smile. It immediately brings back a fond and irrepressible memory.

I am about ten years old, standing at the end of the long hallway in the old house on Fraser Road. It is dark except for the light at the end of the hallway coming in from the window in the top half of the front door. I remember the context of the moment.

Mum and Dad took up ten-pin bowling at the Navy, Army and Air Force Institute's social club or NAAFI. For Mum it was something she could do to alleviate the lonely months while Dad was away at sea. Mum even won many bowling trophies, which was surprising because I didn't think my mum was good at anything. Then Dad decides to buy himself a bowling ball. I remember the day vividly.

Dad brings his ball home from the shop, and he, Mum, and I stand at the kitchen end of the hallway as Dad proudly shows it to us. Dad is delighted with his first custom-made black sphere, ready to show the world that he is a contender on the lanes.

"Look," he explains to me, pointing to the holes in the surface of the ball, "it has finger holes measured for me and is a specific weight designed to optimize my swing and increase my score."

I am impressed. Mum doesn't have her own ball and she has trophies.

The long narrow hallway in the house looks just like a bowling alley and to Dad a tantalizing alternative to the real thing. "I'm goin' tae give it a try," he says, unable to resist the chance to practice his swing and show off his dexterity.

My father rolls his sixteen-pound missile along the hallway with as much energy as he can, aiming for the imaginary ten pins standing in formation at the end of the alley. I watch the black ball rolling away from us at high speed. My father's aim is straight. The ball goes straight down the hallway, straight through the wooden front door, straight through the metal gate beyond the door at the end of the forecourt, and straight into the street beyond. The explosive sound of the ball making contact with wood then metal reverberates around the house and echoes out onto the street, where neighbors come running out of their homes, startled by the explosion and by the sight of what appears to be a black cannonball sitting in the middle of the road.

In the house I stand behind my mum and dad as the three of us look along the hallway to the circle of light entering through the round hole now bored into the front door. I look in disbelief at the sight, scared to say a word, waiting to see how my parents will react. They react as they often did, recognizing the humor in the incident, my father's quiet chuckle and my mother's raucous laugh letting the world know, it is okay. We walk out into the street to explain the incident to the neighbors and to look at the damage, all while having a good laugh. I learn from my parents that sometimes the best thing to do when bad things happen is to laugh them better.

I run my hand one more time over the cool surface of the bowling ball, grateful for the memory. I smile at the ball as if it is a dear friend, then fold the flaps of the box back into place, deciding to leave the ball where it is for the time being.

As I continue my unhurried removal of items from the wardrobe, the void replacing what was my father's tangible presence grows. Where there was once personality within the wardrobe is now emptiness, and it is my doing. I feel like I am throwing away things that had meaning to my father, I feel as though I am betraying my dad, and I don't like it. I take a deep breath and allow rationale to take over my thoughts. Mum doesn't want these items. I cannot take them. Those with value will be given to family members, and the remaining items will go to those in need. I tell myself that logically, this is for the best.

I continue filling the bags with clothing, but not without a final caress of each item in tribute to Dad and the memories each article holds. I look back at the now empty wardrobe. The onerous task is done. I have contributed something to taking care of Dad's affairs, but I still feel unsettled, that what I have done is insufficient, insignificant. I want to contribute more than simply throwing his life away. I need to do more, but what?

Something else to be taken care of is selling Dad's car now sitting forgotten in the tiny garage at the end of the garden. The garage is really more of a shed, just big enough to fit the most compact of cars and nothing more. Dad had to drive the car out to the alley behind the house if he wanted to work in the garage. This last car is smaller than other cars he had owned in the past. A product of the more fuel-efficient and harder financial times I suppose.

The garage will have to be gone through, sorted, and cleared out as well. I have already taken a quick look inside the tiny space, and found a messy assortment of my dad's toys—his old tools from his days as a young carpenter's apprentice, as well as planks of wood everywhere, and PVC pipes, wrenches, pliers, tins of nuts, bolts, screws, light bulbs, and other items he had owned as long as I could remember, all the same hue of dust. Without poking around too much, and not wanting to disturb the spiders I knew would be lurking among the planks of wood, electrical cords, tins of screws, and lord knows what else, I took a general inventory and told Mum that perhaps my cousins will be best at clearing out the garage and taking whatever they want and can use. It will incentivize them to clear out the garage and save me from the onerous task.

I stand one last time in the doorway of the garage, peering into the dim space, aware of the odor of sawdust and grease drifting out past me, happily released into the fresh air, but my mind focuses on the light blue metallic body of the car. I momentarily envision my dad meticulously working under the hood, keeping the engine in good shape, so it could uphold its duty of driving the family around town.

I have fond memories of Dad and his car. When I was a child, it was usual for the family to go for a Sunday drive in the country. My mind flashes back to one Sunday in particular. My dad had retired from the navy and was working for a small engineering company.

It is early morning, and the owner of the company Dad now works for has organized a treasure hunt by car for his employees. We all meet in teams of two in a remote location on the top of a hill in the middle of the Hampshire countryside somewhere north of Portsmouth. Each team is given a map of the local area showing various villages and places of interest, together with two lists: one is a list of anagrams which are the jumbled names of local villages, and the other list is of things to be found in the villages. We have to drive to the villages and look for either the name of a publican, which is typically found above the doorway to a pub, or a telephone number from a public phone box, a name on a gravestone, the name of a cottage, and a few other random things. One item will be found in each village. So we are to unscramble the names of the villages where we will find the items, identify which item is in which village, and then end our trip at a designated country pub for lunch. The key is that whoever found all the items in the villages and got to the final destination, the pub, in as few miles as possible is the winner. Dad's boss records the odometer reading of each car, and off we go.

It doesn't take long for Dad and me to unscramble the village names, find the villages on the map, and determine what we think will be the shortest route to all of the villages and then to the pub for lunch. The tiny village hamlets and country roads are in for a surprise as almost two dozen cars and teams unleash their competitive streak on what should be a quiet Sunday morning.

We all make a funny sight, like something out of an old British comedy. Cars driving madly into unsuspecting villages where they have barely stopped before people jump out and begin running across the village square to the door of the village pub to see if the publican's name matches that on the list. Other team members are falling over each other trying to squeeze into the small space of a public telephone box to find out what the telephone number is and if it is the one on the list. Other people are running around the square looking at the quaint names of the cottages and trying to match the names to the one on the list. Dad and

I are caught running up and down the aisles of a village graveyard trying to find a name on a gravestone just as people begin
coming out of the Sunday service at the village church, no doubt
wondering what these crazy people are doing running around a
graveyard on a Sunday morning.

Cars drive up and down narrow country lanes. At one point,
Dad and I see another team's car coming down the other side of
the road. Both cars stop abruptly, each team looking at the other
and wondering why the other team is going in the opposite direction and does the other team know something we don't? More
than a few times we see cars driving backward along the lanes or
through the villages, the team trying to minimize their mileage
by driving in reverse.

Dad and I complete the treasure hunt and find our way to
the pub for lunch. We are not the winners but that doesn't matter
as the morning event was a fantastic way to do something with my
dad as a team and to have some fun. Dad and I spend little time
together these days, so it is great we had this one Sunday together.
The teams sit in the country pub, having lunch and exchanging
stories of the crazy morning and the reactions by the unsuspecting villagers to the bombardment of their normally sleepy hamlets and the desecration of their Sunday mornings. The moment
and memory stays forefront in my mind for days as I share our
silly Sunday antics with friends and family.

The smell of dust and oil pull my mind back to the present. I run
my hand along the roof of the car, stroking its smooth surface as if
it was a family pet, and not without deserving a little love. I reach
down and slowly open the passenger side door which is the closest
to me and, looking into the shadowy inside, immediately notice
my dad's blue woolen hat sitting innocently on the passenger seat,
left there the last time Dad had driven the car, waiting expectantly
for the next outing—which never came. Bending forward, almost

in deference, I pick up the hat and hold it close to my face so I can see it in the dim light. I study it intently. My fingers play with the woolen knit, feeling its softness in my hands. Dad had left the hat on the seat ready for the next time he drove out into the cold spring air. It is now evidence of a life interrupted midstride. It is a symbol of how our presence can give inanimate objects personalities. It is a personification of my father, and now, left alone in this dark mausoleum, it conveys his recent story. Dad hadn't known that the last time he parked his car in the garage, it was truly the last time. I clutch the woolen hat to my chest. Tears well in my eyes. My chest tightens with the hurt.

CHAPTER

EIGHT

Mum is pregnant. And at her age! She's in her midthirties! I've been an only child for thirteen years, and everything has been just fine as far as I can tell. I am sitting cross-legged on my bed, back against the wall, arms crossed, and my mind in a sulk. Why do my parents want a new baby? Why am I not enough anymore? What's wrong with me that makes them want another child? I know I get into trouble a lot, but I work hard at school and try to make them proud of me. I look across the room at my trophies and other awards won in dancing competitions taking pride of place on my dressing table. I tell myself that I am good at things. Why do they want another child after all this time?

And surely my mum is too old? I shudder with discomfort and my nose wrinkles at the thought of sex and babies. My face muscles contract farther as I add a frown and pursed lips to my expression. I internally shout, "Yuck!" as my thoughts expand to Mum and Dad, and sex and babies. I cover my face with my hands, embarrassed that my mum is having a baby and at her late age.

Mum and Dad tell me the news in a matter-of-fact way as we are all in the kitchen getting ready for tea. I am washing my hands in the sink when Dad mentions that Mum is having a baby, as if it was common information inserted into an everyday conversation. Not believing what I am hearing, I turn to stare at my dad, then at Mum, ignoring the running tap behind me, and the waterdrops falling from my hands onto the kitchen floor. Are they talking to me? They are looking at me, so I assume the news is for my benefit. I stand motionless, saying nothing, my mind in a whirl as it is suddenly clobbered with images of babies and nappies, and baby bottles, and crying, and this baby belonging to my parents, and actually coming to live in this house.

Mum and Dad look at each other and smile. "You'll have to help out more around the house," my dad says. "The ship is off abroad in a couple of months. I won't be around when the baby arrives, so you'll have to help Mum."

And that is that. No explanation as to why this baby is necessary. No interest in whether I have any questions, or how I feel about the news. My input is not required. My feelings are irrelevant. It is a done deal and apparently no concern is given as to how this will impact me.

Going up to the refuge of my bedroom and sitting on my bed, I sigh dramatically, and keel over sideways so I am now lying on my bed staring up at the ceiling. I feel deflated, like the news has pummeled every ounce of air out of my body. A new baby in the house will create a lot of changes. The idea of change worries me; it gnaws at my mind as I fret about what a new baby is going to mean to my home, and my life.

I look at the four walls of my room. This is my domain; this room will still be mine; nothing will change in here. The baby can interrupt life outside of my bedroom, in every other area of the house, but my bedroom is my sanctuary. When the baby comes, I will simply live in my bedroom. Thinking of this drastic and monumental alteration in my life makes my mind flash with every synonym I can think of for change and interruption: upheaval, mayhem, intrusion, disturbance. I think, *cataclysmic*. That's it! That's the perfect word to describe this unprecedented event. I then focus on how to best deal with this incident that is going to change my entire life, rewrite my entire future. After giving it much thought, I rationalize that I will have to take this new wrinkle in my life day by day and see what happens.

Over the next days and weeks, Mum and Dad's focus is on each other and the impending new addition to the family. All they talk about is the baby, names for the baby, doing up the spare bedroom as a nursery for the baby, telling everyone they know about the new baby.

Of course everyone we meet—from family and friends to neighbors and acquaintances—says to me, "Oh you must be so excited about having a little baby brother or sister!"

I'm not excited but dutifully reply with as much enthusiasm as I can muster, "Oh, yes. Very excited." All followed by a wan smile and a desire to immediately escape this confined bastion of new baby-ism.

My parents seem to have momentarily forgotten I exist. They don't seem to notice whether I am in the same room as them or not, so I leave them to their plans and make myself at home in my bedroom away from the pending baby doom. A new baby is coming into the house as I am preparing to leave. Such is life!

As I am not the center of my parents' attention, I turn my focus inward and preoccupy myself with what I am going to do. I am growing up and it is time to start planning my near future. I will be old enough to get a job in just over a year, shortly after the baby arrives. I look forward to earning my own money and being able to buy my own things and not relying on whether I am getting pocket money or not. Then I have to study for and take my General Certificates of Education, or GCEs, and then it will be time to try and get into a college and decide the career path I want to take. I ignore the other occupants of the house, distancing myself from them. I focus instead on my own end goal, my plan to leave home and travel the world.

The discomfort I feel at the thought of a new baby in the family diminishes as I rationalize "what does it matter?" My plan is to leave home as soon as possible and another child will not make a difference if I am not here. I slowly adapt to the impending baby atmosphere now permeating the house.

Mum has been extra moody lately. I try and help out around the house the best I can—do the shopping, do whatever she needs. But it seems I can't do anything right. I could be a million miles away and if something goes wrong, it is my fault. The yolk of her egg is runny. It is my fault. The bus didn't come on time, so it is my fault. I get home from school and Mum yells at me because for some unfathomable reason, and even though I was sitting in a classroom all day, it is my fault the milkman only brought one pint of milk instead of two. It must be her pregnancy, I justify, not liking this woman called Pregnant Mum. If this is what having a baby does to a person, I am never having children!

A week before the baby is due, I am sent to stay with Mum's friend Betty and Betty's daughters, Heather and Nancy, until after the baby is born. I think this is to give Mum some peace and quiet and to get everything ready for the baby's arrival without having me underfoot. Dad is away at sea. We will send him a telegram when the baby is born.

I am at Betty's house, sitting on the living room floor playing a card game with Heather and Nancy, when we get the news by phone that Mum is in the hospital, giving birth. Betty, Heather, and Nancy start twittering excitedly about the baby and if it will be a boy or girl. The card game is abandoned, replaced by gender speculation. I feel a little odd. My heart is racing. I am surprised to think that perhaps I am feeling excited at the impending event. Perhaps I am simply being influenced by others around me, and their months and months of excited and incessant chatter about the new baby. Like them I wonder if I will have a little brother or sister, and not knowing what to expect piques my interest.

A few hours into Mum's labor, Betty's phone rings, and she

relays the message that Mum is having problems giving birth and there might be a problem with the baby. This news is a shock. Not once have I considered that there might be difficulties with the pregnancy, or that there could be health risks involved. No one had told me that. I'm not prepared for bad news. What are the problems? Is Mum going to be okay? Is the baby going to be okay? Betty doesn't have the answers.

I sit myself down on the stairs next to Betty's phone, anxiously waiting for it to ring again and hoping for more news, all while praying everything will be okay. The excitement that had made me jittery has now turned into tight knots in my stomach. I am nervous, worried about my mother and the baby. I realize with some surprise that what happens to my mum and the baby matters to me, that I really care about them. The baby is no longer some generic third person designed to disrupt my life and something to think about in the future tense. The baby is about to be a part of our family, my little brother or sister. I envision a helpless baby struggling its way into the world and I have the responsibility as a big sister to make sure everything is okay. I have always considered family to be people you can count on to be on your side when things get tough. I must live by my own beliefs. I must be someone the baby can always count on to be there when needed. I must step up and embrace the role of big sister.

The phone rings.

I watch as Betty answers it, and I listen carefully to her side of the conversation. I see the frown take over her face. She glances sideways at me with a worried look. She says, "I see," and puts the phone down.

Betty places her hand solicitously on my shoulder and explains softly, "The umbilical cord is wrapped around the baby's neck, and with every contraction your Mum has, the cord tightens around the baby's neck, and it is strangling the baby. The doctor is going to do an emergency C-section to try and save the baby." She pats my shoulder. "It'll all be fine."

All I hear are "strangling" and "emergency" and "try and save the baby." The images in my mind are horrifying, and I feel ashamed and guilty because I had given little thought to my mum or the baby and now they are in trouble. Gut-wrenching knots form in my stomach. I put the palms of my hands together and do something I rarely do. I pray. "Please dear Lord. Keep Mum and the baby safe." What if my mum doesn't make it? What if the baby dies? Oh no! I glare at the phone daring it to ring. Please let everything be okay.

Minutes later the phone rings and Betty hastens from her living room to answer it. I grab the railings of the banister tightly, hoping for better news. Betty puts the phone down and turns to tell me with a smile. "You have a little baby sister and mum and baby are doing fine." I am thrilled. Mum and the baby are fine. I feel the knots in my stomach unravel and the muscles in my body relax. The awful thoughts pounding away at my brain are replaced with sunshine and sheer joy, all feelings I never once thought I could feel about the new baby. A little girl. My baby sister. For the first time in my life I have a sister.

Mum said if the baby is a girl, she will be called Loretta after the actress Loretta Young. Loretta. I like that name for my new sister. Betty goes out to the post office to send Dad a telegram while I sit in the house and discuss the baby news with the other girls. The baby is all I can talk about. She is the only thing I want to talk about.

Mum and the baby arrive home from the hospital. I meet Loretta for the first time, gently taking the baby cocoon into my arms and holding her as my mother shows me. I sit down on the living room couch and stare at this little person who shares the same parentage as me. I study the soft lines of her face, her sleeping eyes, her dark eyelashes, and the shock of dark hair she has already. Mum sits next to me and shares with me that originally she wanted a playmate for me, but it took thirteen years for her to have another baby. For the first time I understand why my parents wanted another child. I look at the sleeping baby and rock her gently. She smells of baby powder and milk. She melts my heart. She won't be a playmate, but I will take very good care of her, and I do.

I become Loretta's second mother, doting on her and taking care of her. Loretta is my real-life doll, and I change her clothes, brush her hair, and dote on her as any big sister would. I take Loretta out in the pram, enjoying this new companion and dimension in my life. I talk to Loretta and play with her, and love it when she falls asleep in my lap. I am just as excited as Mum and Dad when Loretta gets her first tooth, starts crawling, and takes her first steps. I vow to be the best big sister ever and to always be there for my little Loretta.

CHAPTER

NINE

It is early morning as I walk through the thick, damp London fog, kicking moist clumps of rustling leaves beneath my feet and relishing the momentary quiet of these historic streets. I see the ghostly images of the houses standing guard along my route, and the looming shadows of trees peering out of the mist to see who deigns to pass beneath their branches before they dismissively fade back into the grayness of the early morning. I am sixteen years old and finally have left home to come to college in London.

For the first time I taste the independence I have craved for so long. But with the independence, I discover the trials and tribulations of making my own decisions and then having to live with the decisions I make. My proverbial wings begin to grow. The safety net of life my parents once offered me begins to dissipate. My world expands and once expanded, there is no going back.

My moving to London is the conclusion of a whirlwind year of life-changing decisions, decisions I routinely question during my morning walks. I am still not sure I made the right choice. There was no doubt in anyone's mind that I can have a career as a professional dancer and the next step along that path was to study at a full-time theater arts school. My expectation was to audition for a school such as Bush Davies near London. There I can learn to dance, sing, and act—learn everything that I want to do, everything that I have dreamed of doing all these years. I know many dancers who have studied at the school and gone on to be professional performers. But then my dance teachers, Paddy and Susan, add a twist to my options. I am told that I should audition for the Royal Academy of Dance in London.

I know nothing about the Royal Academy. Of course I have heard of the Royal Academy for music and drama, but not for dance. I don't know anyone who has studied there. I discover that the academy focuses on classical dance and related studies. There are no singing or acting classes. The academy only takes about thirty-five students a year from the hundreds who audition from all over the world, putting a student studying there in a prestigious position. The teachers are icons in their fields: former prima ballerinas, historians, the "who's who" of the dance world, and the patron is Her Majesty, the Queen. But in my mind it all sounds very posh, and very unlike me.

Another problem is that I am only sixteen and you have to be seventeen to be a student at the academy. I have just taken my school General Certificate of Education or GCE O-level exams, and have two years until I am eighteen and can take my A-level exams. I wonder if I am to wait until I am seventeen to audition, or spend the next two years studying for my A-levels and then audition for the academy when I am eighteen. Paddy, Susan, and Mum tell me it is silly to wait another year until I am seventeen, that I should audition now, who knows what might happen? I am reluctant to agree to the audition. It seems like it will be a waste of time: they won't accept someone like me, and, besides, I want to sing and act and not just dance. Why can't I just audition for the arts school, which will take me now that I am sixteen?

The adults persist, telling me that anyone can get into the other schools but think of how special it would be if I was successful and accepted into the Royal Academy. Both Paddy and

Susan tell me that I am the first pupil they have ever had that they thought could make it into the Royal Academy. And, I would be the first girl from my hometown to be accepted into this prestigious school. Feeling mentally browbeaten, I agree to go to London to audition.

The audition is on a Saturday. Dad drives Mum and me up to the school located in Battersea in London. I have received information about the audition, what I am to wear, and what the audition will entail. Mum comes into the academy with me while Dad wanders off in his car. Mum sits in the waiting room while I am shown the changing room and change into my pink tights, black leotard, and pink pointe shoes. I pay little attention to my surroundings, finding the whole environment intimidating and not a little austere. I would rather focus on what I have to do, the familiarity of taking a dance class, and put the unfamiliar aside. My hair is already tied up in a bun. I catch a glimpse of myself in the changing room mirror. *I look the part,* I tell myself, *but can I dance the part?*

The audition process begins with the first twenty of us, all girls, taking a ballet class in one of the main studios. The academy building is a converted warehouse, and its studios are large, airy, and light with sprung wooden floors that are a delight to dance on. The ballet class is taught by a Miss Vivienne. A panel of people sit behind a table at the front of the studio, studying our every move as we are taken through a barre, and then brought to the center of the studio for center work and across the floor work. They write notes and whisper to each other from time to time, but nothing is said to us directly. I know that the panel is made up of important balletomanes. I ignore them.

The exercises given to us are made up of familiar steps and movements, and I put every effort into executing the steps with my best technique, including my best posture, and with an element of performance. I point my feet as hard as I can. I lift my legs as high as my strength allows. I force my hips to turn out like they have never turned out before. And I smile. A relaxed, pleasant smile, exuding the appearance of effortless movement, which in actuality is the antithesis to the unnatural pushing and stretching occurring below my waistline. I find myself enjoying the audition because I am not nervous since I have no expectations and nothing to lose.

After we have completed the dance class, we are given a "Thank you" by Miss Vivienne and taken out of the studio. I have no idea how well I did in the dance portion of the audition. I am in automatic mode in this strange environment. I simply follow along with the other girls as I am told, and find myself sitting and waiting outside a trailer in the parking lot of the academy. One by one we are asked to go into the trailer where our physical attributes are evaluated.

I enter the trailer, where I am immediately weighed, my height taken, and then asked to lie down on an examination table. Also in the trailer is Miss Vivienne, a Miss Penny, and a doctor. The doctor lifts and twists my legs, testing my flexibility. Miss Vivienne hovers nearby, scrutinizing the doctor's examination and my physical qualities. A measurement is given to Miss Penny, who writes it down on a notepad. My knees are bent and my leg twisted to the side to determine my turn-out. Again Miss Penny notes the angle of my knee and leg. I know I do not have a dancer's body because my tendons are short, and every inch of flexibility I have developed over the years to allow me to lift my legs high in *arabesques* or *penchés* has taken a lot of work and stretching exercises, unlike those lucky dancers who are born with natural flexibility.

After the physical examination I am asked to sit on a chair, and I am interviewed by Miss Penny and Miss Vivienne. I am asked about my dance background and why I want to study at the academy. I give the appropriate answers.

"Why haven't you auditioned for the Royal Ballet Company?" Miss Penny asks, referencing this other elite ballet school and training ground for the many prima ballerinas of the day.

"I never ever thought I was good enough!" My simple but

true answer generates a look between the two women suggesting an appreciation of my honesty.

The day ends, and the audition is over except for the two hours of interrogation by my mum as we travel back home in the car from London to Portsmouth. "What did you do? How did it go? Were the other girls any good? What did they say to you?"

I respond to Mum's questions with as much patience as my tired mind and body allow. Then finally in a moment of quiet I think to myself that I am glad I did the audition. It was an interesting experience, but I honestly cannot see myself studying at the school. It will be two or three months before the academy makes its selection. I put the audition to the back of my mind.

Early summer comes, and with it madness, as events occur in such a swift sequence they cause me to panic because life-changing decisions have to be made, and made soon. First, I am told by my dance teachers that they received a call from the Bush Davies school to ask if I was applying for the school this year because they would like to have me there. Apparently I am well known to the staff of the school from my years of competitions and exams, oftentimes before adjudicators who teach at Bush Davies. I am delighted with the news. I want to go to the Bush Davies school. It is the epitome of my years of dreams of singing and dancing, and acting.

Paddy and Susan advise that before I make a decision, I wait for the results from the academy. I agree but with no expectation that the Royal Academy will accept me. I am too young and, in my mind, not good enough. Within days I receive a letter from the Royal Academy. I have been accepted into the school for the next term, even though I am only sixteen, and will be one of the youngest students ever to be accepted. The one proviso is that I earn six O-levels. Shortly thereafter I receive my GCE results. I have earned six O-levels.

Suddenly and amazingly my future has great options, and I have a dilemma. Should I attend the school of my dreams, so I can learn to sing, and dance, and act like I have always wanted to do, or should I attend the prestigious Royal Academy?

I am persuaded by the adults in my life to attend the Royal Academy, their urgings enforced by the argument that a position at the Royal Academy is unique and something that should never be turned down. I do not feel exuberant at the prospect. Quite the opposite. I feel as if a high hurdle has been placed before me with everyone expecting me to leap over the hurdle with ease. Only I know how daunting it is to face that seemingly impossible hurdle head-on, and I know that if I fail, it will be me, not anyone else, who is going to be humiliated.

With some misgivings I agree to accept the position at the academy. But I admit that the day I went to the grammar school and told Mrs. Dudgeon, the headmistress, that I will not be studying for my A-levels because I have been accepted to the Royal Academy gave me a feeling of pride. Seeing the look of surprise on her face, and the faces of other teachers and my friends when I told them where I was going to study, helped me better recognize the importance of this unique and prestigious opportunity I have been given.

And here I am, walking along the historic streets of London, kicking orange-hued leaves as I make my way to the prestigious Royal Academy.

I settle into my new life studying at the Royal Academy quite quickly, although having dance classes two or three times a day versus the once a day I am used to requires me to develop more stamina than I have. The days seem overly long during the first weeks as the extreme physicality of the day leaves me exhausted. But I persevere; the other girls, my new friends, are having the same issues, and we motive each other to get through the days.

I find my dancing is on par with that of the other students in my class, who are all girls. Similarly, my agile mind adjusts to my new studies of physiology, anthropology, and psychology along with music, ballet, character and modern dance, and Labanotation, a shorthand notation for dance moves. We are being trained not only on dance and performance, but also how to teach. Hence the classes to help us understand the human body, the mentality of a dancer, how to help those we might teach with disabilities or attributes that make dancing physically difficult. We also have many teaching classes, where we learn syllabi, and how to convey dance exercises or choreography to others. While I still hope to dance professionally once my three years at the academy is over, I see the advantage in taking the teaching classes to give myself options in the years to come.

One of the first things I learn at the academy is the plan for our three years. The first year, we will be pulled apart, our dancing and technique will be criticized, we will find we are doing nothing right, and every flaw that we have in our dancing will be highlighted again and again. The second year, we will be put back together again; our dancing and technique will be exactly as the Royal Academy requires. We will have learned our flaws and be ready to embrace the "proper" technique. During our third year, once we have mastered the required technique of the Royal Academy, we will be allowed to develop our own style and performance quality.

The classes during the first weeks are tough. All I hear is: "You!"—no one has yet learned my name—"Your back is too arched. More turn-out on your right foot. Your foot is sickled. Your arm is too bent. Your arm is too straight. Your weight should be more forward over your big toe. Your weight is too far forward. Your derriere is sticking out. Your posture has collapse. Your body is too stiff." I remind myself this all comes with the territory of becoming a better dancer. I try not to take the constant criticism personally but simply to tune out any harshness in the comments and do as I am told. It is difficult. I am putting two hundred percent into my work. I am trying to make the physical adjustments to my posture and technique shouted at me again and again and again. I am exhausted and my body is sore, yet for all my efforts I do not appear to be making any progress. The criticism keeps on coming.

My one respite from the academy is the girls' hostel I return to at night. It is in Earls Court, a nicer part of London, but the hostel, once the home of a wealthy family, now houses seventy girls. Some of us are students; others are working. There are five of us Royal Academy girls sharing one small room. Our five beds take up almost all of the space in the room, but sharing a room keeps the cost down. We are from different parts of the country, and our parents are from different walks of life. Sharon is from Liverpool and the daughter of a single mum. Anne, Lynn, and Elizabeth are from working-class families like mine. Regardless, at this moment in time we have the same lives and share the same rituals. Every night before we turn off the lights in our room, we have to make sure important possessions are stored away or at least off the floor so the mice that come into the room during the night do not chew or poop on something important.

"Is that James?" Anne points to a gray flash running across the floor from under the wardrobe to under my bed. We have named the mice.

"It might be." I kneel on the floor to look under the bed. "It is hard to tell James and Jasper apart." I see a shadow in the corner with two beady eyes cheekily twinkling at me. "I think it's James." Attending the Royal Academy might seem prestigious, but it comes with living in cramped quarters shared with mice.

Meals at the hostel are challenging. The hostel has two tiny kitchens, each with one stove, to serve the seventy residents. There are no refrigerators. I have a grant from Portsmouth City Council which gives me six pounds a week for my expenses, which include my bus fare to and from the academy—located across the Thames River in Battersea—and money for food and anything I need for my studies at the academy. I believe my parents are supposed to add money for my support, but they do not. They think the council gives me enough to live on, but it is difficult to attend a prestigious school without sufficient funds to obtain the tools I need to maximize my studies.

I find that a can of soup, if watered down, can last a couple of days. That with a loaf of bread will provide three of my evening meals for the week. By lunchtime, and after hours of dance classes, I am hungry. My lunch is usually a can of soda. It fills me up, and gives me enough sugar and caffeine energy to survive the rest of the day without it costing an arm and a leg.

None of us girls have cars so we make our own way in our own time to classes. My bus fare is almost two pounds for the five days, so to save money I start getting up early, and I walk to the academy in the morning and back to the hostel at night. It is about an hour and a half each way, but it is not that much longer than the bus, which can take just as long as it meanders through the busy London traffic.

It is my morning walks to college that give me some semblance of sanity. These moments allow me to visit my thoughts and evaluate my life. I am used to walking, and I like these short moments alone away from my four chatty but nice roommates, and away from the constant oversight of the academy faculty. My route takes me from Earls Court through Kensington, and through areas with big fancy houses and communal parks.

I walk partway along the trendy area of the Kings Road and then turn south to walk over the Battersea Bridge, the four chimneys of the Battersea Power Station reaching high into the sky on my left side. On mornings when the fog is at its thickest, walking across the bridge is eerie. I see only three or four feet in front of me. I see the pavement disappearing into the fog. It is like I am walking into nowhere. The bridge railing on my right side separates me from a gray misty nothingness. Only the images in my mind of what is beyond the fog allow me to continue on in comfort.

The first class of the day is always a ballet class. I am already warm from my lengthy walk and use the exercises to prepare me for the day ahead. Classes are taught by the premier educators of the topic: former prima ballerinas, professors of history, medical doctors. Costume making is taught by a woman who is head of the BBC's costume department. My education is the best. I don't appreciate it. All I know is that I can only buy one pair of pointe shoes a term. I won't have money for a new pair until I get my grant installment for next term. Pointe shoes always go soft within weeks of wearing them every day for ballet classes. Most of the term I am left struggling to dance as perfectly as I can on soft shoes. I don't have access to a sewing machine outside of school, and my efforts at making a handmade tutu and character skirt as part of my costume class are sadly deficient.

I realize that the money my parents have put into my dance career over the years must have seemed like a fortune to them. My parents didn't make a lot of money, but somehow they always came up with the money for class fees, competition entrance fees, exam fees, the pianist fees, or the many tutus and other costumes I needed. They were told they needed to pay for this, or buy that, and they did. As a child I hadn't appreciated what they did for me. I hadn't considered what it took to make sure that the money was always there. I just accepted it all, no questions asked. I appreciate it now as I learn the importance of money and recognizing that it doesn't always go very far. Part of me wishes that Mum and Dad were still taking care of me, that I hadn't been in such a hurry to grow up and leave home.

It is Friday night. Dad is driving me home to Portsmouth. Most weekends I don't go home because I don't have the train fare. Now and again, if Dad is at home, not away at sea, he might drive up to London on Friday night to pick me up for the weekend, then drive me back on Sunday night.

Dad opens the conversation. "I'm sorry, love, but I have sad news."

I turn to look at Dad. "Oh no! What happened?"

"We had to have Schickrys put down yesterday."

"What? Oh no! Why?" I feel as though my heart has stopped beating at the news. My lovely Schickrys is gone. "What happened to him?"

"I took Schickrys to the vet a few days ago because he kept throwing up his food. The vet discovered he had stomach cancer, and it was the humane thing to have him put down." Dad gave me a moment to digest the news. "I didn't want to tell you before. I didn't want to upset your studies, and I thought it better to tell you in person."

"I didn't get to say goodbye."

"I know, love. I'm sorry. It was for the best."

The car continued on along the narrow country roads of Hampshire, but I saw nothing as I stared ahead out of the window. My tears blurred my view. My lovely Schickrys is gone.

My father further explained that he had to immediately report the cat's death to his commanding officer, who then had to report it to the admiral, who in turn had to report the death to Clarence House, the Queen Mother's residence. In due course, through the chain of command, my father was told he needed to get a death certificate from the vet. Not even knowing if such a thing existed for a cat, Dad dutifully returned to the veterinarian's office, where apparently the vet was apoplectic on learning that the cat he had euthanized was a royal cat.

"Oh my God, I've killed the royal cat! I've killed the royal cat!"

My dad relays the vet's funny response to me, trying to lighten the mood, and I offer a wan smile in return. To me the vet's reaction is a reminder that even the simplest of events can have a larger significance than we are aware of, and that even the seemingly most ordinary of persons can have some contact with prominence. My moment with prominence was having a royal cat snuggle with me, giving each other hugs and love. That prominence is now gone. Common sense told me that Dad is right. It is for the best. But I feel oh so sad. The grown-up part of me recognizes that death is the only certainty of life. The child in me isn't ready to accept the inevitable loss of those we love.

It appears my family is not quite done with prominence. During my last year at the academy, I learn that Dad is to be recognized for his long naval career and service to the Queen. He is honored on the New Year's Honor list of 1976. He is to be awarded the Royal Victorian Medal for his services to the Queen. The Royal Victorian Medal was established by Queen Victoria in 1886 as a reward for personal services to the sovereign or royal family, and as a token of royal esteem. I need permission to be excused from my studies at the Royal Academy to attend the ceremony at Buckingham Palace. I take my mother's note to the principal's assistant, a lady called Kim, who wears her hair in an austere knot on the top of her head, and an even more austere expression on her face. This is the Royal Academy, and it is a privilege to study at this edifice of artistry. Even if you have a severe injury, you are expected to drag yourself into class. There are no days off, and no excuses for missing class.

When I go to the office to request a day off, Kim growls at me and asks with her usual sarcasm. "And where do you think you are going? Buckingham Palace?"

I answer sweetly, "Yes, actually."

It is one of those sweet moments of comeuppance that we imagine or wish will happen, but which rarely do. The look on Kim's face as I hand her the note from my mother detailing the ceremony we are to attend at the palace, and could Laraine please have the time away from the academy, is priceless. I savor the moment, enjoying the look of shock on Kim's face and the rare feeling of satisfaction when an annoying person is put in her place. Above all I enjoy making this self-appointed doyenne of the academy's office understand that I might be a nobody attending the school on a council grant, but my dad is worthy of being recognized by the Queen at Buckingham Palace. I get a lot of mileage out of that feeling.

Attending the ceremony at Buckingham Palace is a fascinating experience, not only because it is something few people get to do, but also because it is exciting to be part of the historical ceremonies of the monarch bestowing commendations upon her subjects in appreciation of their service. I see persons being knighted, and of course my father receiving his medal from Her Majesty.

Beforehand, as we drive through the gate into the courtyard of Buckingham Palace, there are guards in red jackets and tall, black bearskin hats standing to attention at the gate. A long line of impressive-looking luxury cars drive through the palace gate ahead of us, all without creating any movement from the guards. But as my dad's little blue car approaches the gate, the guards come to attention and salute him. On the windshield of Dad's car is a pass bearing the insignia "RY" for Royal Yacht, making Dad in his little blue car worthy of the attention and salute that those passing ahead in their Rolls-Royces and Bentleys do not earn. Dad says he is "dead chuffed," pleased at the recognition. I am pleased for my father.

After the ceremony we stand in the courtyard of the palace with other dignitaries for official photographs. The photographer takes a photograph of Dad and his medal, and then with the whole family. Looking around at the surreal scene, I understand that this is a tremendous recognition for my father. Receiving this medal from the Queen is a long way from where Dad began his life. It belied his modest upbringing in Glasgow, living in the tenements, and his limited education after having to leave school when he was fourteen to learn a trade. It is a lesson to us all not to accept difficult circumstances, and low odds of success, and not to give up. With the right effort and attitude, we can all go far in life.

My three years at the academy are over. My time at the academy is without memorable achievement other than being able to add my studies at the academy to my résumé. I don't want to teach; I want to dance, I want to perform, and I want to travel and see the world.

My parents give me a set of bright red leather suitcases as a graduation present. The message is clear. They have done their bit for me. It is time for me to move on and take care of myself. So I do. I am nineteen. I find a professional dancing job abroad. I pack my red suitcases and leave home for good. It is time for me to live my life and do what I want to do: time to leave my family behind.

CHAPTER

TEN

I stand by the bay window in the living room, watching Mum's small figure disappear along the road toward town. She drags her shopping trolley behind her, and I watch it bump along the uneven pavement. It is full of glass bottles and jars Mum is taking to the recycling bin in North End. I offered to go with her, but she declined, stating that she must get used to doing things herself, and without Dad driving her around. She is right that she must adjust to living without Dad, but it shouldn't be too much of an adjustment for her. As a navy wife she spent months on her own responsible for the house, bills, children, and maintaining a job.

Still, I am annoyed that my seventy-two-year-old mother has a fifteen-minute walk to the bin because the local trash services will not pick up glass from the houses. After working and paying taxes for more than fifty, almost sixty years, one would think that the elderly like my mother would be shown some consideration. That she shouldn't have to walk fifteen minutes both to and from a recycling bin just to dispose of glass containers. But that is what life has become here in England. My mum just accepts it as what has to be done these days. I remind myself I do not live here and I am not entitled to an opinion.

Mum turns the corner and disappears from my view. I sigh deeply, my heavy breath the only sound in the now quiet house. For the first time in a long time, I have the house to myself. I move away from the window and sit on what was Dad's chair, leaning back against the soft leather, allowing my muscles to relax and my entire body to sink into the pliant cushions. For a few moments I am going to sit and do nothing, a respite from the long list of projects to be taken care of for Dad, and Mum, before I go back to the States.

Loretta decided to go back to her own flat, apparently unable to deal with Mum, me, or anybody. The taxi is called, and Loretta leaves before Mum or I know she is gone. It seems Loretta wants solitude to grieve in her own way, without impertinent questions from others, and without intrusion into her feelings. I try to be understanding, recognizing my sister's bad mood is the result of her constant struggle with diabetes-related illnesses and the daily buffet of medicines she has to ingest just to stay alive. Mum telephones her every day to check and make sure she is okay, but Loretta won't answer the phone. Mum explains to me almost apologetically that perhaps Loretta doesn't have her prosthetic on and can't get to the phone easily. Or that Loretta is often moody and it is best to just let her be. She will snap out of it when she is ready.

Mum has often told me about Loretta's moods, or that she is often in such a bad or sarcastic frame of mind that her comments to family members are biting. Our father had most often been the recipient of the sharpest jibes: "He was so stupid!" "He was clueless." "C'mon, Dad, you're so bloody slow!"

Loretta forgot or ignored the fact that Dad was there for her day and night, taking her to doctor and hospital appointments, to the store, wherever she wanted to go and when. He put new flooring in her flat, and he redecorated the bathroom and kitchen, making them more manageable for Loretta's disabled state. All Dad got for his efforts was Loretta's disdainful comments, her put-downs, and he took it all with stoicism, and without criticism.

I recognize now that perhaps Loretta's comments to our father, and even my mother's constant scolding of Dad, were simply how the three of them communicated normally, and no offense was meant or taken. But to me, who rarely spent time with my family, and who didn't interact with them on a daily basis, the comments seem harsh, cruel, disturbing. I can't fathom talking to my parents with the malice or the disrespect that Loretta displays and without any embarrassment or apology. I conclude that my long-distance relationship with my family doesn't allow me to understand the dynamics of the family, be privy to the daily challenges they face as the different personalities, the elderly and the disabled, are forced to cohabit. I can't get mad at Loretta. I don't have the right.

Loretta's behavior is excused by the family as being the result of her illnesses, the side effects of the numerous medicines she takes every day, the pain she has to endure, and her frustration at her disabled life. Loretta's day is one long schedule of pills, and she does nothing without considering her location, where the nearest bathroom will be, and when and what she can eat so she doesn't throw up or have diarrhea anywhere outside the house. Over the past few days I have occasionally looked at my sister, noting the contracted body language, the hunched shoulders, drooping head, anxious expression, and wondered if Loretta is in pain. No point in asking, I surmise. Loretta will deny it if she is, or tell me to mind my own business if she is in a mood. But, Loretta's moods are tempered by her infectious laugh, a deep, throaty, dirty laugh unexpectedly emanating from the soul of this little person whose appearance has never aged beyond sixteen, and who looks the picture of innocence. People outside the family think Loretta is a sweet girl. She is, I decide, despite her moments and moods; she wouldn't intentionally hurt anyone, Mum and Dad included.

Still, a small part of me can't help but be frustrated by my sister right now. There are certain times when we all have to garner that extra amp of strength, endurance, energy to get through difficult challenges, particularly times such as now, when we each need to take care of Dad's arrangements. To me the list of things to be done is overwhelming, and I really need help to organize Dad's affairs, his funeral. Loretta has been very vocal about being involved in the arrangements. She has definite ideas about how certain things should be done, the music to be played at the funeral, the prayers to be said, but is now unavailable to help in making those decisions, or to even tell me what Dad's favorite hymns and prayers might be. I know I am being ungracious, churlish, and even childish. I haven't done this before, and I want to get it right, which includes taking as much burden as possible off of Mum's shoulders. But the other side of the story is that I don't want Loretta to be angry at Mum, or me, because the arrangements are not to her liking. I don't want to give Loretta reason to argue that matters were taken care of without her input, that she has been deliberately excluded. But realizing that time is limited, and the sooner the tasks are completed the sooner Mum can settle into her new life as a widow, I put aside the worries about my sister and my own inabilities and move forward to get the job done.

I look across the room and see the messy streaks of paint scribbled on the opposite wall. Decorating the living room was to be Dad's final project although no one knew that at the time. Dad had moved aside the furniture and had begun painting one of the walls. To this day it remains an unfinished series of brush strokes in a slightly different shade of cream from the rest of the wall, evidence of a clear intent to return to the task but not knowing that the opportunity would not be there. Mum makes note of it from time to time. She has made up her mind to eventually sell the house. It is too big for her. She wants to get away from Dad and the memories. But before she can do that, the walls have to be finished being painted.

Earlier this year, I was told that Dad had begun acting strangely. Mum called me one Saturday afternoon as she usually does, and described how the night before, Dad had gone into the kitchen where she had left some pizza for him, and instead of putting a slice of pizza on his plate, he put the dishtowel on his head. He came back into the living room and sat staring at Mum from under the dishtowel, disoriented. Mum had laughed at the incident. She hadn't shown any concern over it to me. But when I heard the story, I found it disturbing. It had worried me. But I couldn't tell if Dad's behavior had truly become odd, or whether Mum was simply exaggerating to tell a good story.

A short time later while I was chatting on the telephone with my sister, Loretta told me that recently Dad had picked her up in the pouring rain to drive her to an appointment. On the way back they had stood outside in the street for forty-five minutes while Dad had searched and searched his pockets but just couldn't find his car keys. The heavy rain thoroughly soaked them both as they stood there waiting for him to find his keys, but he just couldn't coordinate his thoughts with his searching. Loretta told me how she was angry and frustrated because she kept telling Dad to look in a certain pocket, but he just wouldn't look there. I firmly told Loretta that Dad should be taken to the emergency room—immediately. Something was obviously wrong with him. They needed to get a doctor to look at him as soon as possible. Loretta had said, "Oh, he doesn't want to have to spend hours in that place waiting to be seen."

I was angry and frustrated when I heard Loretta's comment because surely sitting for a few hours in the emergency room and getting this bizarre behavior evaluated by a doctor was preferable to Dad doing something to seriously hurt himself. I was shocked at what appeared to be a callous evaluation and dismissal of Dad's very strange and concerning behavior based upon inconvenience, because no one could bother taking him to the emergency room or wanted to sit there for hours with Dad. I had taken a deep breath and again reminded myself how some people see things differently than I do. They don't necessarily understand or agree that waiting a couple of weeks for a doctor's appointment is not always the better way to go.

A few weeks later I received an unexpected telephone call from Mum. She routinely called on a Saturday afternoon. This call came on a Sunday. This Sunday I was told that late the night before, Dad had stood up to go to bed, but he was dizzy and unstable and staggered around the living room, eventually falling down backward and hitting his head on a cabinet. Mum called for an ambulance, and Dad left the house for what would be the final time. The doctors discovered that he was in bad shape. He was very ill. His kidneys were not working, a condition I found out later could have been remedied if he had gotten medical attention earlier than he did. His body was not getting rid of the toxins, and it was affecting his cognition. Dad was also diagnosed with Hodgkin's Lymphoma. He had trouble with his lymph nodes the year before, but was told they were successfully treated. However, this time was different. Because his body was poisoned from his lack of kidney function, he was unable to put up enough of a fight to beat the attack on his body.

Part of me is still angry with my mother and sister. In my mind they were charged with my father's safekeeping, making sure that when he did something odd, they checked it out, or at least showed enough concern to bully Dad into getting it checked out. Talking with them both, I believe that was never done. And my mother was an auxiliary nurse, so surely she had a heightened duty to watch out for them all. The other part of me recognizes that my dad must have had some awareness of what was happening to him and how he was feeling for many months at least.

Mum had once mentioned to me that my father went to his doctor's appointments alone. Mum wasn't allowed to go, and he didn't tell anyone much about the visits. I believed this was true after I saw him in the hospital and saw the way his kidney failure had made his body swell, and saw the fluids secrete through his skin, having nowhere else to go. I could only believe that he did not want to go into the hospital, that perhaps the fight for him was not against the disease, but it was to stay at home in familiar surroundings and with his family for as long as possible because he knew that once he was admitted into the hospital, he would never leave.

When it comes down to it, I can be as judgmental of others as I want, but the truth is, my opinion has no value because I had not been here. My information comes secondhand from others, not from my dad. I had not experienced what Mum and Loretta had experienced, and I have to believe that they were in the better position to judge. All I can do now is to ensure that all moves forward smoothly with no recriminations, regrets, anger, or guilt because any such feelings cannot change what has happened. We each have to live with the past. It is indelibly shaped. But we can still mold the future into something more positive.

I stare at the streaks of paint. They are like bold strokes of graffiti on the wall announcing "Dad was here!" Except that he isn't anymore. I feel sadness begin to infuse my body but then abruptly push it away.

Stop being so morose! I tell myself. *Snap out of it!* In response to my own admonition, I jump out of the chair, leave the heavy atmosphere of the living room to find something more positive to do.

"I'm back!"

I hear Mum at the front door. I go to her to see if she needs help.

"Hi, Mom. Everything all right?"

"Fine, love. I bought some wine and a bottle of Cinzano to take to the party tonight."

Of course. The party. I had forgotten about it, or perhaps deliberately pushed it to the back of my mind, uncertain that going to a party at this time would be a good idea for Mum, for any of us. But my cousins, Karen and Andrew, are known partiers, and they wanted to get the family all together while Mark and I are still here in England.

"I'm looking forward to it," Mum says matter-of-factly, no strain in her voice. "It'll be good to be with the family and do something fun."

I study Mum for signs of forced bravado but see none. I conclude that perhaps Mum is right. A party is just what we all need.

At my cousins' house, the clan gathers en masse. The furniture is pushed to the sides of the room, leaving a space for everyone to dance. The lights are dimmed, the food is prepared, and the drinks flow. The music plays and the dancing begins. The family all sing along to party favorites, both young and old stomping their feet on the floor to a raucous performance of such favorites as Slade and *Mama Weer All Crazee Now.* Everyone is familiar with the moves, and dance in unison, even the babies of the family. The sadness of my dad's passing is momentarily trumped by the triumph of the living, the next generations of the family moving forward as they should.

My parents had always enjoyed a good party and between the navy socials and my mum's work socials, my parents had enjoyed an active party life. When I was a child, there were many occasions when Dad would come home late at night from a "do" with his naval buddies and, after having had a considerable amount to drink, create a good-natured ruckus in the house. Mum was no better. She loved her Cinzano and would watch Saturday night telly with a couple of drinks in her. I remember coming home from a date one Saturday night and finding my tipsy mum lying on the couch watching television and asking no one in particular why they had bowling balls lined up along the front of the telly? They were footlights along the front of a stage, unrecognizable to my mum's intoxicated brain.

But this night at my cousins' party, I watch without criticism as Mum drinks, dances, and sings with the family as we all celebrate our bond, knowing that we can rely on each other, through thick and thin. Mum is her usual funny self, full of piss and vinegar, with a quick retort for every comment. She is the epitome of what we call "cheeky." Mischievous, quick-witted, having fun, and quite intoxicated.

Even Loretta has emerged from her flat and her mood to enjoy the party. I watch as she dances, balancing herself between her prosthetic leg and her cane. I admire how she doesn't let her disability slow her down.

For the first time in many days I allow myself to "let go." I have a few drinks. I dance with my cousins. It has been a long time since I have danced, and despite feeling awkward at first, as I begin to relax, I find myself enjoying the familiarity of moving to the music, my feet following the beat, my body movements accompanying the steps. I watch everyone around me, smiling and dancing. The clan is having a great time. The party was a great idea.

The hours are passing in song and dance and people enjoying each other's company, then, unexpectedly, Mum's Scots brogue cuts into the din.

"Where's Ian? Is he in the kitchen? Where is he? Was that him I just saw?"

Instantly the party comes to a crashing halt.

People stop dancing. They stop singing, ignoring the music as it incongruously plays on. All eyes turn to Mum. She had forgotten. In the fervor of the party and shrouded in an intoxicated haze, she had forgotten that Dad was gone. For more than fifty years they had gone to parties together, as a team. This is the first time she is without him. But, she had been sitting in a big armchair near the door of the living room when out of the corner of her eye she had seen someone walk down the hallway into the kitchen. A man who in her mind looked like Dad and, as was normal for her, she questioned where he was going, what he was doing.

Everyone is silent, and as the reality begins to filter into her intoxicated mind, she begins to cry.

"Where's Ian? Where is he?"

My heart breaks. "Oh Mom!" I don't know what to say to her. I don't know how to make it better.

My mother's face crumples in misery, tears begin running down her cheeks. She shakes her head and closes her eyes.

"I want Ian. I miss Ian."

She is pitiful. My heart weeps with her. The family looks at each other, silently asking each other what to do. I kneel down beside my mother, hugging her tight but saying nothing. I don't know what to say. I simply hope the hug will make up for the missing words of comfort. My mother cries. It is the distressing lament of a woman wanting her man, not wanting to accept he is gone forever, that she isn't going to see him again. Poor Mum. For me it is heartbreaking, gut-wrenching.

The mood has changed. The party is over. People around us begin to move discreetly, turning down the music, grabbing their coats, quietly thanking the hosts, and making arrangements among themselves to get home. I continue to hug my mum, trying to console her. But I need to get her home soon. It is going to be difficult. We have to walk because we have been drinking. One of Mum's friends who doesn't drink has a car and room to drive Loretta to the house. Loretta can't be expected to walk the distance home with her artificial leg. But Mum, Mark, and I will have to walk. I gather Mum's things, and help her put on her coat while fussing over her as if she is a little child, urging her to turn around and put her hands through her sleeves. Mum is still crying, softly now, her cheeks wet with the evidence of her grief. I pick up my mother's handbag and my own, and taking my mother gently by one arm, I guide her to the front door. My cousin Steve and my younger cousin Cameron say they will walk us home to make sure we don't get lost and to make sure we get home safely. It is kind of them. After seeing us to the house, they will then have the return walk back to their own homes. The walk home that should have taken us about ten minutes takes much longer. We are delayed by the impromptu concert in the street.

It is the early hours of the morning as we say our goodbyes and step out into the sharp night air and begin the walk home. We are an odd-looking bunch. Steve and I, both older adults, the young adult Mark, Cameron the teenage boy doing his good deed of escort duty, and the old lady singing at the top of her lungs. I am not sure if it is the fresh air hitting my mother mixed with the alcohol in her system, or what it is, but as soon as we begin walking along the road, my mum's demeanor changes. She begins to giggle and sing, and she is loud. The quiet of the night is shattered by her raucous voice singing—I don't know what—but what should have been a walk in a straight line along the pavement becomes a meandering dance as my mother wiggles and wobbles from side to side with the rest of us tracking along with her, making sure she doesn't fall, while at the same time gently guiding her forward.

I nervously watch the houses around us for signs that we are disrupting the sleep of the occupants, hoping that no one will call the police so we don't have to explain the unfortunate circumstances. We are lucky. No lights suddenly come on in any of the houses. Nor are there signs of movement behind curtains or of people looking out of their windows to see who is making the disturbing racket. Meanwhile Mum keeps singing, loud but surprisingly in tune. More surprising is the strength of the voice coming out of her tiny frame. She is funny, though the circumstances are somewhat tragic. I gently urge my mother homeward. I become the parent chastising the wayward child, my tone serious, my words fruitless, my smile a reflection of my rolling eyes and shaking head. My cousins and son are laughing. Mum is a character.

The April night is cold, brisk. Despite our thick coats the cold finds vulnerable spots on our hands and faces and unkindly cuts into us like a sharp blade. The walk is long. I am more than ready to get back to Mum's house. The alcohol is wearing off, leaving me feeling tired. I want my bed. Mum keeps on singing, oblivious to the time of night or the spectacle she makes. We walk down to the end of the street, past the park, and onto the main road. We turn the corner, and after walking a couple more blocks, we eventually get to the house where Loretta has the lights on ready for us, and the kettle on the boil.

We usher Mum into the living room, and settle her down. I then go to the kitchen to prepare some coffee for my mother, leaving everyone else to keep Mum company. Taking the coffee into the living room, I find Mum surrounded by family, and in a poignant frame of mind. She has reached the fanciful state of drunkenness where everything is good, and she loves everyone. In her slurred Scots accent, she holds court, grandly announcing to those seated on the floor around her how much she loves them all.

I sit down on Dad's chair, leaving the rest of the family to attend to Mum. I look across at the opposite wall and the broad streaks of off-colored paint put there by Dad. I pray that everything remains good and loving in the morning when Mum remembers that her reality has changed forever.

CHAPTER

ELEVEN

"*L*ook there! Out at the horizon. I think that's it sailing in now." The other three girls and I, all dancers, follow the line of Sheila's arm to where she is pointing out across a blue expanse of the Caribbean Sea. It is still very early in the morning in this tropical paradise of San Juan, Puerto Rico; the sun is barely up, but we are too excited to sleep. We four girls and Sheila, the choreographer, are standing on the hotel balcony, waiting for our new home to come sailing into the port. I look out and see something on the horizon. It is shapeless at this distance, but I think I can make out smoke trailing above the object. It will be a while before the shape makes it to shore, but for me it gives me that much more time to stand on the balcony and absorb every element around me, from the salty air blowing in from the sea to the humidity of the tropics. I can't believe I am really here, in San Juan, Puerto Rico, looking out at the Caribbean Sea, looking down on palm trees, and listening to the faint foreign words spoken by persons walking along the sand below the balcony.

Within weeks of leaving the academy, I auditioned and got a job as a dancer on a cruise ship, and after a week of rehearsals in London with Sheila, the other three dancers—Susan, Jenna,

Cunard Countess docked in Grenada, photo © Laraine Denny Burrell

and Julie—and I are here standing on the balcony of a room at the posh El San Juan Hotel, waiting for the cruise ship to reach its home port. I am effused with excitement, unable to contain my sense of exhilaration, wanting to know what my future holds for me. Here I am in the Caribbean. This is my first time abroad. It is the first port of call of many places I hope I will visit. This is the first class in life's edification, and I am ready for it.

I quickly and easily settle into my new life, embracing each new wonderful day bringing its own adventure of new people, places, and experiences. My work on the cruise ship, the *Cunard Countess*, involves dancing opening numbers for the lounge acts throughout the weeklong cruise. On occasion I might do extra cruise staff duties, but I don't mind as it allows me to meet and interact with the passengers and other crew members.

Time off is spent at the crew bar or disco, or ashore with groups of crew members visiting the tropical beaches and tourist attractions of the places we visit each week, such as La Guaira in Venezuela, Grenada, Barbados, St. Thomas in the Virgin Islands, and our home port of San Juan. I have a new boyfriend who I meet on the ship. His name is Marty, and he is an AB or able-bodied seaman. I spend most of my spare time with him. Sometimes late at night when he is on watch, I sneak onto the ship's bridge, and under Marty's guidance, I take the ship's wheel, the fate of its passengers in my hands. I see new things: a lunar eclipse over the Caribbean Sea; dolphins chasing the ship and playing in its bow spray; flying fish jumping high out of the ocean, momentarily free from their briny home.

Now and again at night I take a moment to myself and sit alone out on the back deck. I feel the ship sway beneath me, and the sea breeze tickle my face. I hear the rhythmic crashing of waves against the ship's hull. I remember those many hours of having to stand in the corner and my imaginations of foreign ports, sailing on the ocean, and tropical breezes, and here I am: my imaginations have become reality. I am so lucky.

Sitting looking out over the dark ocean waves dusted with sparkles from the moon, I recognize a parallel between my dad's life and my own. I think of my dad's naval career and his life onboard ship. I think of my father sailing these same waters and feel an affinity with him. We are both travelers, seamen, escaping the boundaries of ordinary life, seeking and accepting each new horizon open to us.

Living on a ship suits me. I share a cabin with another dancer, Susan, and we never have to cook a meal or clean up after ourselves, or change a bed. There are no rent or utility bills to worry about. Our wages are all ours, and we spend them well on visiting tourist attractions, parties on shore, fun clothes from the ports. It is a carefree time, and I absorb every enjoyable moment of it.

Every Monday the ship docks in La Guaira, the port city of Caracus, Venezuela. Today is my first excursion ashore in Venezuela. Following instructions from a leaflet obtained from a ship tour guide, Marty, our friends, and I find the bus stop and the right bus, and manage to work out the correct bus fare to our destination. The temperature is hot and humid. The ride is uncomfortable and dirty. I don't care that the bus is a rusty dilapidated vehicle that hits potholes and jolts me abruptly upward from my seat. Or that the route is dirty and dry, the dust lying on the street disturbed by the bus and finding its way inside the open windows, coating us passengers in a beige film. This is an adventure, and I look out of the windows left and right, wanting to see everything we pass, not wanting to miss a thing. Shops, some mere wooden shacks, and the occasional cart are lined along the street, selling some things that are familiar, some things unrecognizable. The familiar Coca-Cola® sign hangs over more than one doorway. I see various handmade craft items, hats, and bags, all trying to lure the American dollars of the tourists. I make a mental note to buy a souvenir for myself.

Our destination is the cable car where apparently we can ride to the top of the mountain and look down at the port on one side and the city of Caracas on the other. On the bus we are surrounded by passengers dressed in colorful South American clothes, including ponchos and wide straw hats, the colors a contrast to the brown leatherlike faces of the locals. We friends are riding the bus, looking at the map the ship tour guide has given us, while keeping a lookout for our stop.

Suddenly, several people on the bus begin to clap. My friends and I are startled by the sound and look around, wondering why these people are clapping, and then we look at each other without comprehension. I laugh.

"What are they doing?"

Marty shrugs his shoulders. "Dunno."

It happens again, people clapping for no apparent reason; they are not looking at anything in particular, nothing noteworthy is taking place on or off the bus, and still they keep clapping, not the same people, but different groups at different times. Marty asks, "Should we be clapping too?"

I shrug. "No idea."

We watch the people sitting around us, studying what is happening, the people clapping and the stopping and starting of the bus. What are we missing? Within time it clicks. We begin to understand that in Venezuela, clapping is the way to stop the bus. Nothing fancy; no bells or buzzers. It is a simple solution to a basic need. It is one of the first times abroad that I recognize people in other countries do things differently. Arriving at our destination, we all cheerfully clap our hands, and the bus stops, allowing us to get off.

Once on the cable car we take a lengthy, almost perpendicular ride some distance up the Avila mountainside, looking in amazement at the farms we soar over which are literally carved into the steep mountainside. They are man-made horizontal plateaus of grain and bright green pasture cut into the vertical landscape. It is a mystery how the people manage to live on these farms, let alone how they whittled them out of this unlikely farmland in the first place. It is a prime example of people adapting to their environment, and making the environment adapt to their needs. It is humankind and nature working together to sustain life.

As we ascend in the cable car, the temperature drops. The humid, tropical temperature in the port city is replaced by an icy temperature at the top of the mountain, where a restaurant and skating rink offer visitors some distraction.

From the top of the mountain the main attraction is the view. To the north I look down on the Caribbean Sea, where oil tankers sitting outside the port look like minute ants sitting on a blue canvas. To the south lies the capital city of Caracas sprawled in green hues throughout the valley so far below. This is not England. It is not my own port town of Portsmouth. It is a page in my book of reality; a class in my course of life's education. I take a deep breath, inhaling the thin air, the view, a feeling of excitement and elation. I am very lucky.

It is another Monday and the ship is again docked in La Guaira. I am not going ashore today because there is a rehearsal in the lounge for tonight's show. I am in my rehearsal clothes, standing on the marble dance floor, holding a yellow boa, a prop for our dance number, trying hard to focus on the rehearsal. But the lounge windows and doors are open, allowing a light breeze to visit from the outside and bring in a warm tropical scent that tempts us to go outside and enjoy the day. Julie the dance captain calls to us to pay attention and then begins showing us a dance step, but as she is dancing, the rest of us become aware of vehement shouting in Spanish coming from somewhere outside. The loudness and tenor of the shouting suggests something angry and aggressive, and, ignoring Julie, the other dancers and I run out the door of the lounge onto the promenade deck. We find ourselves watching what develops into an international incident involving the ship, her officers, and the Venezuelan army. An incident underlining my acknowledgement that I am no longer in England and that things are different abroad.

I learn that sometime during the morning after the ship had docked and most passengers had gone ashore, some Venezuelan visitors tried to come onboard but were refused permission to do so because their passes were not in order. The ship's security officer, in proper British fashion, refused to bend the rules. "If they don't have the correct papers, they are not going to step foot on the gangway."

As it turns out, the leader of the group was a high-ranking military official in the Venezuelan government. The security officer's refusal to let this official and his party on board is seen as an insult, and despite the security officer's recitation of the rules, and the need for strict adherence to them, there is no appeasing this vocal, hot-tempered South American. The antagonism is heightened further because the ship's captain is standing behind his security officer. There are rules for security purposes, and if the Venezuelans do not have the proper passes, they do not get on his ship.

The military official angrily left the gangplank and called the appropriate authorities and ordered that the ship be impounded, and for all the ship's crew ashore to be rounded up and thrown in jail. The army is called in, and green-uniformed soldiers line the quay shipside, machine guns pointing at the ship's decks. Gunboats line the seaboard side of the ship, preventing the ship from sailing. I am lucky that I had been rehearsing onboard that morning, otherwise my education might have included seeing the inside of a Venezuelan jail.

I go up to the lido deck where I get a better view of what is going on. Other dancers follow. I lean over the wooden rail on the dockside of the ship and point to the soldiers with their guns aimed at the ship. "Wow, this is serious!" I say. I look at the soldiers looking at us. They stand rigid facing the ship, guns raised, their eyes tracking any movement along the decks. The other girls giggle beside me, making comments on the green men and pointing to the object of their comments. Passengers gather around us with comments and questions on what is happening.

Every few minutes Marty comes to find me and gives me updates.

"They won't let the ship leave," he reports, his own voice sharing my excited tone. Sometime later he tells me, "Captain is communicating with London, and the embassy in Caracas. This is being called an international incident!" Marty quickly walks away to return to his work below deck.

I feel important having someone give me knowledgeable information about what is happening to the ship. Each time Marty appears on deck to talk to me, the other dancers and the passengers turn to listen to his reports. It is exciting for us teenage girls to witness an international drama firsthand. It is an exciting and novel story to share back home.

The ship is scheduled to sail at 4:00 p.m., but that time comes and goes. As the hours pass, I learn telefaxes and phone calls are exchanged between Venezuela and the ship's headquarters in Southampton and London. The captain is not going to back down. Rules are rules, his officer is correct. However, the ship carries Venezuelan passengers, and they need to embark and disembark in La Guaira each week as scheduled, so some compromise has to be reached.

I don't know the diplomacy behind the resolution. I only know that around midnight the crew ashore are allowed back onboard and the ship is given leave to sail. However, the cheeky British captain has the last word. We are hours behind schedule. The ship sails away from the port, but without untying the long guy ropes that tether the ship to the quay. The ship pulls out sideways, rotates a hundred and eighty degrees, and then sails forward away from the port—the guy ropes pulling the concrete quay with it. Only once we are out in international waters does the ship slow enough for crew members to cut the ropes from the ship's decks, allowing the concrete quay to sink to the bottom of the Caribbean Sea. Next Monday we are all back in La Guaira as if nothing has happened.

This is my first lesson in foreign diplomacy.

Every Wednesday the *Cunard Countess* visits Barbados, docking in Bridgetown, alongside warehouses packed with sugar cane harvested from the island's farms. Anytime I go ashore, Marty carries me piggyback from the ship's gangplank to the dockyard gate because I absolutely won't walk on the quay. The sugar attracts cockroaches by the tens of thousands, and they scurry across the quay, creating a brown crunchy carpet that makes it impossible to walk without stepping on these offensive creatures. I wrap myself around Marty's back, keeping my legs as high as possible just in case the creatures somehow jump up onto my legs. I know my arms are like an iron vise around Marty's neck as I giggle nervously and "ew" at the sight beneath me.

"Quick, Marty! Let's get out of here!"

"I'm moving as fast as I can. You're a bit of a lump to carry!"

"Ooh they're awful!"

"You're choking me. If I drop you, you'll land right on them."

"Don't you dare!"

We make it to the dockyard gate without Marty dropping me, and to celebrate our success, we head to the nearest bar, where we sit outside under the palm trees and drink tropical drinks with tantalizing names, enjoying the day, our relationship, and the company of friends who join us.

At times I disconnect myself from my companions' conversation and take in the environment. The warm humid air, the fragrance of hibiscus and other flowers I have never seen in England. I think how lucky I am to have this life, to dance and to travel. The fun I have with my friends, the mischief we sometimes get up to. I never imagined when I was growing up that I would get the chance to travel to these places. Had I known, perhaps the dramas and challenges I faced as a child would have been more bearable. My reverie concludes, and I rejoin my companions' conversation, with Marty challenging his mate, "Bet I can down more of these Coco Locos than you!"

A crash course in reality comes one Wednesday afternoon when the ship is docked in Bridgetown. I am lying by the pool, enjoying the quiet of the ship, its hundreds of passengers having been released ashore for a couple hours. Marty is working, painting some divots on another deck, so I decide not to brave the cockroach carpet by myself, but to stay onboard to sunbathe and swim in the relative peace.

It is quiet except for the low hum of the ship's ecosystem at work, and the occasional breeze flapping the flags high above the deck. Suddenly a loud boom echoes around the pool deck, shaking everything from the glassware and bottles behind the pool bar to the sun beds around the deck. Abruptly I sit up. I am confused as I look at what is happening around me. The ship's crew and passengers are running to the ship's port side railing. I get up from my sun bed and follow them across the deck, knowing something has happened but I am not sure what. I see a black cloud of smoke a short way out from the airport, hanging in the sky over the blue Caribbean Sea, dropping bits of something into the water. I am not sure what it is, but I know something is not right.

I retain my place by the railing, wondering what is transpiring out there in the water, unable to walk away from what I instinctively know is a terrible human tragedy. I am aware of the rushed activity around me as a siren sounds and the ship immediately changes into rescue mode as the crew reacts quickly, scrambling to get the lifeboats underway. The doctors and nurses grab supplies and join the crew by the lifeboats, changing from tourist guides to rescuers as the lifeboats are sent over the side and away to pick up survivors.

Matt the bartender pulls out a small transistor radio and places it on the pool bar and fiddles with the dial and turns up the volume. He finds a local news station from which an anxious male voice announces, "There are reports of an explosion on a plane shortly after it took off from Bridgetown International Airport." The scene playing out before me confirms the story. Moments later a news update explains further, "The flight is Cubana de Aviación Flight 455 carrying seventy-three souls, including teenage members of the national Cuban fencing team and five crew members. There are no survivors."

Marty is sent out on one of the lifeboats. When he returns, his voice is subdued as he describes the detritus he saw. He saw pieces of humanity and personal effects—strewn for miles across the ocean—being looted by the locals, who are just as quick on the scene with their own watercraft, going out to find what prizes they could acquire from this tragedy. I hear of watches wrestled from bodiless wrists, and clothing unceremoniously searched for valuables.

For me, the most memorial and nauseating moment comes at the end of the rescue mission. As a crew member I have been summoned to my lifeboat station. I stand on an upper deck, watching as the ship's lifeboats are hoisted back on board. The decks are packed with gawking passengers lining the ship's rail to watch the return of the rescuers. Strips of clothing and other matter are twisted around the lifeboats' propellers, and those on the lifeboat deck and close enough to the hoists reach up to pull pieces of that tragic material from the propeller as a souvenir, something they can share with friends back home, their memento of someone else's loss.

News media worldwide report the story of two bombs being placed on the plane by anti-Castro exiles. The ship is given credit in the newspapers, by local authorities and the authorities in Britain, for being so quick to offer assistance and to step into the rescue role. Still, I cannot forget the images of the pudgy ladies in swimsuits, reaching fat fingers up to the lifeboat's propeller and eagerly snagging a piece of material and slipping it into their bags, gleefully smiling at their companions, sharing the accomplishment. It disgusts me that people are so willing to trivialize tragedy and make it into a carnival sideshow or party piece for their next cocktail hour. Until that day, I had little or no interest in politics or world events, and didn't trouble myself with knowing about anti-this or pro-that groups. It is my first lesson in how quickly life can be extinguished, and part of this lesson is recognizing how harmful intolerance can be. That day I vow to learn tolerance of others no matter how differing their points of view.

CHAPTER

TWELVE

S tepping off the plane, the first thing I feel is the force of the dry heat. Even in the middle of the night, it is pervasive, like a thick invisible barrier of thermal energy, pushing against my body and making movement difficult.

Welcome to Egypt, I think to myself.

The dance group I am now working with, and which I joined after my contract with the ship ended, is The Three Cs, standing for Cool, Calm, and Collected. We have just finished several months of working in Minorca and Barcelona, in Spain. We fly in from Barcelona, landing at the Cairo airport around one o'clock in the morning.

The local agent meets us at the airport terminal and takes us to process work papers, and then brings us to the nightclub at the Mena House Hotel where we are to work. Our first priority is to find out what length of show the hotel wants from us, put together the running order of the show, unpack and set up costumes, and run through music and lighting cues; only once that is all in place are we able to grab a bite to eat. Finding our accommodations and sleeping will come at some later time. Just before sunrise the agent asks us if we would like to see the pyramids when the sun comes up. Naturally we all "ooh" and "aah" at the suggestion and follow the agent out to the Mena House gardens by the pool, where the agent then points out into the dark night.

"Wait," he tells us. "Wait and you will see. When the sun comes up. Soon you will see."

I look out through the dark night toward where I anticipate the horizon will be when the sun rises. In my mind I imagine the pyramids out there somewhere, and I picture them as triangular shapes that will appear out on the dawn horizon. As my friends and I stand there, the black sky lightens, just a shade. I look out, not taking my eyes away for a moment, anticipating this significant sight. The sky lightens little by little as the night slips away, allowing the dawn to take over. I strain my eyes, looking out at eye level, impatient as the sky continues to lighten. But then, instead of a cloth of solid dark, the horizon begins to show silhouettes, shapes of dark and light. And as I stand there watching, waiting, the dawn begins to reveal immense shapes growing right before my eyes, and no more than one hundred yards away, I see blocks forming, and I slowly follow their form upward and lift my gaze as the pyramids are gradually and dramatically revealed to me by the dawn's light. I look up, up, having to lean backward to see the top of these ancient pyramids towering regally above me. I see I am standing at their base. They are so close I feel as if I can reach out and touch them. They have been standing here for thousands of years. And today they now show me my own insignificance as I stand in their dawn shadow.

Every day in Egypt is a learning experience. It might be 1977, but in some parts of the city it is like going back in time, looking at people, ways of life, culture, buildings that have not changed in centuries. In Cairo I see the discrepancy in living conditions between the poor and the rich citizens of Egypt. And, as history would have it, I also have a front row seat to the first Israeli-Egyptian peace talks, being held at the Mena House at the end of 1977. The Mena House is on lockdown and surrounded by high security. While the talks are ongoing, our regular shows are cancelled,

view of Pyramids at Giza, Cairo, Egypt, photo © Laraine Denny Burrell

leaving us to enjoy our days and nights to ride across the desert, visit casinos and nightclubs in the city. One honor bestowed upon us is that The Three Cs is asked to perform shows for dignitaries and the press at the Mena House. The shows are performed at night, on an outdoor stage by the pool and gardens, with the pyramids as our backdrop. To me this is not only a unique performance but also a small way I can be part of this historic step toward peace in the Middle East.

Life in Cairo is different than other places I have lived and worked. I soon learn that in this country the temperatures can soar. Yesterday, the thermometer at the pool recorded 144 degrees Fahrenheit, and the local paper recorded temperatures in Upper Egypt as 156 degrees. Accurate or not, it is bloody hot! What is accurate is that because of the heat, little is accomplished during the day, and the pool is the visitor's best friend.

My practice of tolerance serves me well as living in Cairo,

Egypt, is like living in another world as my history and geography books come to life around me. I see the ancient world playing host to the modern as the pyramids and sphinx and hieroglyphics of the past educate the visitors of the modern resort hotels, the Nile Hilton, the Sheraton. I learn a staple Egyptian term, *Mish Mumkin*, for "impossible" or "no way!"

I learn respect for the Muslim faith, knowing that when the imam calls for prayer from the minaret of the mosque, the faithful will place mats on the floor facing toward Mecca and kneel to pray. I know not to enter a shop during that time as the shopkeeper will be in prayer, his mind somewhere beyond the tangible and commercial function of his store.

The streets are dusty crowds of humanity, camels, goats, and cars and old sand-colored trucks pushing and tooting their way through the masses. I see carts of camel carcasses hauled along the road and wonder whose dinner plate the meat will end up on. Hopefully, not mine. Technology is dated. The apartment building where the other performers and I live has only one telephone number, and every time the phone rings, someone from each of the six apartments answers the phone, and a heated discussion, usually in Arabic, ensues until the proper recipient is identified.

My pale skin, blonde hair, standard jeans and T-shirt tag me as the European woman that I am, and a constant stream of curb-crawlers follow me along the streets, each vehicle moving single file at a walking pace next to the curb. Darker-skinned young men lean out of the car windows, shouting at me in accented English or in Arabic, their hands waving me over to the car. Of course I ignore them, knowing their interest in me is because I am an "uninhibited" western girl and likely to do things that Egyptian women will not do, or are forbidden to do.

Sometimes when I walk through the souk or along the streets, women will come up to me and touch my blonde hair with their tanned hands, sometimes stroking it as if to verify for themselves that my hair is real, and to feel the texture of the light strands. Dark wrinkled faces grin at me and mutter something in

Arabic that I am supposed to understand but don't. I smile nicely at the women, then walk on. I know I stand out; I am different. People here are curious, and entitled to their curiosity. I am the visitor. I have to accept and adhere to local customs, and rather than be offended at the interjections of inquisitiveness, I use them as lessons to help broaden my understanding and acceptance of other people, other cultures.

I see the pyramids on a daily basis since I live on *Shari Al Ahram*, Pyramid Street, and work at the Mena House in Giza across the street from the pyramids themselves. The other dancers and I make many friends, young Egyptian men from wealthy families who pursue the pretty European dancers, knowing we are freer to enjoy life than Egyptian women. We party; we drink. We visit nightclubs and casinos.

The Three Cs's entertainment agent at the time is a tall, handsome Greek impresario named Mimis. He is much older than me, and, despite my travels, is more worldly than I am. He and I are drawn to each other. He knows people and invites me to interesting places both cultural and social. I like that he can take me to nice restaurants, and to see shows by other performers he represents. He makes me feel important. I like that I can have an intelligent conversation with him. When he is in Cairo, we are inseparable.

One night Mimis takes me to play blackjack at the Nile Hilton. At the same table is none other than Egyptian movie star Omar Sharif. I am underage and not permitted to gamble. But who cares? I don't. I am twenty years old and feel quite sophisticated, and I intend to live life to the fullest, and undertake as many different experiences as I can, while I can. I am Laraine, daring, and free, escaping the bonds of my strict upbringing. I am a jet-setter like those women I see photographed in glamour magazines. I travel the world. I play blackjack with celebrities in Cairo. I am feted by men, young and old alike. Life is fantastic.

One evening I am hanging out with a group of friends at an apartment when I am introduced to a Lebanese boy, Tariq, who is known for his palm readings.

"Laraine, let Tariq read your palm. He's very good." Mustafah nudges me toward Tariq.

I laugh, offering minimal resistance. "I don't believe in those things."

"Go on, Laraine, just for fun." This from Elena, another dancer.

After good-natured cajoling I am persuaded to let Tariq read my palm. Intrigued, I give him my hand, palm up. I watch his head bow, and his dark hair falling over his brow as he peers intently at my palm. His long index finger traces the lines etched into my skin. I smile at the gentle tickling feel, enjoying this amusement.

"You will be famous. You are going to make your future husband unhappy. And you will only ever have one child, a son."

I laugh at these prophesies, not knowing whether to believe him or not, but they are notable enough that they stay in my mind.

As special as my nights performing are to me, so are the days where my education expands beyond anything imaginable. I ride camels in the Sahara Desert, including one called Jack Albert, a disgruntled beast doing as he is told only because he is whacked with a stick. Some of the other dancers and I negotiate a deal with the stable owner, and for fifty Egyptian pounds I buy the right to my own Arabian stallion, riding him every day for the time I am in Cairo. My horse is called Prince Philip. I'm not sure why. It is an odd name for a horse, and I have a feeling that the name changes depending on the nationality of the rider. But I am in heaven, my lifelong imaginations coming to life as I gallop flat out across the desert, in front of the Sphinx and the pyramids, and on a beautiful chestnut Arabian horse no less.

My friends and I ride across the Sahara Desert to Sahara City, an open-air nightclub and bar sitting alone among the sand dunes. We take a break at the club, ordering lemonade to quench our dusty thirst before reluctantly returning back across the desert to the stables. For me it is the realization of all those photos I had clipped out of magazines and newspapers as a child. I ride mimicking the forward racing position of the jockeys I had watched for hours on television. But the horse is as untrained as

I am, and the only way I can stop the animal is to ride him into a sand dune where the sandy slope slows down his gait until he is forced to stop.

A guide we befriend from the stable takes our group out for rides beyond the city. We get to know the locals, and we ride out to places tourists never discover. One day we ride south to Sakkara to visit another array of pyramids. The ride there and back takes most of the day, and we ride across the sand hour after hour without meeting another soul. The ride takes us back in time to an era where nomads traveled the desert for days without seeing civilization. I enjoy this experience tremendously. I am pleased to see that there are areas of the planet that are not overcrowded, that are left natural, untouched, even if it is an inhospitable desert.

Another time we ride out into the desert with a local friend acting as a guide, and we come across a sand dune with an incongruous green-painted wooden door placed on its slope. As we dismount from our horses, the guide goes over to the sand dune and opens the door.

"Come inside," he invites with an intriguing smile. "I will show you something special. Few foreigners will see this."

Without hesitation we follow behind him through the door into the sand dune. Inside the door is blackness.

From his pocket, the guide pulls a flashlight, which now offers minimal light.

"We have to go down a ladder and then crawl along a passageway, and then you will see. Follow me."

We follow the beam of the flashlight and are taken down a steep ladder. We are then directed to crawl on hands and knees along a narrow passageway well underground, at the end of which is a room carved out of stone where we are able to stand again. The beam of the flashlight displays a large stone rectangular-shaped object sitting immovably in the center of the small room. It's the tomb of an Egyptian queen. Its existence is something not many locals are aware of, and it's certainly not accessible to tourists. I am awestruck knowing I am one of the few people to have ever visited this queen's tomb. I run my hand along the rough top of the stone tomb, my fingers sweeping the centuries of dust into small piles. I wonder who this queen was, what her life was like, but before I get too involved with my thoughts, the guide says we have to leave. There is too little air in the tomb for us to stay long.

Another ride takes my friends and me out east of the city along an old canal extending away from the River Nile. Here I see people living just as they had thousands of years ago, using zebus hitched to a wheel and walking in circles to grind corn, and fashioning Archimedes' screws to lift water from the canal into the water channels, dirt trenches lining the fields. That same ride takes us back in time to a village untouched by modern day. We are treated like royalty, sitting on mats on the floor in a villager's stone house, drinking a sweet tea. The homeowner is honored to have the European guests. My blonde hair is touched and felt by the women of the village, who are amazed by its color. I am privileged, not because of my own upbringing, but because I have here the unique chance to glimpse these people and their way of life, to be welcomed into their homes, their village, to see and understand that there are different ways of life, and to learn that none are more right or wrong than the next.

"It's time!" Debbie shouts excitedly to the rest of the cast. We all scurry out of the dressing room at the Mena House, ready for the evening's adventure. It is Angelo's birthday, and my castmates, Mimis, and I have collaborated to create a unique Middle Eastern celebration for him. We arrange for a bedouin tent to be set up out in the Sahara Desert near Sahara City. There will be a feast of Egyptian food, we will sit cross-legged on cushions, and there will be a bedouin band and dancing horses as entertainment. Those who have horses will ride across the desert to the site, while others, including Mimis, will drive cars along a dirt road passing near the site.

Now, at two in the morning, after the second show of the night is finished, and costumes put away, the other dancers and I excitedly run across the street to the stables by the pyramids, where our horses are saddled and ready for us. Despite the late hour we are full of vigor and chat excitedly about the party.

"This is great!" I exclaim to no one in particular as I mount up. I feel my horse's own nervous excitement beneath me as he prepares to gallop out at this unusual hour.

Debbie responds, "I am so glad you convinced me to learn to ride, Laraine. What a fun thing to be doing, and in the middle of the night!"

The other riders offer their own similar comments, and as we take off riding around the pyramids and out across the sands of the Sahara under a full moon, the uniqueness of the occasion is not lost on any of us. We ride as a group. The only sound is the pounding of hooves on soft sand. For me this is bliss. It is exotic. I am riding a beautiful Arabian horse at full gallop across an extraordinary piece of the world under a full moon. It is exhilarating, freeing. It is beyond anything I have ever imagined doing.

We arrive at the bedouin tent to find it beautifully decorated with colorful braids, bells, and banners. It is lit with hundreds of candles, and there's not a hint of a breeze to disturb them. A sumptuous array of Egyptian food is laid out for us on low-lying tables inside the tent, and we sit on the plump cushions, eating and drinking as locals kindly serve us, figs, fruit, couscous, taking good care of us even at this late hour. The rhythmic music and beating of the drums add to the excitement of the occasion. Many people had taken the risk and driven along the bumpy desert road, not wanting to miss this exclusive party. The tent is packed with people lounging on the fat cushions, or standing in conversation, all making Angelo's birthday a success.

Guests move outside to continue the celebration under the full moon as the dancing horses raise dainty forelegs in time to the bedouin drums, their harnesses jangling in rhythm to the music. For me this is the most wonderful party I have ever attended. It is an Arabian movie set come to life. I look around at the opulence and extravagance of the party and sadly realize how little it had cost us Europeans to fund. The wages we earn are of a much higher value compared to the low incomes of the Egyptians, so while it cost us only a few pounds each for the party, that would equate to a month's wages for a local. On the positive side, it has put well-needed money into the pockets of the many locals who have assisted in making the party possible. They deserve every penny; it is a wonderful evening.

After living and working for six months in Cairo, the dance group is moving on to Iran. But not me. I realize I have a health problem. It has been plaguing me for a couple of months, making me uneasy, and I decide it will be best to go home to England. I say goodbye to my friends, to my wandering lifestyle, to the fun and freedom, and book my ticket home. With Mimis promising to phone me often and offering me anything that I might need, I go home to face the consequences.

CHAPTER

THIRTEEN

he high-pitched scream unexpectedly cuts into the quiet of the morning, reverberating around the house, its echo bouncing off the walls. It sounds like Mum. It comes from upstairs and is followed by a torrent of cursing in a Scottish brogue: yep, definitely Mum. I bound up the stairs, hastened by the shocking timbre of the cry, and find Mum in her bedroom.

"Would you look at that?" my mother says, pointing toward a drawer at the side of the bed. "Gave me the fright of my life!"

I look into the drawer and laugh. Inside are multiple pairs of false teeth, pink gums and white teeth all grinning up at us as if laughing at the practical joke they had just played.

"He wouldn't throw a thing away." Mum shakes her head. "Well, they're going in the bin now."

She pulls out the drawer and unceremoniously tips its contents into a bin, the act accented by the clatter of hard plastic hitting the metallic side of the bin.

I think to myself, *This was typical Dad, always the comedian, making my childhood a compendium of banter, witticisms, and jokes.* Dad's false teeth would often become the center of much jocularity, particularly when he had had a few drinks. He would amuse us all by playing with his dentures, pulling faces to make us laugh. Here he was still playing the jokester, even after he was gone. I look down at these personal items to be discarded as trash, their usefulness over, their relevance to my father's life and my own memories finished. A twinge of sadness hides below my laugh. Of course we have to let go of the belongings that had accessorized my father's life. We have to physically and permanently remove the tangible evidence of his existence. It is a natural part of the healing process.

The false teeth don't end with the drawer. Over the next couple of days as I help sort through my dad's things, I find more and more pairs: in the pockets of his Mackintosh (why he had a pair there was anyone's guess), in a box stored high on a kitchen shelf, and in a tin in the garage. My father had lost his teeth when he had childhood rheumatic fever; over the next sixty-plus years, he had worn dentures and, apparently, kept every one of the sets he had used during his lifetime. They are an odd historical collection not only of how dentures were made over the years from the 1940s to the present, but of how each set in its own way had traveled part of Dad's journey with him, some to foreign countries, but each allowing my father to speak to us, to smile his handsome smile, and even to joke with us.

The dentures keep appearing in odd places. Each new find is another grin and a reminder of Dad the comedian. I am thankful I found them. Dad's clothing is going to a charity shop. Imagine the shock of the new owner of his Mac finding a pair of false teeth in the pocket.

The false teeth are not the only oddities I find among Dad's belongings. There are containers of all shapes and sizes, including old metallic tobacco tins, and biscuit tins of buttons bearing anchors, cloth badges, and other insignia saved from his old naval uniforms. A plastic Brylcreem container is filled with foreign coins. Apparently, Dad threw nothing away.

In a small cardboard box I find a fake rubber finger, dripping with blood, which I remember from my childhood and which would appear at opportune moments around Mum's vicinity, such as on the shelf in the kitchen cupboard, or in the fridge, in Mum's teapot, or in the biscuit tin. Dad and I would measure the success of the joke by the volume of Mum's scream or curse. I remove the finger from the box and feel its rubbery softness between my own fingers and smile as I study the gruesome digit.

I remember the joke and novelty shop on the corner of Charlotte Street and how on Saturdays I would take my pocket money to the shop and buy some novelty that in those pre-computer days we all thought was very clever. Cat poop was a favorite, with Schickrys getting the undeserved blame and on more than one occasion being "shooshed" out of the house by my mother. The bugs that could be moved with a magnet were another favorite and usually got a good rise out of Mum. Something I definitely inherited from my dad is a love of practical jokes.

Mum asks me to take on the onerous task of clearing out the things Dad had stored in the attic. Unable to ignore this chore any longer, I climb the ladder into the vast archive looming over the house, the brain trust of clutter and memories for the family extending over many generations and over many more decades. As expected, I find it full of boxes, old suitcases, plastic bags, and other miscellaneous containers, and overall the space at first view appears nothing more than a dirty, musty storage area for rarely used, or forgotten items. Probably no different from any other attic in England. At least Dad had rigged a light bulb near the entrance of the attic, making it easier to see what inanimate objects stood ready for my attack.

I'm not thrilled at having to take on this task, especially in this dark, unfriendly, space thick with dust and unrecognizable living organisms. I hate organizing things, especially someone else's clutter. But being the dutiful daughter, and the only one of us three women with two legs and enough youth to climb up the stepladder and hoist myself up into the attic entrance in the ceiling, I know that I am the only person who can take on the task. I look around at the clutter and hear myself sigh heavily. This is going to take me days.

At first I don't know where to start. I take a general inventory of what is immediately visible. I see planks of wood and rolls of wallpaper, bags of Christmas decorations, old lamps, a Hoover from the 1950s, and the old sewing machine and sewing box I remember from my childhood—and tools, all sorts of tools everywhere.

I briefly wonder why Dad had so many tools in the attic when his garage-cum-workshop at the end of the garden is overflowing with tools, accessories, and media such as wooden planks, tiles, PVC piping. Tools epitomized my dad. As long as I can remember, my dad had a long list of projects to do for other people. He would build cabinets, tables, and all sorts of other furniture for anyone and everyone. He would paint and wallpaper rooms, fix cars, do electrical rewiring, do whatever odd jobs a person needed, and he did them well. He even invented a type of safety ladder, and I recall he mentioned a patent, but I had never asked him about it. I make a mental note to research the patent further.

When my dad was on leave from the Navy, he spent his time doing jobs for neighbors, family, and friends. Later after he retired from the Navy and worked in a factory, his workload and the number of jobs he did for others grew as he had more time to give. Mum often complained that he spent too much time working for everyone else: for family and friends, people he worked with, neighbors, even people he didn't know but to whom he had been referred. She complained that he did not have enough time to do things around our house. Dad rarely sat in front of the television at night unless he had a project manual or do-it-yourself book in hand. His evenings and free time were spent in the garage, doing his projects regardless of the weather or temperature.

No matter whose house the family visited, there were always signs of Dad's handiwork, be it in the form of painting, wallpapering, woodwork, handmade furniture, a car sitting outside the house that Dad had worked on. He was generous with his time and his skills, never refusing a request for help. I didn't think much of it until years later after he retired when Mum laughingly told me about the list of jobs she had ready for him to do. I became concerned. I complained to Mum that Dad needed time to rest. He should be allowed to slow down a little at his age. He was not as young as he used to be. High ladders and long hours would take their toll. But Dad couldn't, or wouldn't, say no. Perhaps Mum wouldn't let him. I had to trust that his working so much and so hard doing projects for other people gave him satisfaction.

I am surprised at what I find in the attic; surprised at what had not been thrown away. I see items that had been hidden out of sight for years but that immediately bring back fond memories. Not one to get too fussy about dust and dirt, and just wanting to get the job done, I sit down on a dusty wooden floor beam next to one box and begin sifting through its contents. I take out items one by one, inspecting them and cataloguing them in my mind. At least it is quiet up here. At least this keeps me busy and gives me something to think about other than Dad's passing. At least I am doing something to help the family after being absent for the past thirty years, off gallivanting around the world. Now it is time to organize the family junk and figure out how to get it down from the attic and disposed of appropriately.

But as I begin going through the boxes, pulling out and studying their contents, holding the more intriguing items closer to the light bulb for a better view, and conducting a mental inventory of what I find, it slowly dawns on me that what I am uncovering is not junk; they are not discarded or unused or unwanted items, but an intriguing assortment of objects that my father had gathered and kept over the years. Each item has a personal significance to my father. They are a treasure trove of my dad's life, the things he had wanted to keep. These are mementos from his past, each having a special meaning and value to him; things worth holding on to for sixty, seventy years or more. No wonder he kept them up here, away from Mum who would throw out the lot. "Rubbish" she would call it all.

My organization slows as new discoveries cause me to pause and take a closer look at each of the items I find. There are very old books, dark in color and bound with fabric. There are loose pieces of paper, yellowed with age, together with records from my dad's navy days, and dozens of old tools from a time before they were electric or cordless. I find a theater program for April 1935, for the *Orient Kinema* on Sword Street in Glasgow, announcing the showing of a Shirley Temple film and the next week a film with Laurel and Hardy. I reverently turn the program over to find an information sheet of the time: countries and their capitals, including Ceylon, which later becomes Sri Lanka, and China with its capital city of Nanking. It lists the census figures of 1931. There were less than five million people in Scotland, and England and Wales had just under forty million. This is a brief memorandum of the time. I stare at it intently, wondering how it came into my dad's possession, particularly as he would have been only about four years old in 1935, and I wonder why he had kept it for more than seventy years. Had it some correlation to his birth year—1931? I can wonder all I want; chances are I will never find out. Chagrined, I recognize the blunt fact is that it is too late to ask my father about this, or any of the other items I find here in the attic.

I move to another box, kneeling on the floor beside it, ignoring the aged dust wiping itself against my clothes. I find many notebooks, or exercise books as they are called in England, each with a different and faded colored cover. As I thumb through them, I see each is filled with notes on a different subject, written in a meticulous hand, and with carefully crafted colored diagrams and drawings. The drawings appear to relate to engines, or something mechanical. I think perhaps they have something to do with Dad's career as a marine engineer mechanic with the Royal Navy. Were these notes created as part of his training, during a class? Was he required to have notes of this kind at hand to help with his work in the engine room onboard ship? Or did my father make these notes of his own volition, deciding to diligently make and maintain his own record of the key information on the engines he was working with and servicing? No matter the motivation behind these carefully crafted drawings, they are now a memorial of something central to his life. I run my fingers across the faded red cover of a notebook, thinking of the book in my father's hands, the pages carefully turned, each new page becoming a tangible expression of some task or project he was working on. I hold the book to my chest and close my eyes. I deeply inhale the aged air around me. For a moment I am transported back in time and remember when my father was a young man, lean, eager, full of vigor and motivation. I exhale and open my eyes now moist with the memories. I miss him.

I continue with my inspection of another box in front of me, finding inside some old books and a large wooden cigar box still with colorful, exotic labels attached to it. Inside the cigar box there are hundreds of photographs—all sizes, and ages. Most are black and white, and all collected during the lifetime of my parents. I set the photographs aside. I will visit them later.

I pick up the old books. I hold them reverently, turning them over in my hand and scanning the black leather-bound covers for more information. They are apprenticeship books from my dad's days as an apprentice carpenter. I look inside the cover at the copyright notice for the publication date, and also see my father's name and the year written in pencil: Ian Denny, 1944. Dad had left school at around thirteen or fourteen years of age and was sent to learn a trade: carpentry. Throughout my life Dad had made most of the furniture in the house—the bedroom sets, wardrobes, tables. Older English houses did not have walk-in closets, so wardrobes had to be bought, or built. I scan through the carpentry books and imagine my father as a young lad leafing through the pages, reading, learning his trade all those decades ago.

I put the trade books to one side, then one by one I pick up and scan through some exercise books stacked neatly at the bottom of the box. I carefully turn the yellowed pages, looking with wonderment at my dad's beautiful handwriting. My finger traces the curves and loops of the inked letters. The penmanship would have been extraordinary for a woman, but for a man with little education it is a form of artwork. The meticulous notes show how hard my father must have worked even as a young man to not only improve his writing, but also make sure his work was as good as he could make it. He had held himself to high standards, wanting to improve himself and his lot in life. He had imposed his high standards on me during my years as a young student; he was often relentless with his discipline of me, but I know now that he did not impose on me any more expectation and discipline than he had placed on himself.

I sit back on my heels as my analytical mind begins to connect the dots between events from the past and the items I am now discovering in the attic. Since my father's death I had felt as though I have been wearing a heavy cloak of guilt because during my adult life I had only thought about myself, did what I wanted to do, giving little thought to my dad, my mum, or even my sister. But now my mind goes back to my own childhood and to the books, dictionaries, maps, science manuals, and math books, all of the educational materials my dad had incessantly bought for me. He was strict about me doing my homework, and goodness help me if I didn't get good grades in school. In junior school I was Head Girl and Head Prefect. I was head of my student house. At sixteen I was awarded a full scholarship to the Royal Academy and, at that time, was one of the youngest students to ever attend the Royal Academy. I analyze my thoughts, my education, my father's strictness and firm impetus. As children we think our parents are mean, they don't understand us, they are too strict; they make up unnecessary rules. They make our lives unnecessarily difficult. My father had wanted me to be well educated, to get the education that he never had. He had wanted me to do well in life. I had complained and grumbled at the unfairness of my dad and his always pushing me, punishing me. Nothing was ever good enough; it could always be better. And if I didn't get it right, or if I spoke back and complained, there was the belt or his hand putting me back in my place, or hours spent in the dreaded corner. Actions which by today's standard would seem abusive were many decades ago the signs of a caring parent.

My father was born poor and one would think without prospects. He never complained about his circumstances. He had simply done what he could to educate himself, and to do well in life and provide for his family. He had pushed me as his daughter to take that vision even further and I had. I am well educated. I am well traveled. I have learned much from living with diverse cultures, and through my life experiences. I admit that I am where I am today less because of my own efforts but more because of my father's discipline and impetus. Perhaps my life travels and education were exactly what my dad had wanted for me. Perhaps my dad was proud of what I had accomplished. My cloak of guilt becomes a little lighter, as the burdens I carried are now lifted from my shoulders.

With a renewed vigor I sort through lamps, Christmas decorations, bits and pieces of Dad's navy uniforms. I am astounded at the number of items that I find that I have never seen before but which obviously exist, and have been in my parents' possession for many decades. But then, sorting among all these objects, I find a true treasure. At the bottom of a box and wrapped in grease-proof paper and then again a plastic bag, I find a very old book. I gingerly unwrap the book from the paper. It is a book on household management for running a household at the early part of the twentieth century. It appears to have a wealth of information on what women were expected to know and do during this time in history. The book appears to have belonged to my Granny Denny, who as a young girl had been in service, but the book was passed on to my father at the woman's death. I gingerly turned the pages, but they are crisp, fragile with age, and are falling apart in my hands. The first pages are missing, so there is no copyright notice or indication of a publication date on the book. I have never seen this book before. It has obviously been in the family for decades, possibly for more than a hundred years judging by its content, yet I hadn't even known it existed. I would love to know more about it, ask about its provenance. I realize that there is so much about my family, my heritage that I don't know. Time is running out to get that family history from those elders who can tell it best. I carefully wrap the book back in its paper and plastic bag. This needs to be preserved. I put it to one side, taking stewardship of this piece of family history.

"Laraine! Are you all right up there?" Mum's distant call interrupts my inventory taking.

"I'm fine, Mum. Did you need anything?" I shout down through the two floors of the house.

"No. I'm just checking. You're awfully quiet up there."

"It's all good. I'll be down shortly."

Before calling it quits for the day, I look back through the dusty dimness and take stock of the items I have seen. I look around at Dad's treasures, each memorializing a particular part of his life and the people he encountered. Obscure objects but of such importance to him, he had kept them, some as long as seventy years: each giving a sense of what had been important to Dad.

I smile to myself, now knowing what I can do for my father. I will give his eulogy and here is its theme. I can't speak knowledgeably about my dad per se, because I had spent so little time with him, but I can speak about these treasures he had kept and link them to the timeline of his life. Through these objects I will tell his story and ensure his memory lives on.

CHAPTER

FOURTEEN

I am twenty-one and pregnant, alone, unprepared, unsure of where my own life is going, let alone knowing how to take responsibility for another life.

I return to England from Cairo a few days before my twenty-first birthday, pretending this important milestone is the reason I returned home to be with my family. In cooler England, I am able to hide behind the more casual and bulky clothing I can wear, knowing within time I would not have been able to fit into the tight, revealing show costumes. Better to leave based on my own decision than wait for the embarrassing telltale signs to emerge, which inevitably would create ugly gossip and my firing from the group. The group is contracted to work around the Middle East. Local societies do not tolerate a girl in my condition.

At first, my lean dancer's body does not put on too much weight, and I have been able to laugh with my family and friends that my weight gain is the result of my currently inactive lifestyle. I can't tell my parents what the weight really is. They would be shocked, angry, among other emotions, but happiness would not be one of them.

My naïve mind is convinced that Mimis, the Greek agent, will come through for me, take care of me. My parents will see that everything will be all right, that I have my life organized. After all he loves me, doesn't he? That's what he has told me over and over again. He bought me presents, earrings, a gold ring. We spent every moment we could together in Cairo. When I told Mimis I was pregnant, it was he who suggested I return home to England, to get the best medical care for the baby and me. He said he would make arrangements for us all. His suggestion made sense to me. He is concerned about the baby and me.

For a couple of weeks after I return home, Mimis telephones from wherever he is in Europe to see how I am doing. To me, the calls all the way from Europe are proof that the man loves me, will be there for me. I trust him. The phone is in the hallway by the front door, and each time he calls, I sit on the lower stairs quietly talking to him, keeping my conversation as private as I can, not wanting my parents to hear. Mimis tells me he loves me. I whisper into the phone that I love him too. I become more elated with each call, imaging the life the three of us will live together. Will it be in Spain, in Greece?

But then one day like a shocking splash of ice water on my face, I realize that the calls have stopped. They simply cease to come. During the last call, Mimis told me that he would call me again in a couple of days. I wait and wait, but the call never comes. For weeks afterward, each time the phone rings, I tense, my senses tuning into the shrill ringing in the hallway, hoping, praying, that it is him. It never is.

I am now four months pregnant. I don't sleep. I can't eat. I won't let my mind formulate the obvious. Finding clothes big enough to accommodate the extra bulk is becoming difficult. Hiding my condition from my parents is becoming virtually impossible. My mum has started asking questions about my weight, the tone of the questions suspicious. I laugh off the concern, but in reality I am becoming physically and mentally desperate. Each day that passes without a call is another slap in the face, that I am stupid, that I have it all wrong.

Within time I become resigned to the fact that I have been abandoned. My baby's father conveniently and cowardly taking the "easy way out," disappearing from our lives, leaving me alone to cope with my pregnancy and without coping mechanisms, other than my tears. I don't know what to do. I have no resources. I tell no one.

My life becomes a routine of misery. As soon as my parents leave the house for work in the morning, I release the smiles and easygoing banter I share with them, and walk into the living room, where I take my position on the couch and begin to cry, wailing to myself, my arms wrapped around my body, rocking back and forth, my mind unable to comprehend this awful position that I find myself in.

How did this happen? Why have I been abandoned? What have I done to deserve this? What am I going to do?

I am numb, unable to answer my own questions. I stay there on the couch all day, sitting, doing nothing. I don't eat, don't drink. Penance for my sins. I am oblivious to my surroundings, oblivious to the changing light and shadows in the room as the sun rises throughout the morning and then descends in the afternoon. I don't move, my active mind focusing only on my inner thoughts, reliving the events of the past few months, trying to analyze what went wrong. *What did I do wrong? What had I done for this man to discard me like an inconsequential piece of lint?*

Just before my parents come home in the evening, I finally get up and go to the tap and bathe my red, swollen eyes with the cold water, touching up my face with makeup if needed, trying to hide the shock of my day. By the time my parents arrive home, I have reattached my smile, and the consummate actress in me pretends everything is fine, that I have had a good day.

The weeks pass. It is May and the weather is warmer. I can no longer hide my body behind winter sweaters. The winter sweaters can no longer be used to hide the fact that I keep my pants unzipped at the waist. I know I must eventually go to the doctor. Now seven months pregnant, that time has come. I wait for a day when both my parents are at work. I don't need an appointment. I know the surgery hours and simply just have to show up and sign in. Mustering the little courage that I have, I go to see the doctor.

I sit on a wooden chair in the waiting room, feeling as if

all eyes are on me, as if my shame stands out like a neon light, drawing attention, announcing, "Look at this shameful person!" I don't make eye contact with anyone. I stare at the notices on the wall, listening as names are called and aware of the movements around me as people go back to see the doctor.

I sit motionless, but my mind is running wildly. What am I going to say to the doctor? How am I going to tell my parents? What am I doing here? How did it come to this? My name is called, and as my mind snaps to the present, my nerves take control. I stand up feeling obvious, as if my condition is on display to the world. I am wearing my loosest jeans and largest top, yet know they look too small for me. I slowly follow the nurse through the door to the back rooms and enter the doctor's office as directed. My mind is unfocused; I am in a daze. I see Dr. Brown, an older man, sitting behind his desk. I take a deep breath, but it shudders in my chest, my nerves controlling my entire body.

The doctor doesn't look at me. His gray-haired head is bowed, looking at the notes he is writing on the last patient. I stand in the uncomfortable silence. Staring at the top of the doctor's head, unaware of the makeup of my surroundings, I wait for the doctor's acknowledgement, wondering how to explain my predicament, petrified of the outcome. But, Doctor Brown takes his time, ignoring me. He moves at his own pace, leaving my nerves to grow and take control, shaking me as they rattle around my body.

Finally, the doctor puts his pen down, puts the notes in a tray, takes off his glasses, and looks up at me. Before the doctor even speaks to me, I stammer, "I . . . I . . . I think I'm pregnant."

Doctor Brown takes one look at my belly and immediately says, "I think you are!"

I feel stupid. To the experienced eye my pregnancy is obvious. I wonder who else has realized my condition but has not said anything to me. I momentarily wonder about what might have been said behind my back, but then I quickly push the question aside. It doesn't matter now. My pregnancy is something that can no longer be hidden. I am here to face the consequences.

After examining me, and asking about my circumstances, the doctor dispassionately advises me to put the baby up for adoption. It is clear he doesn't think too much of me, a reckless young woman with no morals. I am told it will be better to give the child up for adoption so I can get on with my life and allow the child to be raised by people who can offer him more than I ever could. I feel cheapened by his words. He clearly assumes I am not going to do much with my life, and that I am more interested in getting on with enjoying my life and that I don't want to be distracted by a baby. But as I sit in the doctor's office, listening to his cold chastisement and assessment of my morality, I think back to my time in Egypt, to the Lebanese palm reader and the three things he had told me: I was going to be famous; I was going to make my future husband unhappy; I was only ever going to have one child, a son.

It does not matter whether the palm reader's predictions are true or not. What does matter is that he told me I was only going to have one child and that thought stayed with me long after I left Egypt and returned to England. It had germinated in my mind over the months. Now listening to the doctor telling me to give my child up for adoption, I wonder, *But what if this is the only child I will ever have? How can I ever give him away?* It is the 1970s, but there is still a stigma attached to being an unwed mother. Can I live with that stigma? I have two months to decide.

I leave the doctor's office with instructions for follow-up care and take a slow walk home up the quiet back streets toward the house. I have survived the first step of my disclosure, but can I survive the second? Once home I go straight into the compact kitchen situated at the front of the house and take a seat on a kitchen stool where I can see out of the window to the street. I will be able to see when my mother arrives home, and I will be able to brace myself and be ready for step two, the confrontation with my mother.

It will be an hour or so before Mum finishes work, and Loretta will go straight to dance classes after school, so for a while I am alone. I don't move. My feet are perched on the rungs of the stool, and my hands are placed in my lap. My posture is upright; my eyes are on the street. I wait, and pray. The house is silent. The tension mounts. My nerves are held tight to my body by the closeness of the kitchen walls, refusing me any escape from what I am about to face.

I see my mother walk along the path by the house, open and close the front gate, and walk across the forecourt. I don't go and open the front door for my mother. I sit motionless, on the stool. The tension in my body makes me nauseous, as my muscles tighten inside me and asphyxiate my core. I sigh deeply, trying to calm my nerves. This is it.

"Laraine? I'm home. Where are you?"

"In the kitchen, Mum." My voice is quiet, calm, belying the turmoil swirling inside my head and body. The walls begin to spin around me.

"What have you been doing all day? Nothing, I suppose."

I hear the door of the hall cupboard open and close as my mother hangs up her coat. I note the annoyance in my mother's voice thinking I had sat on my rear all day doing nothing around the house. My mother comes into the kitchen and puts her shopping bag on the counter. Ignoring me, she takes the kettle off the stove and moves to the sink to fill it with water.

"Mum, I need to tell you something." I take a deep breath. I need to get straight to the point, get it over with. I look down at my hands perched on my lap and say quietly, "I'm pregnant."

"What?" The kettle drops into the sink. Metal hitting metal, the harsh sound reverberating around the little space.

Scottish indignation and righteousness come out in full force as my mother whirls around to face me. The woman screams, "What the hell have you done?" She takes two steps across the floor and slaps my face, the "smacking" sound of skin on skin accenting the anger. The woman begins pummeling me with both hands, hard, again and again, and with all the force her tiny frame can muster. The blows hit my bare arms—*smack, smack*—as I raise them to protect myself from my mother's frantic thrashing. The next few moments go by in a dark blur. I close my eyes, trying to censor the moment. I feel the pain, but it is less than the hurtful sting of shame.

"Oh, my God!" my mother shouts. "Oh, my God!" Each word emphatically spat into my face. The blows suddenly stop and I realize I am alone. I hear running steps thumping up the carpeted stairs. I hear my mother's bedroom door slam above my head and the *whamp* of my mother falling down on the bed, followed by a noisy, pitiful wailing lest anyone should doubt the horror of the news. I open my eyes, sit upright, ignoring the aching in my arms and body, and look around the tiny kitchen. My body involuntarily sighs deeply. My mother's torment is over. But it is best if I go somewhere else to face step three: my father.

Sitting in my own bedroom waiting for my father to return home, I again find myself staring at the walls. It is a full-time occupation these days. I anticipate my mother's dramatic rendition of the news to my dad, and the outrage he will express. There is no going back now, but the certainty of my father's likely reaction—the yelling and maybe the belt—has yet to be endured. I tell myself, *I am ready for it.* I have to be. There is no other option.

My father comes home. I hear my mother's movement in the next room in reaction to the activity at the front door. I hear footsteps descending the stairs, followed by the muffled voices. I am unclear of the words, but can easily interpret the tone. In less than a minute I hear footsteps ascending the stairs, heavier impatient steps. The door to my bedroom flies open and hits the doorstop on the wall with a bang. I involuntarily flinch. My father stands in the doorway. He is looking at me through narrowed eyes; his face is crumpled up as if smelling something repugnant.

"You're a disgrace!" The words are spat at me like refuse thrown at a lowlife.

I do nothing; I say nothing. I brace myself as my father takes a step forward into the room, but he simply grabs the door handle, slams the door shut, and is gone. That is it. Nothing more. Instinctively, I know the worst is over. I have survived. The nerves, the tension flies out of my body as if fleeing from a cage after being imprisoned against their will. My body deflates. All I want to do now is close my eyes. I lean sideways on the bed, tuck up my feet, and lie down, closing my eyes, sinking into the softness, allowing sleep to ease my aches and pain.

For days afterward, I stay in my bedroom while my parents are at home, not wanting to unnecessarily face their disdain. From time to time Loretta comes up to check on me but neither parent will talk to me. I hear activity in the house, including my mother sitting on the bottom stair in the hallway phoning other family members and friends with the terrible news, dramatizing the circumstances, playing the victim; the crying and woeful recitation of the dreadful news is easy to hear everywhere in the small house. How can Laraine bring such disgrace on her, on the family? How can anyone live this down?

In due course, my parents come to terms with the story and circumstances surrounding my pregnancy. I tell my mum that the doctor has advised the child be put up for adoption, hoping that this option might offer her some comfort that this unwelcomed baby might not be a permanent intrusion into her life. But within time, it is my mother who reluctantly asks me to consider keeping the baby. This is, after all, going to be her first grandchild.

While my parents don't forgive my disgrace, the atmosphere in the house becomes less hostile toward me and more resigned to the inevitable. For the times when I have to leave the house to go to the clinic, my mother bought me a huge brown overcoat to wear to cover myself up, even though it is June, July, summertime. My mother is still ashamed of me; she doesn't want people to see my pregnancy. I ask myself over and over, *Can I live with the stigma?* I retreat into myself; it is easier, less confrontational that way. If I don't see people, don't talk to people, I don't have to respond to their questions, their stares.

I have to work with social services, trying to track down the child's father to get support from him. I give them the only photograph of Mimis that I have; in it we are sitting together having dinner at a restaurant in Cairo, leaning toward each other, heads touching, smiling for the camera. Social services can't find Mimis. He is gone from my life with no qualms of leaving me alone to raise his child. I learn how callous people can be, even those who say they love you.

The last two months of my pregnancy pass. My time comes; my labor is induced, some force taking pity on me and granting me a short six-hour labor. While I am in the hospital both before and after giving birth, I watch the other women sharing the joy of a newborn with their husbands and partners. Lying on my bed, or strolling around the wards watching the interplay between the couples, I am envious. I feel very alone. I have no one to share this experience with. And even though I am momentarily resentful of the happiness of these other women, and doubt my own ability to raise a child by myself, I remember the words of Tariq, the Lebanese palm reader, and how I will only have one child. I lie on my hospital bed, my son snuggled in my arms, the sweet scent of baby mixed with the warmth and trust this little one has for me. He is my child. I am no longer alone. I keep my son. I name him Mark. I want him to make his mark on the world.

author and son Mark, photo © Ian Denny

CHAPTER

FIFTEEN

I am now a mother with new responsibilities, the most important of which is supporting my son. The English social services will give me benefits, including housing. I should feel grateful for a system that will look out for me, but the thought is depressing. This isn't where I want my life to go. Not after all the effort I have put into my dancing career and after living abroad and the experiences I have had. I don't want my dreams to fade away just because I made a mistake. I look at my son sleeping in my arms. His eyes closed, his mind innocent. I chastise myself. He is not a mistake. I will never again refer to him as a mistake. He is a gift that I must appreciate and love. But what is the best thing for me to do for him? For us both?

My mother wisely tells me that if I give up my dancing career because of my son, I will blame him for the rest of my life. My mother's words are astute. My mother tells me she will give up her job to care for my son, and I will pay her the salary she would have made at work. I agree, thankful for the good heart and wisdom of my mother.

I contact my agent in London to seek work abroad, knowing I will make more money working for foreign shows than in

England. It is a wrench knowing I have to leave my son so soon, and before bonding with him; it is a difficult balance creating a life that will be good for both of us. But my parents have opened their hearts to their grandson. He will be loved and well taken care of.

Within three weeks of Mark's birth, I have a job as a dancer with a French dance group Les Danceurs d'Amon, named after its founder and producer, Garib Amon, and based in Paris. This new tour abroad has its own challenges. It is my first day of rehearsals with the group, and I find myself standing in the middle of the studio dumbfounded because the rehearsals are in French and beyond my understanding. I studied French in grammar school, but the extent of my knowledge is *"Où est la porte"* or "where is the door."

Two Dutch girls, Lea and Ansje, speak English and guide me through the routines, but clearly I need to learn French quickly. I also need to get back into shape. I tell no one I have just had a child. I am not sure of how people will react to me being a single mother. I avoid the stigma and focus on the job at hand. My work has a new purpose. It is to provide my son everything he will need in life, and to do that I must save my money to pay Mum her salary.

After rehearsing in Paris for a week, the group travels to Lago di Lugano in Switzerland, where we perform in a nightclub for a month before traveling on to a place called Ngor, just outside of Dakar in Senegal. Senegal is a French-speaking country, which explains why a French group is asked to perform at the Ngor resort.

My education continues as I broaden my knowledge of geography and history. I learn that an island just off the Dakar coast called Snake Island was apparently where the African slaves were kept so long ago before being shipped off to the New World. In Ngor, I learn a little of the local language, Wolof, and enjoy basic banter with the locals working at the resort nightclub.

After Senegal, the group travels to Thailand. I see what on first glance look like lakes but which are in fact rice fields. Whole

author in Senegal, family photo

communities live on rivers or *khlongs,* and during my stay I often visit the floating markets to buy fresh, exotic fruits such as rose apples, papaya, and pineapples. The other dancers stay in their rooms or spend the day at the pool. I have to see the culture.

"Hey, Francine," I call to my roommate, "I am off on a tour today."

"*Encore!*" The disinterested French voice is accompanied by the rolling of eyes. She doesn't ask where I am going.

"If Garib asks, I should be back before it gets dark."

"Okay."

Today my tour takes me hours outside of Bangkok to a historic location. I am standing at the site of *The Bridge on the River Kwai,* looking down at the muddy-brown water of the river, and across at where gaps in the green overgrowth show where the original bridge had once spanned. I pull from my memory scenes from the famous film, and the history on which the film was loosely based. Here I am at the actual site and I compare the historic reality with the

Hollywood story. The bridge was built by the Japanese during World War II to connect the Bangkok–Rangoon railway. It was known as the Death Railway because of the large loss of life incurred in its construction, not only of Allied prisoners of war but also of local civilians who were treated with brutality by the Japanese overseers.

Original carriages from the trains that once ran from Burma across the bridge and through Thailand now rest at the side of the river. I study the carriages; they are now rusty, old, but are a historic part of the Second World War as it played in the Asian arena. I look back to the gaps on either side of the river where the original bridge once stood and imagine these carriages rumbling across the river at the expense of so much misery.

A second bridge was built about a hundred yards up river, and I take the time to walk across the now dilapidated bridge with gaps in the railings and wooden sleepers. The holes in the railway show the brown water floating along in the river below. I am careful where I step, but more careful are the Buddhist monks who are also visiting the bridge. I learn the monks are not permitted to touch women, or money. As I prance along the bridge enjoying my firsthand look at history, the monks lean against the bridge's railings, making sure they avoid any connection with my body. My tour also includes a visit to the cemetery where thousands of prisoners of war are buried. I pay my respects, knowing many of them were British and fought for my freedom.

On another day I go to the Rose Garden, a Thai cultural center in the middle of a beautiful park with a lake and large pagoda. I watch elegant Thai court dancers as they perform traditional dances in beautiful and brightly colored sequin costumes with elaborate headdresses and long nails accenting their hand movements. Also part of the entertainment is a cockfight, a typical Thai pastime. I also watch a kickboxing match. After visiting the main arena at the Rose Garden, I go outside where I watch working elephants perform tasks such as moving logs and pulling heavy objects. I take a ride on an elephant, working hard to maintain my balance on top of the lumbering and swaying animal. At the end of each tour I return to the hotel in Bangkok, where the rest of the cast have spent their day lazing around in their rooms or by the pool. *Silly girls,* I think to myself. *You don't know what on earth you are missing!*

After Thailand the group moves on to Singapore. I love Singapore's orderly civility. It is a hot, humid city, sitting barely one-degree north of the equator. Stepping outside the door of the hotel, I can immediately feel the humidity wrap itself around me as I walk along the street, the humidity a constant companion on my outings both day and night. I become used to perspiration running at will down my face, and drenching my body in confined areas under my clothing.

Singapore is a host to many different cultures, including Indian, Chinese, Malaysian, and European. The many cultures are equally present in the food, the dialects spoken by the locals, the artifacts for sale, and the innumerable festivals held to celebrate gods, seasons, the moon, and whatever else. I love the way the local television begins its evening broadcast with women from each of the four cultures greeting the viewers in their native language. The message is that different cultures can live together with respect and in harmony.

Singapore's general culture is one of politeness. Restaurants have signs asking patrons not to tip the staff because it is their pleasure to serve you. Pedestrians don't dare jaywalk after the government has gone to the trouble of creating crosswalks and lights to make crossing the road a safe activity for the pedestrians. And no pedestrian would be rude enough to step onto the road wherever is suitable for them, and cause drivers some inconvenience when there are crosswalks which drivers expect pedestrians to use.

I perform two shows nightly at the Mandarin Hotel on Orchard Street. I also live in the hotel, sharing the luxury of my hotel room with Francine. As usual, most of the dancers like to spend their days lying at the pool, rationalizing their need to do as little as possible to conserve energy for the two shows. But I can't live in this fascinating place and not discover its attractions. Every day I choose a new area to explore.

As I experience the city, I picture my dad being there years before me, walking along the same streets, and visiting the same tourist attractions, finding some common bond we share with these strange, unfamiliar foreign places. I remember Dad's stories of Singapore and the Tiger Balm Gardens. He brought back little jars of Tiger Balm from his visit.

My own visit to the Tiger Balm Gardens is significant because I know my father had visited the gardens many years ago when he was a young sailor and had spoken about their glorious displays. My dad told me the story of the Chinese brothers creating Tiger Balm and using the proceeds from the balm to create a wonderful garden for the people to enjoy and learn about the mythical Chinese culture. I wonder what my father had thought as he walked through the elaborate gardens, infused with bright colored murals and with large statues and exhibitions showing scenes, some of them bizarre, from Chinese mythology, each with a lesson for the visitor. The vibrant education is converse to anything my father would have found in the drab streets of his boyhood Glasgow.

The group moves on to Syria, another French-speaking country. The difference between Singapore and Syria is enormous, with Singapore embracing tourism, beaches, and sun-tanned bodies, and, in contrast and even in the 1970s, the Syrian government and law restricting people's movements, controlling Syrian life and habits. We live and work in Damascus. We stay at the Omayad Hotel on one corner of a large square, a few minutes' walk from the nightclub where we perform.

I keep a photograph of baby Mark at the side of my bed in the hotel where I am staying, and one day the maids cleaning the

author visa photograph taken in Damascus, Syria,
photo © Safar & Vartan

room ask me about him. I quickly fabricate a story about being
married and my son being at home in England with my husband.
If anyone in Syria discovers that I am an unmarried mother, I am
likely to be stoned or subjected to something equally degrading.

One evening an employee at the nightclub tells me that there
had been a public hanging in Damascus that day and that all the
schoolchildren had been taken to watch, to be taught a lesson. I
don't bother verifying the veracity of the story. It isn't something
I need to know in more detail. I just know that life in Syria, in
many countries, is very different.

It is difficult not to be bored during the day in Syria. Other
than the souks there are no real shopping areas. Next to the hotel
is a small bookstore selling materials written only in Arabic or
French. I peruse the cluttered shelves and confused order of the
books, hoping to find something that I can read. About to give
up my search, I pull a small hardbound book from a shelf. I am

relieved to recognize the name *Agatha Christie*. I buy a number of Agatha Christie novels, and a French-to-English dictionary, and I spend my afternoons in the hotel lounge reading the books and improving my French language skills.

I cannot spend my entire time inside the hotel, and so on occasion, I go out just long enough to buy some necessities. The square outside the hotel is always crammed with men, most in uniform. Syria doesn't have much in the way of industry or businesses. The military is a sure way for the men to make a living for their families. Passing through a crowd of Syrian militia makes me nervous. I walk quickly, keep my eyes forward, try to remain inconspicuous, go only where I need to go, and then immediately return to the safety of the hotel.

Today my mind cannot take in another word of Agatha Christie via the arduous translation process, so I have decided to brave the back streets and alleyways of the city and discover what else lies around me. My exploration takes me down narrow passages meandering between dust-colored, stone buildings, all lacking legible signage, and all equally intriguing to me. I ignore the curious stares of the locals, the stray dogs sniffing at my legs, and step aside to avoid the odd cart passing too close to me. I let my curiosity guide me, following sights and smells, all the while looking for out-of-the-way shops selling things I have never seen.

I discover a curious little alcove tucked under a building. The windows don't have glass. It is dark inside but I see sparks of orange light. Curious, I step inside the doorway to take a better look. I see what looks like a blacksmith's shop, with a man bending over some kind of kiln with what I surmise is molten metal. My eyes adjust to the dim interior, and looking around, I see he is not making horseshoes but decorative metal objects. I see incense burners, candle holders, and ashtrays, all a similar hue of orangey-gray metal. Brass? Bronze? I don't know.

"*Mam'selle.*" I feel a tug at the sleeve of my jacket, and turning around, I see an old man standing beside me dressed in nontraditional working garb. He is at least a foot shorter than I am, but is smiling at me with a delightful three-tooth grin. He continues tugging my arm with one hand while beckoning at me to follow him with the other. I do as I am told and follow the man toward shelf after shelf of handcrafted metal objects. The man waves his hand toward the shelf and nods eagerly at me. His intent is as clear as his pride in the display. He wants me to look at his wares and purchase something. I am happy to oblige. I take my time, browsing the shelves, picking up the occasional item to admire the elaborate decoration etched into each piece, while smiling and nodding at the man to show my appreciation for his talents. I choose a couple of small silver trays beautifully decorated with Arabic carvings, and a small incense burner with a removable conical top with engravings and small holes to allow the incense to escape. The man wraps my treasures in newspaper, and I pay him with coins.

"*Merci,*" I say as I take my purchases from him.

"*Au revoir,*" he replies, the three-tooth grin never leaving his face.

My time in Syria includes the month of December, and I use my resourcefulness to go to the souk to find things to create Christmas for the other cast members, even though this holiday does not exist in Muslim Damascus. After a long walk through the souk browsing the hundreds of stalls and small shops, I have not found everything I need. I go out into the streets of Damascus where I know there is a small store that sells some familiar French biscuits that I buy, hoping they are semi-fresh, or at least bug-free. I also find some locally bottled soda which, despite its famous brand name, and because of its local manufacture and inexpensive price of one Syrian pound for a whole crate, tastes like gut rot. I also find some colored paper and other bits and bobs to make decorations for the dressing room, and for each member of the cast I buy some locally made leather purses and bookmarkers, as token gifts. It won't be a grand Christmas, but it is better than letting it pass uncelebrated.

The nightclub in Damascus is different from anything seen in Europe and is the antithesis of life for the average Syrian. After walking up the stone steps at the club's entrance and then through the opulent glass front door, I am in a grand, high-ceilinged foyer garbed in red and gold, more like a palace or a swanky West End theater than a nightclub. Red velvet drapes fall from ceiling to floor. Ornate stone scrolls in white and gold are carved into the walls, framing sections of red velveteen wallpaper. Portraits of important someones line the long and wide passage that leads to the various rooms, including the restaurant and showroom. The nightclub is owned by a relative of a government minister, and the club has conference rooms where the Syrian government sometimes has its meetings; judging by the Russian Embassy cars lining the curb at the nightclub door, these meetings are always attended by persons from the Russian Embassy.

After performing in the show at the Syrian nightclub on Christmas evening, the rest of the cast and I are sitting around a table in the nightclub's restaurant when the owner comes over with a bottle of champagne, saying nonchalantly, "I think it is some kind of holiday in your country. I bring this for you to celebrate."

What does he mean it is some kind of holiday? It is Christmas for heaven's sake!

I receive letters and Christmas cards from my family, every one of which has been opened by the Syrian censors prior to it being delivered to me. Every message and personal good wish meant only for me is intercepted by some anonymous pair of eyes receiving the message before I do, and making a determination as to whether I am entitled to receive it, or not. This indignity, this intrusion into my personal life by faceless, foreign strangers, has to be accepted without question, without complaint. This is a stark reminder that people in different countries live differently and not always with the freedoms we enjoy in England.

Another indignity is frequently being held at gunpoint by the Syrian militia. Damascus has a curfew, and after dark people have to remain inside their homes unless you have permission to be out on the streets. The other performers and I have permission to leave our hotel to go to the nightclub to perform our shows for the Syrian elite. But late every night, when we walk back from the nightclub across the main square in Damascus to our hotel, the armed guards point their rifles at us and stop us and ask for our papers. We are careful to always carry our passes.

But for me life at twenty-one is still a big adventure. I am young, and life is still a game. Being held at gunpoint is simply another exciting story to add to my repertoire to recite to my friends back in England, and something more to extend my education beyond anything in any book I had read at school. I see the cars from the Russian Embassy lined up outside the Damascus nightclub where I work and joke to my friends that I should be a spy. It seems that every day something new is added to my education.

In other Middle Eastern countries, dancers in shows have to wear black body stockings under their colorful, sequined, and very scanty costumes to cover up any skin from the neck down. Performing in Syria does not require the same restrictions. The other dancers and I wear the sometimes-scanty costumes, showing long legs and bare arms and midriffs. The audience, the elite of Damascus permitted out during the curfew hours, enjoy the show. Except for the one occasion when twenty or more men in business suits, presumably at the club for business meetings, sat in the showroom for the duration of the show. The men refused to watch us perform, instead turning their chairs to face the back of the showroom, rebuffing the dishonorable women on the stage. All we performers can see are rigid backs and heads, but we feel the repugnance from these men. Back in the dressing room we girls laughed at them. What these men think simply doesn't matter.

An odd event occurs one evening while I am at the club. Generally, when performing on stage, all I see are silhouettes in the audience; the harsh stage lights shining in my eyes wash out color and distinctive features. This night I am dancing onstage, the bright lights in my eyes preventing me from being able to see the audience clearly, when I see what seems to be a familiar silhouette sitting several rows back in the middle of the theater. The silhouette is bulky and matches Mimis's physique. I think he is looking directly at me and making some comment about me to a man at his side. Surely not. Is it my imagination playing tricks?

After the show as I am putting away costumes and props in the dressing room, and getting changed to go with the other performers to the restaurant, I half-expect Mimis to come into the dressing room, or for someone to mention that they had seen him. I am shaking, afraid to admit to myself that I want to see him again. After all he has put me through, the misery, anger, humiliation, I want him to come back into my life. I want him to want me. No one comes to the dressing room. No one comes into the restaurant after the show. No one mentions the man.

After our show two nights later, I am sitting in the restaurant with the girls when a waiter comes to the table and says there is a phone call from London for the English lady. Since I am the only English girl, everyone presumes the call is for me and all heads turn to look at me, wanting to know what is going on. None of us ever receive telephone calls when we are traveling abroad. My eyes widen. "A phone call for me?" I stop eating, quickly put down my utensils, and leave the table, wondering who could be calling me from London and why. Is there an emergency? I hope not.

Going to the phone located in the foyer, I pick up the receiver. "Hello?" There is no answer. I hear a crackling along the line. "Hello? This is Laraine. Who is it please?" No answer. "Hello? Can you hear me?" Click. The line is disconnected at the other end, leaving me listening to a monotone hum.

I stand alone in the foyer, staring down at the receiver still in my hand, oblivious of my surroundings, my mind replaying the call. I am in no rush to go back to my friends and answer the inevitable questions. "Who was it? What did they want?" I know in my heart who it was. The call didn't come from London. No one in England would know to call me here. There is one person who does know I am here, who is familiar enough with the area to call this number. I take a mental eraser and began removing the memories from my mind. He had abandoned me two years ago. He had taken the coward's way out. Even now he could not approach me or talk to me. He is not worthy. He is not good enough to be my son's father. The eraser completes its job. The memories of this man are gone; he is no one. I replace the receiver in the telephone's cradle. Taking a deep breath to steady my nerves, I return to the restaurant ready to face the inquisition. I simply state to my companions that it must have been a wrong number because no one was on the phone.

CHAPTER

SIXTEEN

𝓙 am standing in the dark, narrow hallway on the ground floor of the block of flats where Loretta has lived for some fifteen to twenty years. All those years and this is the first time I have visited the flat, visited my sister's home. I hadn't even known the address until today when I got it from my mum to tell the taxi driver. Presents and cards for Loretta have always been sent to our parents' address. I excuse my dereliction of duty to my sister by telling myself that at least today I am taking her for a girls' day out. Still, I should have come here, to my sister's home, before now.

From the outside, the complex appears nice enough, a line of joined two- and three-story buildings with a dark modern brick architecture, a series of large picture windows on two or three levels, most with flower boxes offering some form of green and colored flora, and the extra thought of a resident's garden out back. Loretta has a ground-floor flat, a blessing with her disability.

Inside the dark hallway, I can't see very much. I can just make out the paler painted door of my sister's flat at the end of the hall, and as I near the door, I see the identifying metallic number "2" on the left side of the door. My knuckles rap against the wood, which shakes a little at the assault, while my head cocks forward,

author's sister Loretta, photo © Laraine Denny Burrell

listening for movement inside the flat. On the other side I hear steps moving toward the door.

The door opens to show Loretta leaning against her walking cane. She smiles at me.

"Hello, Laraine, come in." Two awkward steps back and Loretta opens the door farther, allowing me room to enter the flat. "The living room's that way." Loretta points with her cane down the small hallway. "I'll be ready in a sec."

I walk the two or three steps toward the living room door, hearing the front door close behind me, and Loretta's syncopated three-step moving along the wooden floor toward the other end of the flat. I pause to take in the sight: the living room is small, the entire flat small, but cozy. The décor is light, the furniture a pale pine wood, with frosted glass paneling and a matching coffee table, with a sofa and armchair of cream leather. A small wooden desk follows the form of the room's back corner. On top is Loretta's computer and phone. Tucked beneath are a printer and some storage boxes.

Taking a seat on the sofa, I look at the large television screen a mere three or four feet in front of me. My sister's eyesight is degenerating rapidly, so Mum bought Loretta a large flat-screen television, large enough to allow Loretta to watch television in spite of her poor vision. There had been an inquiry from the social services woman who routinely came to the flat to check on Loretta. She wanted to know why Loretta, someone living off the state, could afford a large expensive television. Mum showed the woman the receipt from Argos, proving that Mum had bought the television as a birthday present for Loretta because she could barely see. In a nutshell, this is the story of how my sister lives.

Beyond the loss of her leg, her diabetes, and her poor eyesight are the illnesses, infections, liver and pancreatic problems, blood transfusions, the constant nausea and diarrhea, doctors' visits, hospital stays, and the buffet of daily medications and carefully scheduled insulin injections. Loretta can't work, although she is always into one plan or another, taking a course for home accounting and bookkeeping, computer sciences, something, anything so she can be a useful member of society. The courses never result in work. The hundreds of job applications and résumés Loretta has sent out over the years have generated an equal number of rejections, or cold disregard. Few know of the determined little disabled lady, who is trying so hard not to live off the state, and who wants to be a useful member of society. Her good intent and decent heart are simply set aside with formulaic wording in form letters. She isn't wanted.

Disabled and unable to work, Loretta is supported by the state. She receives a certain amount of money to live on, enough to pay her bills but barely. If she has money to buy items such as a television, or if her savings account shows money above a certain amount, the state will think it is giving her too much money, and her payments will be reduced. More simply stated, luxuries are forbidden, and her flat reflects the basic needs approved by the social services, upgraded a little through the generosity of Mum and Dad at Christmas and on birthdays, all with the receipt for Loretta to show the social services the proof that the items are presents and not bought with Loretta's disability money.

Sitting on my sister's sofa and seeing the simplicity of Loretta's lifestyle and comparing it with my own, I recognize I am in a position to help my sister more than I do. I had become a Qualified Solicitor just in case I had to come back to England to take care of my disabled sister if and when our parents passed. It is insurance. I will have some form of qualification to get work in England, if necessary. Meanwhile, there is so much more I can do for Loretta. I see it now, through the guilt and sadness I feel at seeing firsthand my sister's limited life. I vow there and then that I will come back to England more often; I can afford it. And I will take Loretta on a vacation, just the two of us. Anywhere Loretta wants to go. Two sisters spending time together, making a memory for us both. We will go to a luxury hotel or resort in the country, at the seaside, whatever or wherever Loretta wants. I will hire a limousine to drive us to our holiday location so Loretta doesn't have to bother with public transportation, trains or buses, or planes. An image of Loretta passing through airport body scanners with her artificial limb, and its metallic harness, flashes through my mind. There will be questions, discomfort for Loretta, perhaps even a body search. We won't go by plane. It will be by car, or maybe by boat to the Channel Islands, a more southern and weather-friendly location than damp, frigid England.

"Would you like to see the rest of the flat?" Loretta stands at the living room door.

"Of course." I stand up to follow my sister.

"There isn't much to see," Loretta apologizes. "It's small, but works for me. This is the kitchen."

Three steps from the living room door along the wooden floor of the hallway, I find myself looking into a small but pretty kitchen. "This is really nice!" The tone of my voice reflects my approval of the room and its darker wooden cabinets with blue tiled and papered walls. I can see how the smallness creates an advantage for my sister. Loretta doesn't have to move around too much to do her cooking. Everything is within arm's reach.

"Dad decorated it for me. He did my whole flat, including putting a walk-in shower in the bathroom for me."

I follow Loretta another three steps along the hallway to the bathroom. Also in shades of blue tile, I see the practical nature of the setup, the floor-level shower and its metal handrails making access to the utilities easy for a disabled person. "Dad did a great job."

"Yes, he did, bless him." An unspoken sadness at the reminder of Dad encircles us as we stand surrounded by our father's handiwork. There is a moment's pause as each of us fleetingly thinks of our father, before Loretta breaks the silence. "And here's my bedroom." She opens the door into a bright, cheerful room, the counterpart to the warm environment of the living room.

Taking one step to the other side of the hallway, I enter the bedroom. It is an inviting room, the entire far wall consisting of windows draped with curtains in a willowy white fabric with little flowers, matching the comforter and pillow on the slim bed. A wooden wardrobe and matching bookshelf stand along the opposite wall. I can tell the wardrobe is full by the way pieces of fabric are caught in the gaps between the doors and wardrobe itself. The bookshelf is full, and then some, with novels—some of Maeve Binchy's of course, an author we both enjoy—as well as history books and books on computers and other subjects from Loretta's various employment-seeking courses.

Along the wall facing the bed is a vanity—drawers, mirror, and a little stool. The vanity's top is covered by assorted items of makeup and jewelry. I note the small wooden inlaid jewelry box placed in the middle of the vanity. I know it plays "Somewhere in Time." I had given it to Loretta some years ago for Christmas.

I am pleased to recognize something in the flat that I have given my sister.

Next to the vanity in the corner of the room is Loretta's wheelchair, for those times when Loretta is alone and doesn't want to wear her prosthetic limb, and needs more than the wobbly support of a cane. Its oversized shape and significance detracts from the lightness of the room.

"I even have a workout room!"

Surprised, I turned to watch my sister open the door of a small built-in closet tucked behind the bedroom door, perhaps two feet in depth and four to five feet wide. I laugh. There, sitting on the floor under a high shelf stacked with board games, books, and cardboard boxes, is a stationary exercise bike.

"I pull it around so it is facing out and I have a go on it," Loretta explains. "At least one leg gets a good workout." She laughs a deep, cheeky laugh.

I also laugh, both at the joke of the exercise room and because my sister can find humor despite her disability. I lean forward, wrapping my arms around Loretta.

"Oh, Loretta, you do make me laugh. Love you for it."

With the tour of the flat complete, and after giving my approval both to the lovely décor and our father's handiwork, we prepare to leave the flat. The purpose of today's visit is for a girls' day out and for me to take Loretta to lunch.

I offered to get us a taxi to the shopping precinct, but Loretta will have none of it.

"No need, Laraine. I have my bus pass. Being disabled, I get free bus fare. I can go anywhere in town, and anywhere the buses go out of town. Mum, being old, has her bus pass, and sometimes the two of us go for rides in the country, all for free!"

I chuckle at my sister finding the positive among the negative. My expression then turns to one of awe as I try to keep up with my sister as we walk to the bus stop. Loretta's good leg, prosthetic, and walking stick make a faster job of the distance than my two good legs. At times I am almost running to keep up with my sister as Loretta negotiates the uneven slabs of the pavement, the pedestrian crossing, and various obstacles, including trash cans, dogs, and people in our path. Loretta moves with such speed and determination, and since she makes a straight line to wherever she is headed, other people in the street are forced to move out of the little woman's way.

Loretta has her movements and system down pat. The bus approaches. She has her bus pass at the ready, handbag over her arm, walking cane poised for support, waiting for the driver to lower the ramp for the disabled, and then Loretta is on the bus, a quick flash of her pass to the driver, and away to find a seat, leaving me to fiddle awkwardly in my purse for the bus fare, and then to find my own seat. I marvel at my sister's independence.

We have chosen a pleasant Wednesday for our day out. The rain holds off, the sun gently reminds people that it does still exist, and the temperature is in a temperate mood. We sisters walk the precinct in Palmerstone Road, a pleasant shopping area since the traffic had been banned decades earlier, and benches and trees had replaced the tarmac road. A quieter part of town during the weekdays, the modern fashion stores and eateries are observed by St. Jude's, an old stone church completed around 1851, standing tall at the north end of the street. The area is typically English with older prewar buildings standing in line with their postwar contemporaries. I unwillingly acknowledge to myself that I am old enough to remember the days when a road used to run through the shopping area, and when I would get my dance supplies from The Stage Door just around the corner in Marmion Road. As I walk along the street, memories of the area from decades ago pass through my mind, making me feel like an ancient monument myself.

Loretta and I wander from shop to shop. I offer to treat Loretta to something, I ask if I can buy Loretta something, but Loretta won't have it. It is enough she has a day with her big sister, that we can spend this time together. I see outfits I would love to have tried on, business suits different from anything being sold in the States, which would be a plus not only because they are fashionable but because I know I will not meet a colleague wearing the same suit. But they are expensive; affordable for me, but I don't feel right flaunting my money around in front of my state-supported sister. It doesn't seem right. Instead, I ask Loretta to help me choose a present for our Mum, something to cheer her up. After much browsing and discussion, we choose a gold angel brooch for mum, which I purchase on behalf of us both, and Loretta buys some cream buns to take home for our tea.

A bistro pub is chosen for lunch and we wander inside to find a place to rest our legs and grab a bite of British grub. We both have a glass of white wine to help relax our frame of mind. We sisters chat about our lives, each giving the other an apology about not emailing enough and not being a good communicative sister. I apologize to Loretta for letting my work schedule and deadlines take over my life so that visits to England and even telephone calls and emails are always set aside to do another time, that time never coming. My heart breaks when Loretta apologizes that she can't email me because her computer is old and doesn't work very well, sometimes not at all. And sometimes she can't afford the Internet bill. "Whatever you need, Loretta, just let me know. I am working hard because I want to take care of you and Mum. I don't want you going without something you need. You just let me know."

Loretta smiles her wide cheeky grin and sweetly says, "Thank you, Laraine. Thank you very much."

"Another thing"—I put down my wineglass and lean across the table toward my sister, engaging Loretta's gaze, making sure she understands my seriousness—"I want to take you on a vacation, a holiday. Somewhere, anywhere you want to go. Just you and me. We will go off somewhere, give you a nice holiday, and give Mum some peace and quiet. All my treat. Possibly next year, we can plan ahead, and you can take time to think about what you would really love to do, somewhere you really want to go, to the country, or the seaside. And we will go first class. I want to give you a holiday to remember, for us both to always remember."

Loretta puts down her wineglass, her eyes tearful as she

author's sister Loretta, photo © Laraine Denny Burrell

returns my gaze. "Oh, Laraine, that would be lovely." Her voice is breathy, emoting her genuine longing to get away and do something special. "It would be so nice to go on a proper holiday, get away from my boring life, and my boring flat."

"Then that is what we will do. I promise." We grab hands and smile at each other, the pact made.

For the rest of our lunch we talk about our sadness at losing Dad, but then the sadness turns to jokes as we agree that he is probably happy in Heaven, away from Mum and her nagging. The jokes then turn to our mum, and we share funny stories of Mum's antics, bossiness, silliness, and wit. How she has a retort for everything. I share the story of being bullied by a girl in dance class. Mum had spoken to the girl's mum and said, "Your daughter is such a lowlife even the pavement's a step up in the world for her." We laugh.

Loretta says, "She was once at a party and so drunk she was talking to someone's black sweater lying in a ball on a couch, thinking it was the cat." That story makes me double over laughing, almost falling off my chair.

I recall one telephone call from our mum and her telling me about Loretta having a problem with her new leg. I retell it again to Loretta.

"Mum told me about the time you and her were walking down Copnor Road and she couldn't stop laughing. She said you were both laughing and even had to lean on a wall in front of a house to stop yourselves from falling over. A woman came out of the house to find out why you were leaning on her wall and wondered if there was something wrong with you. Apparently you had a new leg on, and it was loose and jiggled around until it ended up facing backward."

Loretta's hand came to her mouth. She laughed. "I remember that! I was walking down the road with one leg facing forward and one leg facing backward. It must have looked a funny sight!" Loretta fell backward in her seat laughing, nodding her head, agreeing with the memory. "It was really, really funny."

The image of Loretta walking along the road with one foot facing forward and one foot facing backward keeps Loretta and me laughing for the rest of the day. Despite her setbacks, Loretta faces adversity head-on. In fact, she kicks it in the groin with her artificial leg. I have nothing but admiration for my sister.

The day is a success. Loretta has put her moodiness aside, and opened up to me. We have spent a wonderful day together. I will remember our pact; I am going to take my sister on the holiday of a lifetime.

author and sister Loretta, photo © Ian Denny

CHAPTER

SEVENTEEN

Mark is writhing in my arms, kicking out with his legs, which are amazingly strong for a baby not quite two. He pushes against my chest with his hands, and his little face is scrunched up as he forces out a teeth-grating scream at the top of his lungs. I wrap my arms around him in a mix of hug and wrestling hold. "Hush, Mark. It's okay." My gentle words are futile against the might of a stubborn baby.

Around us dozens of people are staring our way as we stand in line at Heathrow. They can stare and pull faces all they want. I cannot control this situation, and I cannot blame Mark for being thrust into this confusion. He has just left the arms of his loving grandfather, who is now making a quick exit away from us and leaving me, for the first time, to take care of my son alone.

A woman security officer approaches me. "Miss. If you would like to come this way, we can get you through this gate over here." She points to an area on my right where another officer raises her hand to wave at me. "Thought it might make things a bit easier for you."

"Thank you. I appreciate it." And I do. The option of passing quickly through security is preferable to slowly winding along behind dozens of people who intermittently turn to scowl at me, showing annoyance at my son's wailing. Like they have only known perfectly behaved children!

I adjust Mark, making him straddle my hip, tighten my grip on him with my left arm, throw the straps of my two carry-on bags over my right shoulder, and grab the pushchair with my right hand, dragging the ensemble toward the waiting officer.

"Thank you so much."

"No problem." Her smile suggests she is glad it is me and not her dealing with Mark today. "Hi there," she says to Mark. "Are you going on a plane today?"

Mark stops wailing and cheekily gives the stranger a grin. Great. He is good for her but not for me, but at least he has stopped wriggling so I can get our passports out of my pocket and hand them to the officer.

"Everything is in order." The woman hands me back the passports. "Bye-bye." She waves to Mark as we leave the security area. Still grinning, the cheeky monkey wiggles his fingers back at her.

Heathrow is an enormous airport, in keeping with its status as a major European hub. I know from prior experience that I have miles to walk and I must keep up the pace to make it to the gate on time. Every muscle in my body is working as I walk briskly along the never-ending corridors, carrying child and bags and dragging the pushchair, which, stupidly, when I need it the most, is wrapped up in plastic security wrap courtesy of the check-in agent.

Sweat forms on my forehead and starts dripping down my nose. It seeps into confined spaces beneath my clothes. I keep up the pace, walking in as straight a line as I can, making people step aside for us, not wanting to add the extra feet and maneuvers to accommodate them.

Thankfully, Mark is not crying, his tantrum temporarily replaced by curiosity of the sights and sounds around him. "Hey, Mark, we are going on a plane." He turns to me with a quizzical "Who are you?" look. I smile. "It'll all be okay, son. I promise, it will all be okay."

Arriving at the gate, I see the area is mostly empty, with a few people at the podium giving their boarding passes to the agent, no doubt the last boarders. Good timing. We can get on the plane, get seated, and get on to whatever lies ahead for us both in Italy.

I hand the agent my boarding pass.

"Only one pass? This is for you. Do you have a pass for the baby?"

"The baby?" I am confused. "No."

"You need a separate boarding pass for the baby. You each have to have your own."

"We have our own passports."

"The airline requires every passenger have their own boarding pass."

"But I called the airline a couple of days ago to see if I needed a ticket for him and the woman said no, and the agent at check-in didn't say I needed a ticket or boarding pass for him."

"I'm sorry, ma'am, but you'll have to go back to the ticketing area and get a boarding pass. And the plane is due to leave."

"Jeez!"

As I evaluated the long trek back though Heathrow's corridors to the check-in area, simple logic took over. I hand Mark over to the agent, pushing him into her arms, dump the pushchair and bags at her feet, grab my handbag, making sure the passports are accessible, and before the agent can react, I turn and bolt. I run from the gate, run back along the corridors, causing a stir and a parting of the populace as my athleticism propels me at top speed back toward security, out to the check-in area, and directly to the front of the line to interrupt the ticketing agent.

"I'm s . . . so sorry." I take a deep breath, trying to find my voice, leaning on the counter to recover from the exertion. "My apologies, but this is an emergency." I turn to the confused passenger in the middle of her check-in. "Sorry."

Turning back to the agent, I say, "My baby son is at the gate with the gate agent, the plane is about to leave, she says I need a boarding pass for my son. When I was checked in, I wasn't told that." I push the two passports across the counter. "I need a pass for him please."

The agent understands and immediately checks the passports and issues a pass for Mark. "Thank you so much." I turn to the passenger again. "So sorry to interrupt."

Niceties over, I turn and reverse my run through the airport. At the security gate I see the officer who had let Mark and me through. I run to her. "Hi, do you remember me? I came through with my son? I had to come back and get another pass for him." I showed her the pass.

"Oh yes. Okay." She allows me through, no fuss, no bother. "Thank you!"

I continue on, familiar with the route. No time to be bothered with the madcap appearance I make. At last I reach the finishing line of my marathon, running up to the gate agent still holding Mark, almost exactly as I had left her, as if still in shock at being handed custody of my son.

"Boarding . . . pass." I push the words out. I am utterly exhausted. "Thank you . . . so . . . much." I take Mark from her arms and see that her medium blue dress now has a darker patch around her stomach area where she had been holding Mark. He had wet himself all over her. Oh well! Nothing I can do about that.

"Let me help you onboard." She grabs a bag and the pushchair.

"Thank you so much. I'm sorry, I didn't know . . ."

"It's okay. Let's get you onboard. Everyone is waiting."

Mark and I are settled in our seats. I feel his damp trousers and feel bad. I do not have a change of clothing for him. It is packed in the suitcase. He no longer wears nappies, my mum having potty-trained him as soon as he could sit up by himself. All I can do is make him as comfortable as possible. I wrap a blanket around him and around his trouser legs, hoping it will absorb the moisture. Mark's eyes are closing. The adventure has tired him out. Good. We will both need our strength for whatever comes next.

With Mark now asleep, I take a moment to look around. The plane is almost empty. Not many people going to Rome today, or at least not on this flight. Good. The last thing I need is a crowded four-hour flight. I tilt my seat back and close my eyes. Life is such a challenge.

Mark had stayed with my parents for almost two years while I worked in the Middle East and Europe. My mother recently announced that she had had enough of looking after Mark and it is time for me to take on the responsibility of caring for Mark myself and to take him with me on my travels. She wrongly thinks I am away enjoying life, leaving her to take care of my son. It is not like that. I am working hard, earning and saving my money to pay my mum's salary and to provide for my son. My mother simply doesn't comprehend my life.

With Angelo's agreement that I can return to The Three Cs with my son, I made arrangements to go back to England to pick up Mark. Here we are on our way to meet the group in Rome.

Arriving in Rome, I meet up with The Three Cs again at the airport. They have just flown in from Spain. The girls, who all know Mimis, make a fuss over Mark, who looks unsure of the new faces. At least he doesn't cry. The Italian agent meets us all at the airport and, after storing luggage, bags, and costume trunks into the van, drives us all several hours north from Rome to Viareggio on the Italian coast, where we are scheduled to perform our first shows.

Thankfully, no performance is scheduled for tonight, allowing us to recover from a long day of travel, which for me spanned several countries and involved a dramatic departure from London, a long drive in the crammed confines of a van, and a baby whose demeanor fluctuated from cranky to petrified. Poor little soul. My on-the-job-training as a mother had no respite as I tried to focus on my responsibilities to my employer and fellow castmates, while making sure Mark had everything he needed, including hugs from me, someone who garnered strange stares from him as he looked at me with questioning big brown eyes. An intangible but heavy weight lands on my shoulders; I want to cry. I dare not; I may never stop.

We arrive in Viareggio, a pretty seaside town and find the pensione where we are to stay for a couple of weeks at least. Despite the length of the day, the sun is still up, but I want nothing more than to sleep and absorb this new life I have unwittingly chosen— and to evaluate how I am going to make it all work.

With Mark in my arms and my bags and suitcase dragging and bumping up the wooden stairs behind me, I find the room we are assigned. I make a mental note that no one offered to help carry Mark or my luggage up the stairs; my "friends" were not interested in my situation, but why should they be? They are young people, responsible for leading their own lives, not mine. I realize I cannot expect their help at any time.

I open the door and walk into the room with Mark still in my arms, my luggage abandoned outside in the hallway. I walk around the room, taking in the tableau of austerity. This is the most barren room I have ever seen. The room is sparse with a wooden, unvarnished floor. There is a full bed in one corner, with clean white linens, and a sink with cold running water in another. The one window has no curtains or blinds, allowing the evening sun to offer its illumination on the otherwise dismal space. A wire hangs from the middle of the ceiling, dangling a light bulb, but no lampshade. There is nothing else in the room, no closet, no chair, no table. Nothing. I lie down on the bed with Mark still in my arms, his little body trembling against me, still not certain of who I am, and uncomprehending of the strange environment. I hug him tight, engulfing him in my arms against my chest, saying soothing words and stroking his forehead. I want him to feel my love, the security I will offer him. I will take care of him. His big brown eyes stare up at me with a mixture of fear and inquiry. His little petted lip quivers, but he is not crying.

What have I done? I ask myself. *Why did I come here? Why did I bring my son to this foreign place? I should have stayed in England.* I chastise myself. It is too late for regrets. I cannot change my life back to how it was. My only option is for me—I look into Mark's brown eyes and correct my thoughts—for us to be strong in going forward and facing the challenges coming our way.

Outside the room in the hallway, I hear the clopping of shoes on the wooden floor and the excited chatter of my fellow performers as they make their way out to celebrate their first night in Italy. I recognize that my nights of celebration are over for a while. As a mother I have other responsibilities, another focus. Life is no longer about me, about what I want, or about my dreams, my goals. My life is about being the best mother I can be for my son, and giving him the only things that I have: a promise of security, that I will always be there for him and take care of him, and, above all, that he has my love.

CHAPTER

EIGHTEEN

"You are dancing like shit!" Angelo shouts at me, his frustration evident from the scowl thrown at me before he turns his back and walks away.

The other dancers look embarrassed for me and also step away, as if avoiding contamination with my less than stellar performance. We are rehearsing a new number to offer the regular patrons of the nightclub something new to see. I don't respond to the admonition. I will not tell him that I am giving one hundred percent of what I have to give even though I am tired and hungry. Angelo, like the other dancers, only focuses on himself, what he needs, what he wants. Like the others, his awareness doesn't extend to recognizing the struggle in others.

I close my eyes and halt my churlish thoughts. These people have no obligation to think of me. My circumstances are of my creation, and I alone am responsible for the life I have created for myself and for Mark. They have given me work. In return I owe them my best performance. I take a deep breath.

"From the top!" Angelo's instructions set the cast and crew in motion. I take my place in the wings, ready to give the number everything I have.

My contract in Italy is for six months. The group travels from city to city to perform at the direction of our Italian agent, who is purportedly a member of a mafia family. We're working in nightclubs and gaming venues, and it makes sense that these establishments might be under a certain control. We travel with the "son" and his bodyguard, who drive us around the country from town to town, venue to venue. The other members of the cast and I enjoy the dramatic circumstances of working for a supposed mafia family. It adds to the stories we can tell those back home. But, the drama is tempered with humor. The DJ in the Caprice nightclub in Viareggio is the antithesis of what one expects. An enormous block of a man, he stands stoically behind his turntable while undeftly changing records on the player and sending the occasional glare out over the dance floor. We learn he is not a real DJ, but another "bodyguard" placed in a position to watch over the club and its personnel.

My room and a daily meal are provided as part of my contract, but I have to pay for board and meals for Mark, even though he sleeps in the same small bed as me. Some places charge me as if Mark is an adult. I find that unfair. *Won't anyone give me a break?*

For each new town we perform in, the first thing is always to check the showroom, get the dance numbers and costumes in order, then worry about rooms and food. I have the additional worry of finding a babysitter, an almost impossible task considering I know no one in any of the towns we travel to and I do not speak the language well. Occasionally I get lucky and find someone associated with the nightclub who helps me find a babysitter. The majority of my wages go to paying some strange woman to sit with my son during the night. Mark often panics and cries at the sight of the strange face, so I always try to have him asleep before the babysitter arrives. Every night after I feed my son, I put him to bed and rub his forehead and sing him songs. "The Gypsy Rover," an old English folk song, is his favorite, and he asks me to sing it for him over and over.

But in most towns I cannot find a babysitter and have to risk leaving Mark locked alone in our room, hoping if he wakes up he will not get out of bed, or will not cry because I am not there. It is a risk. It is always forefront in my mind. Every night, during every show, and as soon as the show is over, and the costumes put away, I run through the Italian streets and alleyways back to the hotel, always with a sense of panic and foreboding that someone or something will hurt my baby, and with the guilty knowledge that what I am doing is so very wrong, but I have no alternative. I am thankful that someone is watching over us. My baby is always okay. We manage.

I become a different person in Italy. I am a single parent, working long hours, for little pay, making sure my son doesn't go without, even to the extent of going without and going hungry myself in order to give Mark my one meal of the day.

It's okay, I tell myself. I am strong. I can manage. But trying to take care of a baby, feeding him, giving him everything he needs, finding babysitters, or not, the worry about whether he is okay while I am miles away working all hours of the night, the panic as I run back to the guesthouse every night after the show, all while never being able to make my money last to the next payday—it all takes its toll. I feel physically and mentally battered.

There are times I have to ask Angelo if he can advance my wages, or spare a little extra because I need to feed my son, and my money has been spent on babysitters or the extra room payment for Mark. I'm not proud of the circumstances making me beg for extra money. But it is what I have to do. There are times I am so tired because I am working long hours as a dancer at night and then trying to stay awake with my son during the day and keeping him occupied, taking him to the beach or to the park.

Today, Mark and I are walking to the beach across the street from the guesthouse. Each pensione has its own private stretch of beach and its own distinctively colored beach chairs and umbrellas for its guests uniformly lined along the sand, down to the water's edge. But because Angelo got a reduced rate on our rooms, I am not considered a real guest, so I have to find an area of sand away from the chairs and umbrellas where I can lie down without harassment from the overzealous beach attendants. I sit Mark on the sand with his bucket and spade, hoping it keeps him occupied at least for a while. I lay out my towel, kick off my sandals, and lie down. My muscles relax; my body sinks into the sand. I feel the solar warmth on my face, hear the white noise of the waves, and . . .

I open my eyes. I hear waves crashing a distance from me, and people shouting in vibrant Italian. Confused, I ask myself, *Where am I?* I sit up. I look around me. "Oh my God!" I shout out. I must have fallen asleep. My heart races. Where is Mark? I don't see him. I look at my watch. I must have been asleep a good hour. "Oh my God!"

I scramble to my feet, scanning the scene around me, trying to find my baby. My eyes filter through the beachgoers, looking for a little person in blue shorts and T-shirt. The numerous multicolored chairs and umbrellas interspersed with adults obstruct my view. I don't see him. I run down to the edge of the water and look back along the sand up toward the road. I don't see him. *Oh my God! Where is Mark? Where is my son? Did he go up to the road? Did someone take him? What have I done?*

My eyes scan down the beach, analyzing every object and person until thankfully I see a little blue figure sitting in the sand at the edge of the water about fifty feet away from me. He is quietly playing with his bucket and spade, apparently not bothered by the bustle around him. My knees buckle with relief. "Mark!" I shout to him as I run toward him. "Mark!"

He sees me and smiles. His chubby fingers wiggle at me in his version of a wave. "Mum-mum," he calls to me.

I kneel beside him on the sand and wrap him in my arms, hugging him tight. "Oh, Marky. I am so sorry!" I am comforted by the feel of his little body next to mine, the salty smell of his hair, the sandy clutch of his fingers around my neck. This is the love of my life and I cannot lose him. I don't deserve him. I am a terrible, awful mother. I give Mark a big kiss on his cheek.

"Mum-mum."

I look down at the trusting face of my son and for the first time realize we have made our bond. He hadn't gone far from me because instinctively he knew he had to stay close to me, his Mum-mum. My life might be impossibly difficult right now, but it is balanced with the love of my son.

Resourcefulness, or dogged determination to succeed despite the odds, can be a burden because with it comes an obligation to at least try to do something when most other people wouldn't bother. It's Mark's second birthday, and I am briskly walking and pushing Mark's pushchair along the edge of a busy freeway for what might be several miles toward a town. Even though I am in Italy, I am determined to create some semblance of English normalcy and to find a birthday cake for Mark. It is a long walk to and from a strange town where I assume there must be some kind of bakery, or somewhere I can find something to pass off as a birthday cake. And despite the incongruity of the circumstances, that I am traveling with my baby son around Europe from show to show with a small cast of performers, my mind is set that my son's birthday is going to be properly celebrated as if we were in England.

I must look an odd sight. A young woman with a stroller and child, shopping bag at the ready, long legs striding along the tarmac at the side of the highway or *autostrada*, ignoring the cars speeding by, focusing only on the rooftops of the village in the distance. Horns toot at me, the fast swoosh of air pushes me sideways as a speeding car passes at close range, taking ownership of the road and ignoring the pedestrian on the shoulder. Mark's eyes are wide. He hears the toot of the car horns and most times jumps a little, startled at the unexpected interjection into his stroll with Mum. I have pulled the top of the pushchair cover all the way up and over, shielding Mark from the sight of the various colored vehicles passing at speed. Still, I can't dampen the sound.

I talk to him cheerily. "It's your birthday. You're a big boy now! Two years old today." We tilt a little sideways as another

author and son Mark celebrating Mark's second birthday, family photo

push of air bowls into us. I straighten the stroller. "We are going to get you a lovely cake for your birthday. There must be somewhere in this village we can get something nice for you." I keep my focus on my son; I smile at him. Mark looks uncertain, giving me a dubious look. He does not smile back.

For more than an hour I stride on, my sneakers pounding the pavement in a rhythmic "left right, left right." I want a birthday cake for my son. I am going to get a birthday cake for my son. My determination pays off. Mark gets his cake. Later that afternoon in my room, the other dancers and I sit in a circle on the floor, surrounding the birthday cake now lit with a candle I had borrowed from the manager. We sing "Happy Birthday" as an embarrassed Mark runs and buries his head in my shoulder. I think to myself, *Finally I did something right as a mum. I gave my son a nice birthday.*

As Mark becomes more accustomed to our nomadic way of life and the more he settles down, the more he turns into a little devil. This is never more apparent than during our stay in Florence. The hotel is near a large two-story indoor market that I visit almost daily to buy fresh fruit and vegetables, which can be easily cooked on the little electric stove in my room. I found the stove a couple of months ago in another town and now discreetly cook as much as I can to avoid the expense of eating out, all while trying not to cause a fire in my room or incur the wrath of the management.

Walking along the streets with Mark is always a delight. The streets are traditional Italian, narrow, cobbled roads aligned with chic boutiques. Once at the market, I walk and Mark toddles along the aisles between the stalls offering cheeses, sliced meats, fruits, candies, bread. In my mind I am deciding what I want to buy today, and practice the Italian words to make the purchase. As much as I always try to keep a hold of Mark's hand, as soon as I let go to take money out of my purse to pay for my purchase, Mark runs off like a shot. This is his new thing, running around as fast as his little legs can carry him, his face a grin of freedom and delight. He doesn't care where he goes; he just runs, and expects me to find him when he is ready.

Over time the market people come to know him. I hear messages over the loudspeaker in Italian but roughly translated as, "Would the English lady come to such and such a stall to pick up her son." I invariably go to the stall and find Mark standing there among the doting stallkeepers, all smiles and always with a handful of candy. The naughty boy knows that if he runs away and makes it to this stall, he will get candy.

I find the Italians very kind to me and my son. The Italians love boys and Mark is a good-looking little charmer. It is not unusual for Mark and me to walk down the street in Viveroni, Montecatini, or Moderno and have strangers thrust candy or an ice-cream cone into Mark's hand, or have someone tell me my son is *"Molto bello."* I am pleased people like Mark. But that doesn't give him license to be the devil that he is.

Interestingly, perhaps the nicest group of people I meet in Italy is a colorful and gregarious group of prostitutes. The company is contracted to perform in a nightclub in Moderno for a few weeks. The agent has arranged for us performers to live in a large guesthouse, a multistory brick building in the middle of the town. I soon learn that most of the residents are in fact prostitutes. They don't work in the building, they work at the various nightclubs around town, but the guesthouse is where they live. Once these ladies hear that a group of dancers are moving in and that one girl is a single parent with a little boy, a couple of them go to the manager and ask that I be given a particular room. It is a room with a large French window opening out onto its own private courtyard. The ladies then commandeer buckets of soap and water from the manager and with no qualms about getting down on their knees, start scrubbing the courtyard so it is clean enough for baby Mark to play in. I stand by with awe and watch the aggressive attacks on the paving stones as the ladies put bristle to stone, refusing to let me help. They are adamant that they want to do this themselves. Mark sits on the floor of the room, staring out the French doors, mesmerized by the voluptuous bottoms and bosoms jiggling as their owners scrub the flagstone beneath them. I am astounded by this gracious act. I learn not to judge a person by their profession.

The ladies and I become good friends. I particularly bond with Sofia, who lives in the room next to mine, and Lena, who has a room one floor above me. They bring Mark toys and candy. They also babysit him so I can get some sleep during the day. This is something the English dancers I work with never offer to do. In the evening as I try to get Mark to sleep before I go to work, I sing the old English folks songs to him and rub his forehead as I sing. I learn that Sofia in the next room lies on her bed listening to the singing because it reminds her of when she was little and her own mother sang to her.

I am constantly reminded that it isn't easy being a single parent, especially traveling abroad with a small child. I hear my fellow dancers in adjoining rooms getting ready to go out on the

Mark in Italian Courtyard, family photo

author, son Mark, and Lena outside Pensione in Italy, family photo

town and to have fun, while I have to stay in my room looking after my son. They find Italian boyfriends. I don't. They enjoy life. I can't. But somehow, with the help and kindness of strangers, I manage. The life I am leading is far different from anything I had imagined. I could have stopped myself from going through the hardships; I could have stayed in England where social services would have taken care of Mark and me. But I didn't. I chose the most difficult road available. It is a character-building education and teaches me strength and endurance and the extent of my capabilities both as a mother and person.

I begin presetting my costumes and accessories for tonight's show in the area assigned to me. I hang the costumes in order of appearance on the hook; put gloves, bracelets, and other adornments on the seat of a chair; and place my change of shoes with straps undone and ready to wear under the chair. The other girls are doing their own preparations around me.

I hear Angelo come into the dressing room. "Hey, guess what!"

We turn to face Angelo, giving him the courtesy of our attention.

"I got a letter from Elena. Remember her?"

The other girls and I nod. Elena had been part of the group in Egypt.

"She wants to rejoin the group." Angelo holds up the letter as proof.

"You're not going to let her, are you?" The disdainful response coming from Debbie, Angelo's partner. "She was such a trouble-maker, saying nasty things about everyone. I was glad to see the back of her."

"Oh, she wasn't that bad," Angelo offers in defense.

"Not to you, perhaps, because you're a guy and the boss. She was horrible to the rest of us."

I take a step toward Debbie. "She was nice enough to me."

"Oh, Laraine! You should have heard her after you left the group in Egypt and went home to England to have Mark. Do you know she told Mimis that you slept with loads of men when he was away on his trips to Europe, and that your baby probably wasn't his?"

"What?" I freeze in shock. "She said that to Mimis?" Feathers and sequins start spinning around me. I reach back to grab the wall to stop myself from keeling over. I lean forward. My forehead is sweaty. I feel sick.

I hear Debbie say, "We are well rid of her. Angelo, if you hire her, I'm quitting."

A chorus of "Me too!" echoes from around the room as the other dancers voice objections to Elena's return.

I fall back onto my chair, inattentively crushing my costume parts as I give in to gravity. Mimis had disappeared from my life without explanation, until now. He had been told that I had slept with many men to the extent that he didn't think Mark was his son. If that had been true, that I had slept with many men, then I would have deserved Mimis's abandonment. But it was not true. It was not true!

This girl's malicious gossip, done without thought or consideration, had caused me tremendous pain. It made me a single parent, struggling alone to raise my son, and sometimes in desperate financial circumstances. I do not know what is worse, the fact that someone I worked closely with and considered my friend would gossip and even lie about me. Or that Mimis's Mediterranean hot-bloodedness and ego believed the girl's story versus asking me directly if the rumor was true. The girl had lied and Mimis had removed himself from my life. Because of this girl's reckless lies, my son will never know his father. I vow, that from this day forward, I will never lie. I never want to inflict this type of pain on another living soul.

CHAPTER

NINETEEN

I lean against the seawall, feeling the damp, salty wind splash against my face, enjoying the moment as I am embraced by all I remember as being wonderful about my hometown, Portsmouth. The sea, the pebbly beach, the gardens and common along the seaside, the promenade linking the timeline of the city's history with naval monuments and memorials, old churches, and military fortifications. I look out at the choppy stretch of water known as the Solent. I can just make out the Isle of Wight on the other side because today the salty mist is obscuring the view. I see numerous ships cutting through the gray water, creating cresting waves beneath their bow and ribbons of white foam trailing behind them. Flags of different nations flap rapidly from mastheads, and a variety of red and blue ensigns flutter from the aft deck.

"Hey, Mom, look at that!" Mark jolts me from my reverie. He is pointing to a gray hull emerging from the harbor somewhere to our right. "I think that's a navy destroyer."

"You are probably right. We should see plenty of navy ships today, including historic ones, once we get closer to the dockyard."

author and son Mark, family photo

I decided to have a day out with Mark. My purpose is two-fold. I think we both need to get away from the somber mood at home. I hope the fresh air will blow away the cobwebs of melancholy hanging in our minds. I also want to take Mark to visit my old haunts and to share some of my childhood memories with him, the passing on of knowledge and family history, the way my dad had passed some of our family history on to me.

Canoe Lake was our starting point earlier this morning, where I pointed out to Mark the old boathouse, still there housing the wooden boats and my memories. The surrounding flower gardens are a riotous display of color and so very English and appropriate for the damp climate. I had grabbed a few slices of bread from Mum's kitchen, and Mark and I had spent a few minutes feeding the swans, the birds descendants of many generations of these graceful creatures which for decades could be found gliding across this lake, and no doubt descendants of those I had fed when visiting this lake as a baby with my mum.

After walking around the lake, we climb a hill and find the

crossing to take us over the road to the promenade, a wide long path extending for miles along the seaside. Now standing on the promenade, we look out at a vast expanse of the gray-green and slightly choppy water of the Solent, dotted with buoys to guide the extensive array of ships sailing in and out of the harbor to our west.

From the beach you can also see the old sea forts rising from the waters of the Solent. These forts had been built in the 1880s to protect Portsmouth's naval base and harbor, and during the World War II, submarine nets had been placed to stop the German U-boats from sneaking into the harbor. Portsmouth had been a naval community for centuries, its commerce designed to support the navy and its sailors. It is still the home of HMS *Victory*, Nelson's flagship, and other historic vessels, as well as the home port of many of Britain's modern fighting warships.

"Have you ever been over to one of those forts, Mom?"

"No, I haven't." I had often wondered what these old sea forts looked like up close, what they were like inside, but I hadn't ever made the effort to find out. I think tours might go out there, but I don't know for sure. "Perhaps another time we can go out and take a closer look."

"That would be so cool!

"Hey, look, Mom, is that a hovercraft?" Mark's inquisitive mind has moved on to another topic.

I look toward where he is pointing, seeing an orange craft on a gray cushion gliding along the top of the water. "Yep, it is."

"Have you ever been on one?"

"When I was a little girl, I went across to the Isle of Wight on one. It is cool when it starts up. You feel yourself lifted up into the air before the craft moves backward into the water."

"Cool. Maybe we can do that someday too."

"Maybe."

We move away from the seawall, now walking along the promenade to the west along the common, a vast expanse of parkland set aside for public use, with ornate flower gardens and park benches for anyone to enjoy. In the old days, the common land was where anybody could graze their sheep or cattle, but today it is where people picnic, play ball, enjoy the fresh air. I tell Mark that his grandfather would bring him down here when Mark was a baby and they would play football.

Mark is fascinated with history, and I do my best to act as a tour guide, passing on my knowledge of this deeply historic place where we were both born. Mark soaks it all in with a fervent curiosity. Along the beach is Southsea Castle built by King Henry VIII, with its black-and-white striped lighthouse tower and its surrounding moat. Although it is quite impressive having an actual castle here on the beach, as a child the main attraction was the steep hill on its northern side. The hill was high enough and steep enough so you could roll down it, building up great speed and causing a giddy sensation equal to anything the Fun Fair at Clarence Pier could offer. I smile thinking back to those moments of me tumbling down the hill with my friends. A part of me wants to give it one last try. Common sense tells me, "No! Not at your age!"

We walk on to the War Memorial, and spend a few moments reading the plaques and visiting the names of those local men and women who had died for their country. There are so many names, and many were so young. Even today we find both fresh and dried flowers and an occasional memento placed next to a name. I watch Mark as he traces names with his fingers, his interest in World War II coming to life, and death, before him.

"Hey, Mom! Do you think any of these people might be our ancestors?"

"I don't think so. Our family is from Scotland, with some Irish thrown in for good measure. As far as I know, I am the first person in our family to be raised in England."

"I see. Maybe we can find our ancestors in Scotland one day."

I nod. "That would be very cool!"

After a final respectful glance at the memorial, we walk on past the Royal Garrison Church, also called the "British Military Cathedral," with its stained glass windows depicting soldiers from history, including the world wars. A church had been standing on that site since 1212. After being restored in the 1800s, it was firebombed by the Germans in 1941, and today the nave of the church is just a roofless shell, its stone walls angled upward, like arms raised to the heavens. As a schoolgirl I had played field hockey and competed in school sports days on Governor's Green, next to the church. It was a prime example of history living side by side with modern-day life, a reminder to all that no matter what has happened in the past, life still goes on.

Further to the west I can see the tower of Portsmouth Cathedral, first built around 1180, peeking above the rooftops of the old row houses, now historical landmarks, some with ornate plaques proudly announcing they were built in the 1600s and stood to this day. Close by are the Round Tower and Square Tower, standing tall along the edge of the seawall. These fortifications with their thick stone walls had changed little over the centuries and their cannons still guard the entrance to the harbor.

Mark playfully runs between the cannons. "Kboom, kboom," he shouts in a deep voice, pretending to arm and fire them at the French and the Spanish, no doubt imagining himself as part of a battle scene from two hundred years ago. I take photographs of Mark next to the cannons and then we walk up the old stone steps to the top of the towers, where we are presented with a view of the busy mouth of the harbor.

All sizes and types of watercraft are entering and leaving the harbor, following the guidance of the buoys and the maritime laws. A large car ferry is coming in from the Channel Islands, passing by a ferry headed over to the Isle of Wight. Each boat slicing through the green water, causing white waves to dance their way to the rocks at the foot of the towers, where they splash in one last "hoorah" before melting back into the green brine. Ships' horns can be heard: three solemn blasts to say "Goodbye" to the port.

"Hey, Mom. We're not in Vegas anymore."

The comment makes me laugh. "That's for sure!"

Continuing on, we walk on through Old Portsmouth past

small, narrow row houses, and then on through Spice Island, an area of marine warehouses, and finally through the, Gunwharf abutting the naval dockyard. All around us is the aroma of salt, fish, aged musty and historical buildings. Within the dockyard is the *Mary Rose* and her museum. She was a naval ship built in the early 1500s and was a favorite of King Henry VIII. She had sunk in 1545 during a battle valiantly defending Portsmouth from the French but had been retrieved from her sea grave in 1982. That she had been recovered from the sea floor and now had a museum to tell her story is a testament to how important it is to recover history and put it on display versus leaving it to decay at the bottom of the ocean.

Walking through the Gunewharf we see the masts of another ship, the HMS *Warrior*, berthed at the dockyard gate. She was the first iron-hulled, armored warship built for the Royal Navy in 1860, and she was the pride of Queen Victoria's fleet. Beyond the *Warrior* in the dockyard itself, we see the masts of the Admiral Lord Nelson's famous flagship, HMS *Victory*, the iconic representation of Britain's victory at the Battle of Trafalgar in 1805. Our British heritage is carefully maintained as a reminder of what it took for us to become who we are today. I appreciate it. I miss it. Mark is right. It is vastly different to our current hometown, Las Vegas, the home of neon signs flashing along the Strip, punctuated with artificial lakes, Disneyesque castles, pirate ships, palaces, canals, palm trees, and fake turf. There is nothing artificial about the brisk sea air, the sound of the waves crashing against the seawalls as they had done for hundreds of years, or the sight of these historical fighting vessels.

Mark and I end our tour with a ride up to the observation deck at the top of the Spinnaker Tower, Portsmouth's millennium landmark, from where we are able to look down not only at Portsmouth and Southsea, but across to Gosport on the other side of the harbor, and as far north as Portsdown Hill. This new tower gives me a view and perspective of my hometown that I have never seen before, and while Mark spends time taking photo-

*view up Spinnaker Tower in Portsmouth from quayside,
photo © Laraine Denny Burrell*

*view of Spinnaker Tower in Portsmouth from across Portsmouth Harbour,
photo © Laraine Denny Burrell*

graphs looking down through the glass floor, I take a moment to myself and stand by a window to reflect on how much my city has changed since I was a child, as have I. In some ways it is the same. The historical areas of the city have been preserved; they are as I remember them. They represent the parts of me that are the same, that will never change. Other areas are foreign to me, such as this marina where we are now, with its modern condominium towers and shopping area with restaurants. These changes reflect the changes in my own life. Even the royal naval barracks along the waterfront have been converted into luxury flats. I don't like the changes. I want my memories of my hometown to be accurate. I see now that they are not. It is disconcerting. It makes me feel old.

I turn around to check on Mark and find him lying on his belly next to the glass floor, his camera pointed down. The typical American, no qualms about propriety, wanting to get the best shot he could of the ground below the tower. I smile at the sight. Then my smile fades. He had a good life in the States, but would he have had a better life if I had stayed in England? I don't know the answer, and the uncertainly is unnerving. Over the past few days, as I have revisited my memories, my doubts about leaving England have become niggling, annoying fears that I had not made the right choices in life. Had my choices messed up my son's life? Have I failed him?

I look around me at the display visible through the windows of the tower and go back to spend a few more moments with my memories. I look across the harbor toward Gosport and visualize the numerous trips I had made across the harbor on the ferry, mostly for dancing competitions and exams. I would practice my routines on the ferry crossing, not caring who was watching. I was a ballet dancer on tiptoe, or a Greek maiden making offerings to a god, a tap dancer or singer in a modern musical.

I look down to my left back to the Round and Square Tower fortifications and beyond to the promenade, remembering the beach days and picnics on the common with my family, seeing myself in a green-and-white gingham-checked dress and pigtails bobbing behind me as I played ball, ran, roller-skated, played hide-and-seek. I feel myself smile at the warm thoughts, wanting, wishing to remain with that child.

But as I stand at the window looking back in time, the sun emerges from behind a cloud and highlights the window before me. An image appears, not of a child but of an older woman. I look at the reflection, the woman's face, her eyes, the furrow running across her brow. This is who the child has become. The reflection looks as sad as I now feel. With empathy I reach out to touch her cheek. She feels as hard as the glass, but I also feel the warmth of the sun shining within her. The child is long gone. So much time has passed. I don't have the power to bring them back. All that is left is this woman standing with me now.

The reflection disappears, as does the sun behind another cloud, leaving the world below me now shrouded in gray. I part ways with my memories and the little girl I once knew, and turn to face the present. Mark is still lying on his belly on the glass floor, now joined by other folks wanting to get their own photographs of the land below. The scene makes me smile. I realize that my life was made up of choices. The different paths I had opted to take and the doors I had selected to go through had brought me to this point in my life today. I could debate with myself forever on whether I had made the right choices, and if my life would have been better if I had gone in other directions. But one thing I know with certainty. The one absolutely right choice I've made in my life was the most important choice, and that was keeping my baby Mark.

CHAPTER

TWENTY

The houselights of the theater dim, the overture begins, a hush falls over the audience. The massive red curtain—expanding across what the *Guinness Book of World Records* recognizes as the largest set stage in the world—begins to rise. I watch as it folds upon itself, ascending beyond the gold-mirrored proscenium and revealing a dark cavernous space broken only by a few lights upstage representing a city skyline. The image of a plane flying across the backdrop is accompanied by a narrator.

"Ladies and gentlemen. Welcome to Reno!"

The audience is suddenly doused with the powerful landing lights shining out from a three-quarter-scale DC-10 traveling downstage toward the audience. Six girls in white-and-blue air-hostess costumes are dancing on each of the wings. Dozens of other dancers and singers appear onstage, and as the main stage lights come up, revealing an airport scene, everyone starts singing the title song of the show, "Hello Hollywood, Hello. The show that really is a show . . ."

"Oh my gosh!" I am amazed at the glitz, the glamour, the feathers, the sequins, the over-the-top creativity performing in front of me.

"It's amazing!" Another dancer sitting on my right echoes my awe.

I am sitting several stories up in the theater's light booth, watching the most amazing *spectacular* I have ever seen unfold before me. Not only is there an incredible theater set to marvel at, but there are more than a hundred dancers and singers performing in choreographed unison to the show's theme song. I am astounded because I have been hired to perform as a dancer in this show of which I have never seen the like. I am both excited and petrified.

I arrived in Reno, Nevada, only yesterday, ready to begin my one-year contract for the MGM Grand in the show *Hello Holly-wood, Hello*. I had no concept of what lies ahead as I made the long journey from London to Los Angeles, and finally on to Reno. There were hundreds of British female dancers on the flight from London to Los Angeles, and MGM hired an entire Boeing 747 just for us dancers. We are to be the American equivalent of the famous Parisian *Bluebell Girls*. We are called the *Kelly Girls* after Miss Bluebell's real name, Barbara Kelly. Some girls left the group in Los Angeles, traveling on to dance in the new MGM show in Las Vegas. The Vegas show is to replace the one that was closed because of the tragic MGM fire. The rest of us are here to dance at the sister property in Reno.

For the next two hours I am mesmerized by what is truly and properly categorized as a *spectacular*. Other scenes in the show include the San Francisco earthquake of 1906, with the entire set of a San Francisco street crumbling and falling from the shaking and rumblings of the earthquake while performers, inhabitants of San Francisco, frantically run around the stage trying to evade the falling buildings. Even an old-fashioned, firefighting pump rushes across the stage to douse a fire.

In another scene, space people and aliens dance before the Space Queen in her court, and a "living curtain" drops from the proscenium, carrying dozens of dancers gyrating to space disco music. The finale is a tribute to MGM musicals, with real horses and of course a real MGM lion on the center platform above the performers. There are approximately a hundred and thirty performers, dancers, singers, and variety acts in the cast. I am used to dancing with eight or nine other performers. Sitting watching the show this first night, I begin to doubt my ability to perform at this high professional level and in such an astonishing extravaganza.

At five foot eight I am placed in the Pony Line, the group of shorter female dancers. We pride ourselves on being the true female dancers in the show and not just walking coat hangers for extravagant feather and sequined costumes. I quickly learn the "showgirl walk" and how to elegantly carry an enormous feather and jeweled backpack while walking up and down a staircase and across the stage, and then how to do a costume quick-change in the wings between numbers and, with the help of my dresser, how to fly the backpack up onto the rail for storage.

A week later, after long days and nights of rehearsals, I am to make my first appearance in the show. Nicola, the ponies' dance captain, gives us the nightly preshow instructions in the dressing room.

"All right, ladies, I have posted the schedule on my mirror for both stage left and stage right. Tonight we're five and five. Swings, check your positions, we have Linda and Kim off tonight. New ladies, double-check your positions on the list. Finale, Mary and Jill do Bubble Girls, Gayle and Liza do Arabians, rest of you are Drummers. Any questions, ask me."

My first show is a blur, from my first position standing in my Bluesleeves costume on the grand staircase as it rises from below the stage through enormous elevator doors to unveil itself to the audience, through dancing in red feathers in the heatwave number and escaping falling debris in the San Francisco earthquake number, and to the final number, marching out in my drummer costume, keeping the beat with my fellow ponies as we accent the classic Hollywood circus show tunes. After the show there is little time to reflect on how it went because we have to preset for the second show, but I do get a "good job" and a pat on the shoulder from Nicola.

I quickly become comfortable in the show as if I have been performing in it for years.

I become comfortable descending down from a height of several stories above the stage on the living curtain while gyrating and disco-dancing around a pole. I am a drummer in the finale and thankful not to be a principal performer during that number because all the principals are presented on the center stage set with the uncaged MGM lion, who sits atop the main platform above the other performers. To keep him docile, the poor boy is given tranquilizers, which has the unfortunate effect of lack of muscle control. So from time to time, a lion-sized gush of pee waterfalls its way down the set, splashing the unfortunate performers and their sequins but never dousing their smiles.

A month after my first performance in the show, I have found my own apartment, and a babysitter, and I am ready for Dad to bring Mark from England to live with me. Dad arranges to fly to Reno with Mark, and to stay for a week to help me get organized. My company manager kindly gives me the week off, understanding my need as a single parent to get my two-year-old son acclimatized to his new environment. Mark is happy to see me. He gives me a big hug and cheerfully says, "Mum-mum!"

Dad, Mark, and I spend the week organizing my apartment, helped by my dad generously buying us a few things we need. We rent a car and explore the Biggest Little City of Reno, and drive up through the mountains, to Lake Tahoe. Not only am I happy to see Mark, but it is good to see Dad, and have the momentary shoulder to lean on. I go out of the way to ask my dad his opinion and advice.

"I'm saving up to buy a car, Dad. Do you think I should go with something smaller and more affordable, or something bigger which might be safer if I'm in an accident?"

"I'm not familiar with these America cars, but I'd think safety is more important."

I nod in agreement.

"You'll want to save your money too. Be disciplined. Ye never know when a rainy day might come, and ye've a bairn who will be relying on you."

I nod. "You're right, Dad, of course."

On Dad's second-to-last night, I go in and do the show, and the company manager comps Dad into the theater to watch me perform in something I know he couldn't before imagine. I'm on stage watching my dad in the audience tracking my every move through every number.

"You've done well," Dad says to me after the show. "You've done well."

With Dad's approval I believe my life is finally on the right track.

Inevitably the week passes too quickly, and after a tearful goodbye, Dad is gone, leaving Mark and me to carve out this new life of ours. Two days later Dad telephones to check we are doing okay. "We're fine, Dad. Thank you for your help. I appreciate what you did, bringing Mark out to me, buying us the things we needed."

"You're welcome, love."

"How was the flight back?"

"It was . . ."

Dad halts mid-sentence, leaving an electric silence over the airwaves. I wait for him to continue.

"Leaving Mark behind, it was probably the loneliest and saddest day of my life."

I sense the raw emotion in my dad's voice.

"I know I reacted badly when you were first pregnant."

The direct comment surprises me. I say nothing, recognizing the gravity of the moment.

Dad continues, "It was a natural reaction, I suppose. I love Mark. He's a bonny wee lad. He's the best thing you could've given me. I miss him. I miss you both."

The words are heartfelt, not only because of their message but perhaps more because I recognize how difficult it is for my dad to open up like this. "Thanks, Dad. We miss you too." I hang up the receiver. Dad and I have made our peace.

"Here, Mark, throw the birds some bread." I hand Mark small pieces of bread pulled from the loaf I am carrying, and then demonstrate to him how to throw the bread out toward the ducks and swans floating on the edge of the lake. I toss the bits of bread onto the water, causing a synchronized turning of avian heads and a mass paddle of feathered bodies chasing toward the treats.

Mark chuckles at the scene and delights at how the birds react to him throwing bread at them. "Birds."

"Good boy! That's right, birds."

As often as I can, I follow the habit Mark and I developed in Europe of going out for walks and fresh air whenever we can. Today we are walking around Virginia Lake, a small but lovely lake in the middle of Reno. A path runs around the lake, making the walk easy. The birds offer additional entertainment for young Mark, making my job easier.

When I first arrived in Reno, I despaired on how I was going to live here for a whole year. The town seemed small and had little to offer as compared with the other more exotic places I have lived across the globe. But I have learned to be adaptable and with the help of friends, including my new best friend Jill, I learn to take advantage of everything the area has to offer. I learn to ski up at Mount Rose, at Boreal Ridge, and at other ski resorts. I hike around the Sierras. Mark learns how to swim and to ride a bike, and makes friends of his own age. Our staid English personas are slowly replaced by more outgoing American personalities.

My social life starts around two in the morning once the second show has finished. There is plenty of late-night fun. My friends and I perform in charity shows in various clubs around town, including at IT or Imagine That, a gay bar across the street from the MGM. Many of the dressers from my show are gay, adding a wonderfully extravagant dimension to life backstage. The gay community has its own court, and I am asked to choreograph a routine for the queen's coronation. For my efforts I am awarded the title Princess of Patience, complete with a scroll commemorating the title.

The company manager routinely asks dancers such as me to do additional publicity events. The extra pay goes a long way to supplement my income. I have done television commercials and print advertisements, and posed in my showgirl costumes at cocktail parties and charity events. Last week I was dressed in my showgirl costume, complete with G-string, diamond-studded bra, and high heels, all to walk around an arena leading a prize bull at the start of a livestock auction event. My high heels were lost in the thick straw lining the arena, and I was thankful that it fell to our dressers to get the cow poop off of my shoes. My first year with MGM passes quickly. I audition to stay on in the show and continue onto my second year in Reno.

Not all of the male dancers are gay, thank goodness! The fabulous male physiques are an attraction to any woman, and I have my eye on a particularly fine-looking man called Stuart, who recently joined the show. But with such a large cast, and with every movement both onstage and off choreographed to ensure performers do not get run over by forklifts, or clobbered by falling drops, I am never near Stuart at any time during the show. I have to amuse myself by admiring him from the wings, or atop a flight of stairs, or while dancing on a moving set piece. Fortunately for me, a fellow dancer leaves the show and my finale position is changed. I am no longer a drummer but now an Arabian dancer, and I make my entrance from the downstage right wing right next to Stuart, who is a gladiator. I twirl and gyrate, jiggling the gold coins on my Arabian costume as I make my way across the front of the stage as part of the parade of Hollywood characters. Behind me Stuart the Gladiator struts purposefully, smiling at me as I cheekily use my character to flirt with him.

Show after show, as we meet in the wings before the finale, we chat and get to know each other and find we have a lot in common. Not the least being that we were born on the same day. I decide it is kismet. Happily, within time Stuart and I start dating. He is very good to Mark, and eventually Mark and I move into Stuart's house. For a while we play happy family.

The MGM Grand becomes Bally's. Despite the change in the hotel name, the show stays largely the same. However, more high-end talent is brought in to star in the show. Our first big celebrity is Carol Channing. No one knows what to expect from her the first night of rehearsals with the full cast and crew.

The second show finishes at 2:00 a.m. Rehearsals start around 3:00 a.m., once the sets, scenery, costumes, and everything else is either put away or preset for the next day's show. We take our places ready for a full run-through of each of the numbers in which Carol is performing.

After the first run, Carol grabs her mike, walks out to the center of the stage, and shouts out to the producer sitting in the house.

"Donn. Can you hear me?"

The entire cast and crew come to a standstill, and turn to look at Carol. What is going on? What does she want?

"Sure, Carol, I can hear you. Something wrong?"

"Let the kids go home. They don't need to rehearse. They know what they are doing. I don't. I'm the one that needs to rehearse. Let the kids go home."

"Er . . . okay."

And with that simple and thoughtful gesture, Carol Channing earns the respect of every performer and crew member in the show.

After Carol Channing, Suzanne Somers brings her stage act into the Hello Hollywood show. I am one of the dancers chosen to be a backup singer and dancer for Suzanne Somers's act, which includes filming a television special with her and other cast members. I get a copy of the television special and send it back home for Mum and Dad to see their daughter on American television.

We finish the second show during the early morning hours. The routine becomes staying up to get Mark, who stays the night with a babysitter, off to school in the morning and then going to sleep during the day until it is time to pick him up from school. We become night people, socializing until sunrise.

Tonight Stuart and I are at Jerry's house, relaxing in his pool with some others from the show. It is a gorgeous summer night, warm temperatures and a clear sky. I am leaning against the side of the pool, looking up at the stars. "I wish I could fly up there," I say to no one in particular.

Stuart is next to me. "I can toss you up there, and you can fly back down into the pool."

I give him an odd look.

"Pretend we are a dance team and I am lifting you into an angel," he says, describing a dance lift.

"I've never done adagio, or any lifts."

"Come, I'll show you. You'll be safe falling into the pool."

For the next hour or so, Stuart and I play around in the pool, trying to do "lifts," him holding me up in the air in various positions. This is what we dancers call *adagio*, the partnership of a male and female dancer performing graceful lifts. We discover we have an affinity for adagio. Stuart lifts me up above his head, and I learn to balance in various positions, using the water as a safety net. Stuart is extraordinary strong and can lift me easily. I am also strong and can balance in graceful positions on Stuart's hands as he lifts me above his head. We work on the angel, the star, some basic seated positions. It isn't as hard as I thought. I point my toes gracefully, place my arms into fifth position above my head, hold my posture erect to make me both light and strong.

"She looks good up there," says Paul, another dancer. "You guys should try forming an adagio team, aim for the principal spot in the Space Ballet."

Stuart and I both laugh at the thought. The space number in the show includes the revered Space Ballet performed to the queen and her court. Only the main principal ballet dancers perform the ballet. I am a chorus dancer, not a principal dancer. Performing the ballet is an unattainable goal. But Stuart and I discuss the idea of working on more lifts. Perhaps we can form an adagio team. It would make us more valuable as performers and give us more career options.

Stuart and I begin practicing lifts between shows. The huge stage offers many nooks and crannies where we can fumble and stumble our way through some basic moves. We share hearty laughs at our many graceless falls. It takes a lot of work and extra physical exertion on top of our two two-hour shows a night, but within time we learn each other's bodies, weight distribution, and best hand placement, and we can do the most well-known lifts consistently.

"We are well suited in body types, height, and strength. We work well together."

I nod at Stuart's assessment as I lean forward to catch my breath after holding it for the duration of practicing the wheel. Holding my breath keeps my body firm, allows me to carry my own weight, and makes me lighter for Stuart.

"Do you think we could be an adagio team?"

I look at Stuart mopping his face with a hand towel as the exertion from lifting me up and down for the past hour shows itself. I nod. "I think we could." I think the idea through a little more and compare what we can do to the abilities of the other adagio teams we know, including those in the show. "We would have to come up with our own lifts. Do different moves from everyone else out there."

"But it's worth a try. Right?"

"Right!"

And so Stuart and I intensify our training to become an adagio team. Instead of hiding behind set pieces, we begin practicing on the main stage so we have more room to do the running stand and a lift where I change position from a standing arabesque to a forward attitude while Stuart gracefully carries me around the stage in a circle. We still have our clumsy moments, but our efforts are now more successful than not. We recognize that our compatibility is special. Not every couple that tries adagio can master the lifts as well as Stuart and I have.

To build up stamina, we begin to practice our lifts during the day in a studio we rent, but still continue to practice between the two shows at night. We create new lifts that no other adagio team can do. Other members of the cast come out to watch us rehearse and give us ideas and encouragement. Our lifts are difficult, and we know we have to learn how to be consistent and able to perform them again and again. We start putting our lifts to music, choreographing highly difficult routines. One of our greatest supporters is Carol Channing, who brings her chair out of her dressing room, plops it down on the front of the stage, and watches us rehearse, giving encouragement, support, and ideas.

author and partner, family photo

Stuart and I become a great team both onstage and off. We marry in July 1984, and shortly thereafter Stuart legally adopts Mark. Stuart brings a new dimension to my life. For the first time, I feel as if I do not have to shoulder life's burden alone. I have a partner by my side, and we can offer each other support and guidance. Stuart introduces Mark and me to new and varied activities, including sailing and fishing. We buy a boat and I learn to water ski. I like this all-American persona I am developing, and I like learning to do activities I would never have thought I could do, or would enjoy. Mark is now six years old and growing up into a fine-looking American boy.

But the dedication and practice and determination to do lifts that no other team performs comes at a price. First I fall and break my right forearm, a compound fracture requiring surgery to place metal plates and screws into the bone to help it mend. The breaks do not mend. The doctor tells me the bone at the break on my ulna is dead. I then endure a bone and bone-marrow transplant in a second surgery, together with the replacement of plates and screws. Before I am recovered from the second surgery, Stuart and I commence practicing our lifts again. It isn't long before I fall and break bones in both feet right across each set of metatarsals. My injuries do not make me popular with the company managers and the other girls who have to fill in my spots on stage as I spend weeks away from the show, healing my injuries. I might have been fired if it had not been for Carol Channing taking me under her wing and shooing away anyone from any management likely to do me harm.

For the first couple of weeks after breaking the bones in my feet, I wear a plaster-of-Paris cast on both lower legs, and I have to crawl on my hands and knees to get around. Once I am able to put weight on my feet again, Stuart and I go back into the studio and continue practicing our lifts. We ignore the casts on my legs, working on the time I am in the air and off my feet, gaining strength, improving balance, and working on choreography.

Another year has passed, and it is time to reaudition for the show. Stuart and I ask to audition as an adagio team, hoping the producer, Donn Arden, might allow us to perform our act in the show. Our audition is on the main stage, in front of the entire cast and crew, and is to the music from *Somewhere in Time*. By now we have mastered never- before-seen lifts, including a reverse bird that ends in me doing a slow-motion and very controlled somersault from above Stuart's head to land on my knees on the floor. Our repertoire also includes the kiss lift, a lovely moment where I am held upside down above Stuart's head and our lips meet, and our most difficult lift, the forward flip, where I am standing in Stuart's hand extended up above his head, he flips me forward into a somersault, and I land in his arms in an embrace as he kneels down and returns the embrace.

Other than the music, not a sound disturbs our performance as the entire theater holds its breath, watching intently as we perform our intricate and dangerous moves. The number is athletic, requiring strength, control, stamina—all with the appearance of effortless movement. We have trained well. Our bodies are well conditioned to this artistic discipline. We finish our routine with an elegant lift. Stuart holds me above his head while I am posing in an arabesque, my leg extended straight out behind me. Moving with the music, I change my position, bringing my raised leg down and into a front attitude as Stuart walks us off stage while the music fades away. Immediately the silence is replaced by an eruption of applause and cheers. Finally, feet firmly on the ground again, I try to catch my breath, all while taking in the stunning accolades from the cast and crew. We walk hand-in-hand back out on stage to face Donn Arden, known for his diva personality and acerbic tongue.

"Wow!" he says to us over the microphone he is holding. The applause quiets as people wait to see what he says. "Wow!" he repeats. "It is rare for me to see something I have never seen before, and your lifts were not only new and unique, your entire routine was stunning!" He turns around to the people in the theater behind him. "Don't you agree?"

We receive more raucous cheers and applause. Stuart slips his arm around my shoulders and hugs me tight. Our months and months of sacrifice, effort, and determination have paid off. We have even wowed Donn Arden! Not only that, we learn that our audition is successful. The producer and company manager allow us to perform our act a couple of times a week as part of the fabulous Space Ballet in the space scene.

"Wow!" I say to Stuart. "The Space Ballet!"

"The Space Ballet!" Stuart's excitement and surprise mirrors my own.

What was once believed to be unattainable, through hard work and perseverance became routine. Stuart and I choreograph our own adagio number to perform in the Space Ballet. We perform on those nights when the regular ballet dancers have nights off, or are on vacation. There is one point during our number when I am leaning backward and looking up at the living curtain suspended high above the stage, waiting for the space disco number in the next scene. I see my fellow ponies leaning over the edge of the curtain, waving down at me as I look up. My smile widens as I see the support of my fellow ponies.

Performing our adagio before a live audience and garnering great appreciation and applause for our lifts, Stuart and I decide that we have a skill set we can use to advance our careers, and we decide to become our own act. We travel down to Los Angeles and audition for producer Jerry Jackson, well known for his shows such as the *Folies-Bergere* at the Tropicana in Las Vegas. We are offered roles as principal dancers and adagio team at the Princess Hotel and Casino in the Bahamas. Stuart and I are ready to leave *Hello Hollywood Hello* and take our act on the road. On our last night with *Hello Hollywood Hello*, the cast gives us the most stunning tribute a performer can be given.

It is our last performance in the Space Ballet. Stuart and I run from the wings, down the long silver ramp, across the huge stage to front center stage to begin the ballet. We take our positions, facing the audience, waiting for the music to start. The stage lights dim, ready to focus their glow only on the ballet. For a moment there is complete silence. We wait.

The music begins, we start our ballet, we grab hands and pull away from each other as our arms move through fifth position above our heads, and we turn away from each other to face the back of the stage. As I turn, I am surprised at what I see. The largest set stage in the world behind us is empty. The entire cast of dancers and singers, even the Space Queen, have left, leaving the entire stage to Stuart and me.

As we dance together, as I am lifted high and smoothly brought down low, as we embrace, kiss, and create lyrical art with our bodies, the enormity of the moment hits me. It is as if the entire world is focused only on us. We are the center of the spotlight universe, the only life-forms in the dark cavern of the theater. Dancing our ballet alone on this massive stage feels incredible, and having the entire cast step away to give us the sole spotlight creates one of the most memorable moments of my dancing career. The scenes and dreams I once imagined as a child have come to life. As I am held aloft in the black space with the bright glow of the spotlight illuminating only me, I feel like a star.

CHAPTER

TWENTY-ONE

"You're the dancer in the show!" A woman stops me as I am walking along the waterfront in Hamilton, Bermuda. "You are fantastic!"

"Thank you very much." I smile in appreciation of the recognition.

"Can I have my photo taken with you? Please?" The woman thrusts her camera at a man I presume is her husband. "Here, honey, take my photo." The woman turns and poses next to me.

"Would you like my partner and husband in the shot?" I motion toward Stuart standing to the side with a sour look on his face, no doubt because he wasn't recognized or complimented.

"He's your partner? Oh sure, sure. Come on, honey." She grabs Stuart's arm, pulling him next to her, and the photo is taken. "Thank you! Are you performing again during the cruise?"

"Yes. Friday night."

"Great! We look forward to seeing you again." She points a finger toward me. "You guys are great!"

The woman grabs her husband's arm and pulls him toward the next store.

Stuart and I continue on our own route along Front Street back to the cruise ship. I throw my arm around his shoulder. "You're a great partner. We're a great team."

"Yeah, we are." Stuart looks at me and smiles.

My dancing career has come full circle as I am back working on cruise ships, this time as a lead performer for Norwegian Cruise Line. After leaving Reno, Stuart and I took our act to the Princess Resort in Freeport, Bahamas, using the time there to hone our craft, develop the strength and stamina needed to perform our dozens of complicated lifts in two shows nightly.

Living the island life was different from anything I had previously experienced and a great respite from city life. Our condo was on the waterway leading in past the Xanadu Hotel from the Caribbean Sea. We bought our own boat, embracing a life of fishing, snorkeling, and scuba diving. With an excellent stable on the island, I rode horses every day, taking lessons, jumping, working on dressage movements, and sometimes taking the tourists out on the beach rides.

Our Chevy Impala station wagon, painted with lime green house paint and with extra air-conditioning by way of the holes rusted through the car floor, epitomized the character of the island. It was common for a friend driving along the road in the opposite direction to cross over into our lane to say "Hello." Red traffic lights were mere suggestions as were the stop signs and speed limits. Tooting one's car horn was an acceptable greeting to a friend or neighbor. Rather than laugh at the culture, we embraced it.

Mark attended a private catholic school, Saint Mary's of the Sea. We are not Catholics, but it was the only decent school on the island. He was the only white child in class, but that didn't seem to faze him. I hope it always stays that way. But as always, life's status quo is but a fleeting moment until pushed aside by the inevitable change. Mark was growing up quickly and no longer getting the education he needed in the Bahamas. I felt he was falling behind his counterparts in the States. Talking to other ex-pats, I learned they sent their sons to a naval prep school, the Almirante Farragut,

author in Bahamas Show Costume, photo courtesy of a family friend

author's sister Loretta with cutout of author in dance costume, photo © Ian Denny

author riding Eleuthera in Bahamas, photo courtesy of a family friend

author's son Mark becoming US Citizen in Miami,
family photo

in St. Petersburg, Florida. Stuart and I submitted an application for
Mark to study at the school, which was followed by an in-person
visit with Mark, who was impressed with the "really cool" naval
aircraft displayed at the entrance to the school grounds. Mark was
accepted into Farragut, meaning it was time for Stuart and me to
readjust our own lives. We had honed our skills as an adagio team,
and it was time to move forward with our act.

Life in the Bahamas was history, and we got a job performing for Norwegian Cruise Line, first on the grande dame of cruise
ships, the SS *Norway* and now on the MS *Dreamward,* sailing
from the home port of Fort Lauderdale to Nassau, Grand Cay-
man, Cozumel, Cancun, and the private island. Twice a year we
do a repositioning cruise that takes us to additional ports, such as
Aruba and through the Panama Canal, until we arrive at our summer home port of New York for the New York to Bermuda run.

We are still the main act in the Las Vegas review show but also have roles in the Broadway production show *Dreamgirls,* which has an integrated cast. I perform the role of Michelle Morris, a replacement for Effie in The Dreams. I also sing and dance in the Broadway tribute show. I may not be a well-known performer, but I am a big fish in my little pond.

photo of author, photo © Mark Burrell

author as Bride in Stage Show, photo © Mark Burrell

Now a young teenager, Mark spends his vacation time from the naval academy onboard the *Dreamward,* learning to do spotlights for the shows, earning money for a guitar and for lessons from the guitarist with the ship's band. With Stuart and I living on the cruise ship, we don't own our own home. Imagine my chagrin when I discover that Mark told his schoolmates at the prestigious naval academy—most of whom are the sons of ambassadors, businessmen, and other notables—that his parents are homeless!

"The lounge should be quiet with everyone ashore." Stuart interrupts my thoughts. "Why don't we get in some practice now?"

"Sure. Sounds good."

We change into rehearsal gear, do some stretches to get the body warmed up and supple, and meet each other center stage. Stuart takes the rosin bag, rubs rosin on his hands, and then hands the bag to me. I rub my legs liberally with the white sticky dust intended to prevent me from slipping through Stuart's fingers when I am lifted high into the air. For the show I add a layer of hairspray to give the extra "stick" that is needed to combat the layer of sweat created by the exertion and bright stage lights. Stuart takes back the bag and rubs rosin behind my neck, on the front of my hips, and on other areas where he will grab me during a lift and wants the extra adhesiveness.

We start our practice with simple back lifts, Stuart standing behind me, grabbing my waist and lifting me up above his head. With my arms in fifth position, I arch back, liking the stretched feeling as my muscles start to perform as trained. I point my feet hard, pushing out the kinks in my lower extremities.

"Down." Stuart's direction for bringing me down to the floor. "Let's run through each of the lifts in order."

I nod. We have our standard practice routine, itself a choreographed series of movements preparing us for the next show.

"The bird," Stuart directs as he does a couple of squats, readying his legs to plié low beneath me, using the impetus to lift me over his head.

I take my position opposite him. I lift my arms to my side,

dégagé my right foot in front, and take three steps toward Stuart, leading with my hips. On my third step our movements and weight coordinate as Stuart places his hands on my hips, and I roll my hips forward into his hands, lifting my legs behind me, transferring my weight from the floor into the cradle of Stuart's hands while he simultaneously lifts me above his head, a careful balance of timing and weight distribution. We hold the bird for about ten seconds, enough time to allow Stuart to play with his position and placement of my body above his head, and for me to tighten every muscle in my body, making me one solid part as Stuart moves me around to test the stability of the lift.

"Down." We reverse the moves until I have both feet back on the ground.

"How about the stand?" Stuart removes his shirt and adds rosin to his upper chest.

"Okay." I add extra rosin to the shin on my left leg. The area has permanent indentations of Stuart's fingermarks from the years of my shin hitting his hand and him grabbing my leg as I run toward him. I present my left leg to Stuart, who then grabs it and lifts me into an arabesque as I stand high on his chest. The lift goes well.

"The kiss lift." We continue our practice for the next show.

Show after show we perform our complicated and somewhat dangerous lifts, sometimes battling the rocking effect of the waves on the ship's stage, but always with success. Our performances garner standing ovations, the ultimate recognition of the hours, years of work Stuart and I have put into our art, not only to be able to offer stunning performances for our audiences but also to develop unique lifts that no one else can do. The hard work, the exhaustion, the injuries are worth those brief moments of an audience rising to their feet in your honor.

"Hey! You're the dancer in the show!"

Stuart and I are walking along Fifth Avenue in New York. New York is our summer home port for the Bermuda cruises.

I turn toward the female voice.

author and partner, photo © Mark Burrell

photo of author and partner, photo © Mark Burrell

She points at my head. "I recognize you by your short hair." She leans in closer to me. "You are my favorite dancer. I could watch you all day. And those moves you do are fantastic!" She waves her hands above her head, replicating her idea of the lifts. "I don't know how you do it!"

I feel a seething wave of hostility coming from behind me. I turn and grab Stuart's arm and drag him closer. "Actually, I couldn't do any of it without my husband, Stuart." I pat his chest, making sure the woman sees him. "He deserves all the credit. He has incredible strength and ensures the lifts always work. He is the best adagio partner in the business."

Stuart offers a courtesy smile.

"You guys are great. Well done! Hope to see you on my next cruise." The woman walks on.

Stuart is unusually quiet the rest of the day.

A few days later I am running on the treadmill in the ship's gym when something tears on the outside of my left ankle and, crying out in pain, I fall into an unceremonious heap onto the gym floor. I am taken to a doctor in Bermuda.

"You've pulled tendons away from your heel and lower leg. You can't dance for some time. You'll need a cast for at least six weeks."

The news is devastating, but Stuart, the company manager, and other performers assure me that it is best that I take the doctor's advice and rest so I can heal quickly.

As the show must go on, it is decided that Jane the dance captain will fill in for me. Stuart rehearses with Jane to teach her some basic lifts.

"What can I do to help?" I offer, hobbling into the rehearsal lounge on crutches. Stuart and Jane are on stage, trying to choreograph the adagio routines for the show. They are working on the angel, a basic lift, but one that can only be done with the understanding of how the female partner must distribute her weight to ensure balance.

I move closer to the stage and offer help. "Jane. You have to walk forward leading with your hips because your weight has to be—"

"We don't need your help," Stuart snarls at me, giving me a disdainful look. I am astonished and hurt by his attitude. "Go away! You are not the star of this act. I can do this and make it look just as good without you!"

Jane looks embarrassed. "Okay," I say softly, forcing a smile, not wanting to show how much his stinging words hurt, and I hobble out of the lounge, leaving them to it.

It is the evening of the first show with Stuart and Jane dancing the adagio numbers. I sit in the back of the audience with my left leg in a cast. Passengers who recognize me come and inquire as to how I was injured and tell me how disappointed they are because I am not performing. I appreciate their comments, but I am here to show my support for Stuart and Jane.

The curtain rises, the music begins, and Stuart and Jane begin to dance. Jane looks nervous, uncomfortable, awkward, balancing in the air, held by Stuart, who has a look of determination backdropped against his stiff, artificial smile. They do a fair job under the circumstances, but it is nothing as compared to the skill level of Stuart and me, who have worked together for years. The number ends, and there is lukewarm applause from the audience. Stuart does not look happy as he takes his bow. After the show, as the passengers leave the showroom, several of them stop and tell me that the show wasn't the same without me. I am thankful for their comments, but they don't know how hard Stuart and Jane have worked in trying to give them a good performance.

I go backstage to the dressing room and congratulate Stuart and Jane on a great job. Stuart tells me in no uncertain terms to "get lost!" Later that night in our cabin, he doesn't talk to me. I can't think of anything that I have done wrong.

My injury is not healing, and we are coming to the end of our contract. Stuart and I agree it is time to leave ship life and go back ashore to perform. I am hoping that getting away from the ship might improve our relationship again. Also, it is Mark's last year of high school, and I would like for us to spend one last year leading a normal family life before Mark ventures out toward his future. Stuart is offered a job in Las Vegas. We buy a brand-new house there and move into the house the week before Christmas.

It is Valentine's Day. Things have been more amicable between Stuart and me over the past couple weeks, and I am in a good mood as I sit out on the back patio, enjoying my morning caffeine. I still cannot dance, but put every effort into making our new house a home.

Stuart comes out, puts a potted plant on the ground in front of me, and walks away back into the house. I follow him into the house. "Is that for me?"

"It's for Valentine's Day." Stuart walks out to the garage.

"Thank you, it's great!" I shout after him, but my thanks is ignored, as is my card and gift to him, sitting on the mantel in the living room, waiting for his attention. They sit there the entire day while Stuart and his buddy John do some carpentry in the garage. My day is spent sitting out on the porch holding back tears, not understanding why Stuart is being so mean to me.

Stuart is about to leave for the evening show, and I go to the foyer to see him off. "I hope you have a great show," I say cheerfully.

He opens the front door and then turns back to me. "I want a divorce. We'll talk about it Friday on my day off." With his announcement made, he leaves, slamming the door behind him.

I am standing alone in our new living room, in the lovely dream house we have worked so hard to earn. I replay Stuart's unexpected words again and again in my mind, and feel the impact from the heartlessness in his tone.

Stuart refuses to talk to me until Friday comes, and then his discussion involves handing me four hundred dollars for child support for Mark and a comment that he is done being a father.

He exits my life with his job and paycheck, leaving me with no income, no unemployment benefits, and with a mortgage to pay. So much for "in sickness and in health." I tacitly understand that my dancing career has unceremoniously come to an end, as has my marriage and my quest for an ideal life. Those dreams are to be set aside to be replaced by the utter devastation I feel. Between the bouts of heartache, depression, and alcohol-induced stupors, I recognize that I have new challenges in my life. I pray I am up to those challenges.

CHAPTER

TWENTY-TWO

*O*ut of all of Dad's things I still need to sort out in the attic, I leave the photographs until last. I instinctively know that once I open the old wooden cigar box and other miscellaneous boxes housing the family photographs, I will want to take the time to look at them carefully and in doing so will become immersed in the images. Lifting the cigar box from the dusty attic floor, I feel the coarse wood against my fingertips. I run my thumb down the jagged seams of the box, allowing the roughness to scrape my skin as if it is penance for my sin of abandonment. The box is larger than those typically used for its original purpose, packaging cigars, but now the mellow brown-colored panels guard a cache of memories. I blow the dust from its top, the particles gently rising then falling at the disturbance. I sit down on the attic floor, under the light hanging from the ceiling, which now becomes the spotlight for the exhibition.

I push the lid of the box sideways along its tracks, forcing this gatekeeper of family memories to reveal its treasures. Hundreds of black-and-white images are squished tightly within the confines of the box. I begin pulling the images out of the box one by one, revisiting the memories frozen in time by the simple click of a camera shutter. I appreciate the preservation of those moments so I can remember them, and relive them now.

The first photographs that I study in detail are of my father as a youth. One is a very small headshot picture of him with two other boys. They wore suits. Incongruous for a period in my father's life when I knew his family lived on, if not below, the poverty line. Perhaps a hint that regardless of the income level, standards were still to be maintained. The three youths all faced to the right, the staged pose no doubt typical of the time but odd for three cheeky-looking boys each showing the hint of a grin. *What was going through their minds?* I wonder. *What was the occasion that allowed money to be spent on the photograph? Who was the photographer?*

My father's voice joins my thoughts, telling a familiar childhood story. "Ah was a wee lad barely old enough to go tae school. Ma, me, an' my brothers Joe an' Russell lived in one of the auld tenements in Glasgow. We had nae dad. I got rheumatic fever and couldnae go tae school and so was left on ma ain all day. The tenement was miserable. Rather than stay on ma ain I'd get up, gather ma clothes and shoes, and go oot tae the street, just wearing my jammies. I'd say to a passerby, 'Scuse me. Can ye help me get dressed?' I'd stand in the street wi' some stranger helping me get dressed, and then I'd wander doon tae the school looking for Joe and Russell. I'd sit ootside in the playground until they came oot."

As my father reminds me of his story, I picture the scene of a small boy, from a poor, depressed area of Glasgow in the 1930s, having to stand out on the dirty street, clothes clutched to his chest, a wee voice asking a stranger passing by to help him get dressed. The image I see is pitiful. I feel bad for my father. Dad had been left to fend for himself and at such a young age. In those days it was not considered wrong to leave a young lad on his own all day to take care of himself. But my father had been resourceful. He had managed. He had risen to the challenges. He had come a long way in life.

Turning the small photograph over, I see the names of Dad's companions written on the back of the photograph in my father's handwriting: Simpsons. I don't recognize the name or the images of the other boys. I wonder who they are. Are they relatives? Are they my dad's friends? I wish Dad was there to ask. I look at the image of my dad's face. He was a handsome boy, with a cheeky grin. I grin myself. I wonder what his life was like back then. What were his hopes and dreams? Did he ever reach them? Was he happy with his life? Did he ever have any regrets? Questions I have that I know will never be answered.

Another black-and-white photograph is of my mother as a young girl in an overcoat, standing outside the Wills Tobacco Factory in Glasgow. My mother had started work at the factory when she was fifteen. I pull the next photograph from the box, and it shows my mum holding a greyhound on a leash. My Grandma Campbell had once owned greyhounds and would race them in tracks around Scotland. The war changed things as Grandma Campbell was forced to turn the once grand house into rental accommodations.

Moving on, I look at other photographs from around the same era that show Dad as a sailor, on HMS *Bermuda* in 1950. There are black-and-white photos of him next to a gun turret, with other sailors on the deck of the ship. In with the photographs

author's dad as young matelot,
photo courtesy of a family friend

there is a postcard entitled "HMS *Bermuda* West African Tour 1950." In 1950, Dad would have been nineteen years old. I analyze those circumstances with wonderment, thinking, *What an experience that must have been for him, having the opportunity to travel and see the world, and to see places and things that many people never get the chance to see.* The family never took holidays abroad because Dad would say he's seen everything he needs to see in foreign countries.

I start looking at the smaller, older black-and-white photographs, seeing myself as a baby, three weeks old, four months old. There is a photograph of me as a baby with my parents outside St. Andrew's Church on my christening day. I recall my last visit to the church: the day I vowed never to go to church again.

I'm six years old. Sitting on the pew in Saint Andrew's Presbyterian Church of Scotland with the Gilchrist family, neighbors from across our street who bring me to church with them every Sunday. The minister's voice and his long sermon are making me sleepy. Usually I watch the sun shining through the stained-glass windows, making them sparkly and pretty, but there is no sun today. I can't find anything to amuse my six-year-old mind. I stare at hats on the ladies in front of me for a while, deciding which hats I like and those I don't. Soon bored with the hats, I look around for something new, and along the pew I catch Ian Gilchrist's eye. He is a year older than me. He sees me looking and sticks his tongue out at me. I stick my tongue out at him. Mrs. Gilchrist catches Ian sticking out his tongue and gives him a hearty thump on the arm. I quickly sit back against the wooden pew, hiding behind Mr. Gilchrist's big chest, hoping Mrs. Gilchrist didn't see me sticking out my tongue.

I think it is funny that Ian was caught and I wasn't. When I think it is safe again, I lean forward and carefully peer around Mr. Gilchrist to see what Ian is doing. Ian sees me peeking and scowls. I give him a silent laugh. Our antics are interrupted by a comment from the minister. In the Presbyterian Church the first part of the service is for the whole family, and then halfway through the service, the children leave for Sunday school, which is in a hall at the back of the church.

We children dutifully stand and make our way out of the pews into the center aisle of the church. I am the last out of my pew and follow Ian into the aisle. His brothers are already walking toward the door at the side of the altar. Ian waits for me at the end of the pew. I know he is ready for some mischief to get back at me. We walk down the aisle together, children in front of us and behind us. The cheeky monkey in me wants to get Ian before he gets me, and I mischievously stick my leg out, trying to trip him up. Wise to my game, he in turn sticks his leg out to trip me up—and he does. I trip over his leg and fall hard onto the flint stones lining the aisle. I am smacked with an awful pain shooting up my lower leg. I can't stop myself. "Aaaaaargh!" I cry out with an alarming, unholy yell not found in any prayer book, and which reverberates up and around the ancient church rafters. I forget it is the middle of the church service, and I continue my loud wailing—"Owee it hurts!"—unaware of anything but the dagger of pain in my leg. A man picks me up and carries me out of the main door at the back of the church.

Somewhere through my haze of pain, I am aware of being driven home, and once home my mother yells at me. "If I have to spend money we can't afford to get a taxi to take you to the hospital, I'm going to thump you!"

I have to go to the hospital. My shin bone is broken. My leg is put in a plaster-of-Paris cast. I can't go to school until it is settled. I can't go to dancing. I can't do much of anything except sit. Sit and play with my dolls. Sit and read. Sit and watch television. Sit and think about how I am never going back to church again!

Smiling at my childishness, I return my thoughts to the present and pull another photograph out of the pile and intently study the image of myself as a baby. I am probably less than a year old, and I am sitting on the grass in the back garden of the house in St. Augustin Road. I have a big grin on my chubby face. It is a picture of innocence. This baby didn't yet know of the trials and tribulations that lay ahead for her. She didn't know that she was going to meet people who would be mean to her, who would break her heart. She didn't yet know that she had a family that would love her unconditionally no matter the mistakes she made. She didn't know of the dreams and wishes that would never be fulfilled, or of the accomplishments that lay ahead. I want to hug this baby tight. I desperately want to let her know that life was going to be okay; she will get through it.

Putting the photograph back into the pile, I look through other photographs from my childhood and the family holidays in Scotland. I find a picture of Mum and me when I was about nine or ten, putting a stone on the cairn as we entered into Glen Coe in Scotland.

The glen is infamous for the massacre of the McDonalds by the Campbells in 1692. There are different versions of the legend, but my mum told me that the Campbells and the McDonalds were longtime warring clans. According to legend, and my mother, the Campbells offered hospitality to the McDonald clan when the McDonalds were in Glen Coe. They drank a lot of whiskey as the clans celebrated the truce around the campfires long into the night, until the McDonalds fell into a drunken stupor and slept obliviously. As the McDonalds slept, the Campbells, who had only been pretending to get drunk, slit the throats of the McDonalds. Such is the charming warrior, take-no-prisoners legacy of my family. Mum and I have to put a stone on the cairn to give us safe passage through the glen because we are both Campbells on Mum's side of the family. According to legend, if any Campbell spends the night in Glen Coe, the ghosts of the McDonalds will slit their throat.

Staring at the photograph, I remember the day well. It is late afternoon, and we are driving back to Glasgow through Glen Coe. The fan belt in Dad's car breaks. We pull over to the side of the road, and Dad tries to fix the car. We are in the middle of the most desolate area of the glen, surrounded only by mountains and with no sign of human life. It is getting late, and the sky around us

author as young girl, photo © Ian Denny

author putting stone on Cairn in Glencoe Scotland, photo © Ian Denny

begins to darken; gray clouds ominously begin to descend down the mountains, filling up the glen around us. Mum begins to panic, convinced that if we do not get out of the glen immediately, the ghosts of the McDonalds will come and slit our throats. Her panic is making me nervous. She frantically shouts at Dad, who has his head under the bonnet, seeing to the fan belt.

"Och! Hurry up, Ian. Can yae no go any faster? What's takin' yae sae long?" Mum is pacing beside the car, looking up into the darkening sky and wringing her hands.

I watch my mum watching the sky and the growing darkness. I am getting nervous. I don't like the moan of the wind as it creeps along the ground, its sweeping tentacles brushing against the bracken and whipping around my face like some invisible specter able to move objects and be felt but not be seen. Something tickled the back of my neck. Was it just the wind or some other force causing my hair to stand on end?

"Ian! Ye need tae hurry up! It's getting dark. We cannae spend the night in the glen!" Mum's raised voice and panic are as unnerving as the wind.

Dad, as good-natured as always, is not bothered and continues his work under the bonnet with an unhurried pace. He is not a Campbell. If the ghosts come to get Mum, so be it. He has nothing to worry about.

I look one last time at the black-and-white picture of me placing a stone on the cairn. My hair hung down my back in a long pigtail. I wore an anorak and skirt. I was wearing two-toned flat, lace-up shoes. I smile, remembering those shoes. They were my favorites. I remember that moment of putting the stone on the cairn. My life was just beginning then. Parents were taken for granted. I had eternity to do the things I wanted to do. It has to be forty years ago at least. Where have those years gone?

Changing my focus, I find some more recent color photographs, including a color print from my time in Italy. The dancers from The Three Cs and I are sitting on the floor of the pensione, watching Mark blow out a candle I had placed on his second birthday cake—the same cake I had found after my brave walk along the shoulder of the Italian motorway. The cake is white with little cherries on top; that detail I had forgotten. Had I sent these photos to Dad? Had I left them behind when I moved to the States? I can't remember. It doesn't matter as I begin pulling them out, one by one, spending a moment revisiting the people, the scenery, and the events they captured.

Another photograph is Mark and me standing outside the pensione in Moderno, Italy. I did remember that this photo was taken by Lena, one of the ladies who also lived in the pensione. Lena had a Polaroid instant camera and was always taking photographs of Mark and me. I also find a photograph of me posing by the dusty roadside in Senegal, another of me riding my horse in Egypt, a picture of the River Kwai in Thailand, and one of me riding a horse over an upright show-jumping fence in the Bahamas. Here are tangible images of the memories I have been visiting these past couple of weeks as I reflect on the decades of my life and the choices, good or bad, that I made.

I pull out another handful of photographs and see they are pictures of myself and other cast members from *Hello Hollywood Hello*. I smile, recognizing the costumes and sets, and scan the familiar faces, trying to remember names, but then realize with sadness that many of these bright, talented people were long gone, lost to the scourge of the 1980s, AIDS. "Such a shame," I whisper to the attic.

As I see my own photographs mixed in with those of the family, I realize that in spirit I have never really left. My life is, and always has been, an integral part of the family unit. Like these photographs, the events of my life naturally fit between the affairs and experiences of my parents and sister. My recent overthinking and worrying that I had abandoned my family were one directional. To my family, I am, and always have been, a part of them. I realize that no matter where I went, or how long I was away, my family readily embraced my return as if I had never left. The thought sends a warmth flowing through me, melting the burden I had been carrying.

Immersed in a renewed sense of well-being, I continue my review of the family photographic archives. I pull out a photo of Schickrys. I remember him as a sweet, docile animal. As was typical for his Manx breed, he didn't have a tail. A student from the Royal Academy of Art was commissioned to design his pedigree certificate, which resulted in the creation of a large, colorful piece with drawings of the cat and a castle, and with the text handwritten in an artistic font. It grandly proclaimed that the cat's owner was Her Majesty, The Queen Mother. For a while, the pedigree certificate hung in a passageway on the royal yacht, sailing across the globe, on display to the numerous visitors who were given tours onboard. Later this pedigree hung in my childhood bedroom, and I would stare at it as I fell asleep. Today this pedigree certificate hangs in my home office, a reminder of so many things, not the least of which was that sunny summer day when Schickrys came into my life.

photo of Schickrys' Pedigree, photo © Laraine Denny Burrell

More recently, historian Richard Johnston-Bryden wrote a book on the royal yacht. Page 104 shows a picture of Schickrys in a little basket being carried by the Queen Mother on that day in 1963 when he was first presented to Her Majesty. I now reach down into the photographs in front of me, find the original of that photograph, and stare at it intently. I will put this in a frame and keep it in a cabinet, right beside my own copy of the book opened to the page showing the same photograph. The book also has a photograph of my father celebrating the yacht's twenty-first birthday. He is leaning over a large birthday cake made for the occasion and surrounded by other yachtsmen. The book also mentions my father by name, as a yachtsman, and for having stewardship of Schickrys. I take a moment to reflect on the significance of the

Rear Admiral P.D. MADDEN CB CBE LVO DSC*
Served in the Royal Yacht Britannia as the Commander(N) when the ship entered service in the Royal Navy 1953/4

Warrant Officer A. (DIXIE) DEANE MBE RVM
Served in Britannia between 1957 and 1985 as a Leading Telegraphist, Leading Radio Operator(G), Radio Supervisor, Chief Radio Supervisor, Fleet Chief Petty Officer and Warrant Officer

Chief Petty Officer(M)E IAN DENNY RVM
Served in Britannia between 1954 and 1976 as a Stoker, Leading Stoker, Petty Officer(M)E and Chief Petty Officer(M)E

Royal Naval
Philatelic Society
H.M. Naval Base
PORTSMOUTH

photograph of stamps showing author's father's signature, photo © Laraine Denny Burrell

book and its contents. My father is memorialized in a book by both his photograph and name. How many people can say that?

I pull more naval photographs from the box, all black and white, all showing the yacht, the crew, my father. My father's naval career was linked to other interesting facets of his life. When the royal yacht was decommissioned in December 1997, commemorative stamps were issued, and the first day edition envelopes included the signature of three yotties chosen to represent the ship. Out of the many hundreds of men who had served on the yacht over the years since 1954, my dad was one of the three chosen, and his neat signature—the result of his efforts of self-improvement—graces the envelope of these special first edition stamps, another way in which this boy from Glasgow is forever memorialized. My parents had given me a set of the first edition stamps, and I make a mental note to put the set on display in my home as it deserves. Today the royal yacht is a museum located near Edinburgh in Scotland, and my father's photo and information is displayed as an eternal reminder to the public of his life given for Queen and country. To me, it is a personal reminder of his extraordinary achievements. I have never been to the museum. *I will go one day,* I promise myself.

Dad's long naval career and service to the Queen did not go unrecognized. He was honored on the New Year's Honor list in 1976. He was awarded the Royal Victorian Medal for his services to the Queen, and I recall the memory of that visit to Buckingham Palace. I find a photograph in the box of my dad in his uniform, proudly showing off his medal.

One of the last royal events my parents attended was the Queen's eightieth birthday party held in a garden at Buckingham Palace. I think it a testament to us as people, and what we can do with our lives, that ordinary, unassuming people like my parents could get dressed up a couple of times a year and go to balls and important events at the palace or at Windsor Castle. Who would think looking at Dad pottering around his garden in shabby overalls, or Mum sitting with her feet up, having a cuppa in front of the telly and watching her westerns, that they would be invited to royal balls and tea at palaces and castles? For Mum, each event required a new outfit, but it was always about the hat and the drama of finding something suitable for the event, with this pre-event preparation often taking months to finalize. The royal family didn't forget

The Lord Chamberlain is
commanded by Her Majesty to invite

Mr. and Mrs. Ian Denny

to a Garden Party
at Buckingham Palace
on Thursday, 20th July 2006 from 4 to 6 pm

This card does not admit

photograph of invitation to Palace to author's mum and dad, photo © Laraine Denny Burrell the ordinary citizen, and I appreciate the fact that an invitation to an auxiliary nurse, such as my mother, or a factory worker, which Dad became after retiring from the navy, marks a person's life as notable. I am pleased that my parents had experiences that few others could share.

I had found an envelope among my father's belongings and inside was a letter dated August 11, 1976. It was on Royal Yacht *Britannia* letterhead and was written by the rear admiral. It was a recommendation letter for my father for when he left the yacht and naval service in November of that year. A few sentences summed up my dad perfectly:

". . . he was a most efficient, smart and above all loyal and trusted royal yachtsman . . . He has a quiet personality, a fine sense of humour and is respected by all on board, his superiors and subordinates alike. He is very tactful and a man with a calm temperament which is rarely disturbed even when under intense pressure."

My father was loyal, to the royal yacht, to the navy and his country. He lost two fingers in an engine room accident on HMS *Bermuda* in 1950, but never complained about the loss, or the risks of his job. In later years it was discovered that the old engine rooms were coated with asbestos, and as asbestos litigation hit a fervor in the United Kingdom, Dad was interviewed by prominent lawyers from London and asked to testify about the asbestos use in the navy. Even though he might have been entitled to monetary compensation, Dad refused. He didn't want to say a bad word against the navy, or against the royal yacht. For him it simply wasn't the right thing to do. Such was my dad's loyalty and integrity.

Looking through the photographs, I find more photos of the royal family, the Duke of Edinburgh and Princess Anne on the deck of the yacht, leaning casually against the ship's rail, having a chat. Another one is of Prince Charles as a young man dressed in a tuxedo and blowing bubbles through a plastic ring, and another is a picture of the Duke of Edinburgh putting on a silly hat as part of the Crossing the Equator ceremony being held on board the yacht. There is a picture of the Queen in a long ball gown, and another of the Queen and the duke with Eisenhower standing casually on the deck of the royal yacht. These are all modestly tucked away among my dad's possessions, as if everyone has photographs of royals or American presidents in their attic.

The final photograph in this group is one that was published in the local *Portsmouth Evening News*. It is of my father standing on the quay at the side of the yacht on the day he was paid off, leaving the navy. Behind him, the decks of the yacht are lined with yachtsmen, all with their caps in the air, cheering him. It was the end of an era for him, although the yachtsmen always remain in contact through their organization. My mother has heard from numerous yotties sending their condolences on Dad's passing. It is expected that some will attend Dad's funeral.

In with the photographs are some old pieces of paper, and opening each folded leaf, I find sheet music with old Scots songs, and a book called *51 Beauties of Scottish Song*, priced sixpence. Dad loved his Scots music and songs, and that is why we have arranged for a Scots piper to play some of Dad's favorite ballads at his funeral. I also find an old piece of paper with the typewritten words of a prayer. It is by Winifred Holtby and reads: "God give me work 'til my life shall end, and life 'til my work is done." I read those words over and over. I absorb them. It is providence that I have found this paper. The prayer epitomizes Dad's life and work. I will use it in his eulogy.

Smiling, I gather up the photographs. Dad was a quiet, humble man, with no hint of an extraordinary life. Yet, the wee lad from Glasgow had "gone to sea" as a boy and been given the opportunity to join the royal yacht family, travel the world with the royal family, attend many significant events both on the ship and in palaces and castles, and have his services recognized by the monarch. He had been given the responsibility of caring for a royal cat. There is a photograph of him and he is mentioned by name in a book, as well as being memorialized in a first edition stamp collection. His name and photograph are displayed in a museum in recognition for his contribution to Queen and country. I think my dad's life was very extraordinary indeed.

I take a final look around the attic, at all the things I have seen and learned over the past few days, Dad's treasures, his keepsakes, the images all capturing parts of his life. They tell his story in a way that he had been too quiet to tell himself. I will use all of these things to tell my dad's story at his funeral because they relate to him, and to the people who have been part of his life. He had led an extraordinary life. But because of his quiet and humble demeanor, and modest reporting of his accomplishments, it is unlikely that people will understand, or even recognize all that he had done. The one thing I can do for him is to put all of his life events and achievements together and make sure they are memorialized at his funeral so everyone can see what I see in these photographs, documents, and treasures. I can make sure that my dad's life, his achievements, and his journey are not forgotten.

TWENTY-THREE

I find my seat, one of a few hundred in the large exam hall. I unpack my computer, plug it into the grid of electrical outlets and surge protectors criss-crossing across the floor below my desk and beyond. I check that the plug connection is good, the computer on, and set it up on the desk allotted to me. I lay out my permitted pens and pencils on the desk, and then remove any impermissible objects, including my computer bag, to an area at the side of the room. Around me the other bar exam takers are doing the same. Some chatting amicably, nervously, excitedly. Some like me: silent, contemplative, serious.

Today is the last day of the three-day bar exam. It is my birthday, but I am not celebrating. Not yet. I need to get through the next few hours and the final tests designed to challenge my worthiness to become a lawyer before I can exhale the breath I have been holding for what seems like days.

The proctor brings around computer discs for us to insert into our drives. I write my exam identification number on the disc and insert it into the computer. The program will lock access to anything other than the exam: no Internet, no saved files, no cheat sheets. I have only my brain to rely on. My brain is in top form.

Studying for the bar exam has been my full-time job, with overtime, for the last six weeks. My brain is now the fittest it has ever been. I am prompted by the computer program to log in. I do so.

Booklets of the exam questions are distributed and placed face down next to each examinee. I notice it is quite thick. I will have four hours to answer all of the four essay questions. I look toward the clock at the front of the hall. Almost nine o'clock.

After giving us general instructions, the proctor says to the quiet room, "You may begin." There is a "wooshing" sound as hundreds of paper booklets are turned and opened.

I open my booklet, do a quick assessment of the length of the questions, and the subject areas, and then do a quick calculation of the time I have to spend on each question. That done, I turn back to the first question. It is on contract law. The first thing I do is grab the scratch paper provided for notes and write out my contracts outline, a well-prepared series of orderly abbreviations setting out every element of every contract and Uniform Commercial Code issue garnered from my law school classes, exam preparation classes, and my own studies. I have prepared and practiced this outline as much as any other part of my bar preparation, and now, in less than thirty seconds, I write my checklist of everything that could be relevant to a contracts question. Feeling confident the extra time spent on writing the outline will save me time later on by helping me quickly order and draft my answer, I now turn to the question.

The next four hours are a mental race between the pages of the booklet, the clock, and my brain. Not one will cede to the others as I methodically make my way through the questions, identify the issues, and draft analysis after analysis of the issues, the elements of each issue, the facts to support or rebut an issue, and my final conclusion. With one eye always on the clock, I master my time management. I am confident I am winning the race.

"Two minutes." The proctor warns of the time remaining.

I do a quick check of my exam booklet, and my answers typed into the computer, and confirm there is nothing I have missed and nothing more I can add. I sit back in my seat, waiting for the final call.

"Time! Please stand and step away from your computers."

There is a scraping of chairs as we examinees stand up and back away from our computers and raise our hands into the air. The proctor and assistants scan the room for compliance. I look around the room at all the would-be lawyers standing with hands in the air, looking like criminals. I smile, finding some irony in that. I inhale deeply, and exhale sharply. It's over. I wait patiently as the proctor and assistants systematically gather first the computer discs and then the booklets and scratch paper.

Knowing the last day of the exam was my birthday, I thought it would be the perfect day to celebrate my completion of the many years of metamorphosis from feather- and diamond-wearing dancer, to advocate. My fellow law students and I often discussed how we will celebrate that moment after the bar exam is over and we are finally released from that cell of study we have locked ourselves into for too many years. I anticipated that I would dance out of the room, along the hallway to the parking lot and my car, getting away from the exam, the other students, and all memories of the arduous challenges I have been adhered to for the past four years. I will go home and celebrate all night long, the bottle of Veuve Cliquot already chilling nicely in my fridge. I will talk to no one; I don't want to see a soul. It is to be my moment of self-celebration; my eight years of sacrifice are over. I have done all I can to succeed, and I have exceeded my own expectations. I have amazed myself.

It takes about twenty minutes for the examination materials to be retrieved from the two hundred or so examinees in the large ballroom. Finally, it is all over, and the proctor tells us we can go.

My desk is next to the right-hand wall of the room, near the exit doors. I am the first to grab my bag left on the floor at the side of the room, bundle my computer into it, and exit the side door to the hallway outside. I walk slowly to the exit and into the hallway; it is still quiet, the chatter of the other examinees yet to come.

I'm not dancing. My brow furrows. I don't feel right. I don't feel happy. Where is the ecstatic sense that it is all over and that I am free? Why is my mind not doing cartwheels and shouting hallelujahs? Instead, an unmistakable sadness infiltrates my whole body. It follows me to the car; it drives home with me. It stays with me all night. The Veuve Clicquot is ignored.

I sit on the couch in my living room, doing nothing but staring outside the window at the fading light. As the room darkens, so does my mood. I don't understand it. I try self-diagnosis. I feel as though I have suffered a terrible loss. Perhaps it is simply fatigue from eight long years of sacrifices, and that I am no longer compelled to spend hours studying, and that I now have my life back. Perhaps it is the stress of the bar exam itself, the last two months of intense studying and taking extra bar courses at nights and on the weekends. I have not chosen an easy profession. I ignore phone calls from my boss and friends, no doubt wanting to ask how I am, how the exam went.

Still sitting on the couch, I retreat into my mind, my memories, and the eight long years of reinventing myself, starting when Stuart walked out of my life, which left me trying to find work with no job skills. Eight years of what it took to bring me to this point, my completion of the bar exam . . .

"*Variety*! *Variety*!" I shout as I am standing at the door of the Bally's Las Vegas Convention Hall, holding copies of the *Variety* newspaper in my left hand, ready to distribute them to passersby with my right hand. I have a two-day temp job at minimum wage handing out newspapers to the attendees of ShoWest. It is all I am qualified to do. I've lost my marriage, my career, and because of my injury, I am unable to do the one thing I am skilled at, dancing.

"Good to see you doing something useful." The sarcasm from the familiar voice makes me involuntarily shudder. It is Stuart. "Not the star of the show now, are you?"

"I see you have come to gloat." I hand a newspaper to a woman passing by.

"Well, I thought it would be rude of me to be in the building but not come see how you are doing. I am on my way to rehearsal. For the show." Stuart emphasizes the word "show." He has a job as a chorus dancer in *Jubilee*.

I want to get in my own dig that as a chorus dancer he is not exactly the star of the show either. But I take the high road and turn my back on him instead, smiling as I hand a newspaper to another attendee.

I am embarrassed at what I have to do to make a living. I recognize that to change my situation, I need to go back to school to get another skill set with some type of certification or degree. With no educational history in the United States, and with no record of a high-school diploma because of the different English educational system, I am forty years old and have to argue my way into a college and into a classroom for the first time in almost twenty-five years. I decide that working in the legal field will be a worthwhile profession. I see a new school has opened up in Las Vegas and offers a two-year associate degree in paralegal studies. I apply and I am eventually accepted after having to jump through hoops to register because I am not an American citizen.

After completing the very first class, I decide I should quit the school because I am apparently wasting my time. My teacher hands me my course report card showing that I only scored four points in the class. I am horrified, embarrassed. I pull my friend to the side and ask her quietly so no one else can hear, "Is the score out of ten?" I show her my pink slip. "Did I only get four out of ten?"

"Oh, Laraine! Four point oh is a perfect score." She shows me her slip with her score of three point one and explains the grading system. I am delighted. I have a perfect score! Then I think, *What a stupid system! Who thought of this daft way to score a class?* I don't quit school but carry on to graduate with a four point oh and to become the valedictorian.

I decide it is a good time to apply for citizenship because

for the first time in my adult life, I intend to live somewhere long enough to go through the citizenship process, which can take as long as two years. I become a citizen in June 2000. It is a proud moment in my life as I am sworn in at the Federal Courthouse. But I don't take time to stop and think of the significance because I am busy. After attaining my two-year degree in eighteen months, all while working full time, I enroll for a bachelor of science degree in business management. I complete this four-year degree in just over two years, again while working full time. The only class I miss during my first two degrees is a Saturday morning class. I miss it because I am taking the LSAT at the university. A law school has just opened in Las Vegas, and I want to give it a try.

I astound myself and get early admission into law school to attend the four-year night program. This allows me to continue working full time during the day. I am now a law clerk with a prestigious law firm. But not a day goes by as I walk into the law school, passing the sign WILLIAM S. BOYD SCHOOL OF LAW, that I don't feel amazed at my accomplishment. I often find myself sitting in class with wonderment that I am able to articulate legal arguments with law professors and discuss the law on equal footing with my scholarly classmates; I find my mind is at home in this analytical legal arena. Never in a million years as I danced around the stage in high heels and feathers, would I have credited myself with the ability to become a lawyer.

After eight years of school, taking and doubling up on accelerated classes, all while working full time, I graduate law school a semester early, so the graduation ceremony is being held in December just before Christmas.

Loretta and my parents travel to Las Vegas to attend the ceremony. Graduation from law school, or any university, is a big event for the family, as I am the first person in my family to get a degree of any kind. The fact that the event coincides with Christmas and the New Year creates a perfect opportunity for the family to celebrate the holidays together, something we haven't done in many years.

Among the celebration and happy times are snippets of less than happy moments. By the time my family comes to visit for my graduation, Loretta has lost a couple of toes on her right foot, the result of the gangrene that diabetics constantly battle. On this one December morning, Loretta is slow to come downstairs, and when she does, she sits hunched on the couch in my living room. Loretta's petite frame is contracted as if enduring an unbearable stomachache. The corners of her mouth are turned up in a false smile, but her eyes are narrowed; she looks focused on something other than the present. She won't look at the family directly.

"Are you all right, love?" Mum asks, used to Loretta's illnesses and health-related problems. It is a question asked several times a day; it is an automatic communication with Loretta.

"I'm fine, thanks." The soft, sweet response fools us all.

Loretta's gait is slow as we visit sites in Las Vegas, see the Fountains of Bellagio, have dinner at the top of the Stratosphere, and walk through the Fashion Show Mall. Loretta doesn't walk much. She sits down when she can, waiting for us to go into the various stores and meeting us on the way out. Dad often sits with Loretta, his lack of interest in shopping allowing him to keep Loretta company.

"Are your shoes too tight?" Mum asks, watching her daughter's struggled steps, and the wince as Loretta puts weight on each foot. The nurse in Mum takes over. "Do you want me to take a look at your feet, love? I'll treat you to a new pair of shoes if you like, if those ones hurt."

"No, no. I'm fine, thanks. Just a bit tired is all." A faint smile tries to show itself but isn't convincing.

One evening the family goes to the Fremont Street Experience, a million colored light bulbs flashing across the street-long ceiling as computer-generated images are choreographed to appear with the accompanying music. Loretta sits on a stone bench in the middle of the street, not looking up at the show but hunched over looking down at the ground. Seeing my sister's collapsed posture, I realize she is not well but is braving the evening, saying nothing, not wanting to spoil the family fun. I sit down next to Loretta and put my arms around my sister, drawing the younger woman to me, holding her tight and rubbing Loretta's head with my hand. It must look odd, two women sitting in the middle of the busy street hugging each other tight, but I don't care. Loretta is not well. I don't understand what is wrong, but as the older sister I want to make my sister better. Not able to offer any medical help, I do the next best thing. I close my eyes, feel the warm body against me, and take a deep breath, trying to draw the pain away from Loretta. I hug Loretta for many minutes, hoping she understands that even though I rarely take the time to visit her and our parents, the love is always present. That hug, that moment, becomes significant.

My mind releases me from my memories, and I find myself still sitting on the couch, the room now completely dark. I lie down along the length of the cushions. Thinking of Loretta, the challenges, the sacrifices, I cry myself to sleep, still not understanding my sadness and sense of loss.

An annoying buzzing sound interrupts my sleep. Opening my eyes, I see daylight. I have been asleep on the couch all night. I reach for the buzzing phone and see it is my mum. Flipping it open, I say, "Hi, Mum. How are you?"

"How was it?" Mum asks about the exam, and I give a condensed version of the process and how I am glad it is over.

After letting me say my piece, Mum says, "I have some sad news for you."

The hairs on my neck rise, my heart sinks. "Sad news? What's happened?"

Mum softly and slowly explains that two weeks earlier on February 14, Loretta had her leg amputated. "We didn't want to tell you," Mum says, "because we didn't want to upset you and for the news to get in the way of your exam studies."

"Poor Loretta," I whisper into the phone as tears express my reaction to the news.

Mum continues, "Loretta's foot had been bad for months, it had become gangrenous, and the gangrene had spread. She had been in terrible pain during our visit to Las Vegas in December but didn't tell a soul."

Mum continues to explain that Loretta has an additional complication. "Her stump, her wound, is infected by the super bug, MRSA, prevalent in British hospitals. Specially raised maggots have been brought in and wrapped around Loretta's stump to eat away the infected flesh." Mum explains that the seemingly medieval and somewhat barbaric treatment is apparently the best remedy for the infection, but still it makes me shudder; my stomach heaves at the image and what my sister is enduring. "Until the MRSA is cured, and her wound healed, Loretta can't be fitted for a prosthetic. It might take months."

I think back to December. We had walked along the Las Vegas Strip, among the neon lights, pirate ships, and palm trees, while Loretta was silently suffering to herself. She had traveled to the States from England and back again while experiencing excruciating pain but not wanting to ruin my graduation, the family's Christmas holiday. Each day the gangrene went untreated, unattended, the more it spread. Only when she was back in England did Loretta disclose the circumstances. Even then she thought of me before herself, not wanting the family to say anything to me lest the news should impede my exam study and affect my ability to focus on the bar exam.

More prevalent is my awareness that I had been able to sense the loss, even before the telephone call from my mother. From thousands of miles away, as soon as my mind had been released from the focus of exam study, it opened up to the pain my sister was facing. The loss I feel is Loretta's loss. The sisterly bonds are close and unbroken despite the distance between us.

CHAPTER

TWENTY-FOUR

The day of Dad's funeral arrives, and it is both sunny and rainy, as if highlighting the bright moments of Dad's life yet crying because it is over. Mum is stoic, knowing the day will come sometime but clearly not ready for it to be now, today. I know what the plans are. I have worked with the people from the funeral home, talked to the minister, and coordinated events with the family. Mum has booked an events room with a bar at the sports center across the street, where everyone will meet for the wake after the funeral. Mum and I fuss and fret with our black outfits, wanting to look our best for Dad, a daft thought under the circumstances.

Family and friends have started gathering at the house, having a drink in Dad's honor, the conversation focusing on my father.

"Laraine." I hear my mother's soft voice call me from the top of the stairs. "Will you come up here with me, love?"

I go upstairs to her bedroom. Mum doesn't want to be downstairs with everyone right now. She doesn't want to talk to anyone right now. She wants peace and quiet.

"We are going to wait here for the hearse to come because this bedroom window has a clear view along the road."

I sense this is important to my mother, as important as the funeral service itself, because of the ceremony involved, and Mum wants to witness it done for Dad. I look down at the woman. She looks uncharacteristically vulnerable. I sense my mum needs all her strength to help her get through this day. I will be here for her.

We two women stand at the bedroom window, watching as the hearse finally comes down the road and approaches the house. It is the middle of the day, and despite the busy traffic on the two-lane road, the hearse stops about a hundred feet from the house; the attendant gets out, dons his top hat, and solemnly begins the slow walk in front of the hearse to the house. Family and friends step outside to watch the hearse approach, to pay their respects. Other drivers on the road slow in deference. Through the large windows of the hearse, I see it is full of flower tributes to my dad, including a rectangular arrangement depicting Scotland's white-and-blue flag of St. Andrew. He loved flowers. He would have been pleased.

My mother, Loretta, Mark, Uncle Colin, Uncle Russell, and I ride in the funeral cars to the chapel while other friends and family make their own way to Portchester. The hearse with Dad leads the procession, and I take the time during the drive to go over the words of the eulogy in my head. I have spent several days crafting the words, the story, until it sounds just right. Family members had come together for dinners and events in the evenings, but I had excused myself to sit alone in the old conservatory at the back of the house to write. I didn't care what anyone thought about me not joining in. I didn't want to be sociable. I had something more important to do, and I wanted to get it right.

The hearse and cars arrive at the entrance to the crematorium. They drive slowly through the ornate iron gates, and I look around at the manicured gardens and the vibrant display of color provided by the flowers. I haven't been here before, and I am pleased that it is as pretty as I had hoped. The cars slow down even more and a piper in full kilt regalia steps in front of the hearse to pipe Dad's journey to the chapel, the lament of the bagpipes echoing the lament in everyone's heart this day. As the cars near the chapel, I see many dozens of people gathered around, dark forms dressed in black, but as they come closer, the forms are crowned with familiar faces, all come to pay tribute to my dad. As the family gets out of the car, I am even more surprised to see dozens more people emerge from a large shed across the way as the coffin is carried from the car and placed on the shoulders of the pallbearers, Mark included. The turnout is tremendous. I am pleased to see so many people making the effort and giving up their time to pay their respects to my father.

The piper continues to play the Scots ballads and Dad's favorites. The coffin is carried into the chapel, down the aisle, and placed in front of the altar. The chapel is pretty, tastefully decorated with white flowers and greenery. I had ordered two large photographs of Dad, one of him as a young matelot, and one of him in later years, to be placed in front of the coffin so the mourners can see his cheeky grin as they pay him tribute. I take a moment to look at those photographs and acknowledge the disparity of the circumstances. This quiet, unassuming man, who had always sat quietly on life's sidelines, is to be the center of our attention today. He deserves it. For a brief moment I wonder if as many people would come to my funeral as have come to his. I look around at the large number of people coming into the chapel. *Probably not.*

Family and friends fill the pews of the chapel, and still many more people have to stand against the back wall. I know some people have traveled hundreds of miles to attend Dad's funeral, including yotties, who have made the journey from across England and Scotland, all come to pay tribute to one of their own. I am grateful. Dad's brother, my Uncle Rusty, arrived last night from Glasgow. I haven't seen him in about thirty-five years, and I am still not over the shock of how much Uncle Rusty looks like Dad. He even has the same blue eyes and cheeky grin. It is as though Dad is back with us, and I want to hug him tight and never let him go. As the family of the deceased, we take our seats in the front rows of the chapel. I sit at the end of the row closest to the aisle so I can move more easily to the lectern to give the eulogy.

The service begins, the congregation sings a hymn, and the vicar says the appropriate words for someone who had lived in her parish but whom she had never met, who had never attended one of her services. Like me, my father had been baptized in the Presbyterian Church of Scotland. Dad had attended church every Sunday at St. Andrews, the Presbyterian Church in Portsmouth, and when I was old enough, I joined him, going to the Sunday school held behind the church. Some years ago St. Andrews was closed. The family would attend Church of England services at St. Mary's on special occasions, but it was the vicar of the parish where my parents lived who had to conduct the funeral service. Even though they had never attended the vicar's church, I am grateful the vicar has agreed to do the funeral service today.

I hear the vicar's words, but am not really listening to them. I am mentally preparing myself for the tribute I am about to give. It will be my job to take the genericness of the service and turn it into something more meaningful and personal to those present. The vicar nods at me when my turn comes to give the eulogy. I calmly rise from my seat, walk unhurriedly to the lectern, prepare my notes, and look out at my audience.

I take a deep breath and then exhale, allowing my muscles to relax, and to place myself within an intangible calming cocoon. Now is the time to put my own emotions aside, to be the consummate performer I have learned to be. Time to show my strength, as no matter how sad I am, and how moved I am by the words I am to speak, I must not cry. I have to rise above human emotions and hold myself together. Because only by putting my own emotions aside and speaking with a clear, true voice, and without faltering, can I properly deliver the eulogy and let people hear and learn of the person who was my father.

I have memorized every word of the eulogy, as I had learned as a performer to rehearse and rehearse until the steps or the lyrics were automatic, because only then can you forget about them and concentrate on their delivery, on communicating their message to the audience. All eyes on me, I begin to speak.

"I want to speak for my father today because it is important for us to take a moment to pay our respects. It is the least we can do for him, after all he did for so many of us. Everyone here has their own special memories of my dad, and I know that the tribute I now pay him doesn't come from my heart alone."

I pause; take another calming breath.

"Dad was born in 1931 and came from a very humble background, living in one of the poorest areas of Glasgow. He never knew his father. His mum worked long hours to give Dad and his two brothers the most basic of needs. Dad didn't have much. He didn't expect much. He would tell the story of when he was a small boy and had rheumatic fever. He was left home alone all day to fend for himself. He would wake up in the morning and his mother was already at work, his brothers on their way to school. But rather than lay in bed all day, Dad would gather his clothes and, in pajamas and bare feet, go out into the street to ask a passerby to help him get dressed. He wanted to go to school with his brothers. He wanted to do something useful. To me there was something tragic in this image of a small boy standing on the street asking strangers to help him get dressed because he wanted to be with his brothers, and I share it with you now so you can understand how far Dad had come in life; from his humble origins in Glasgow, to invitations to Buckingham Palace. We can take comfort in knowing that Dad's life was far from tragic but was instead a truly amazing journey.

"Each of us here has shared a part of Dad's journey. He was a brother, father, grandfather, uncle, and friend. My mother shared Dad's journey through friendship and marriage for sixty-two years. Dad was a mentor to many of us. I attribute the person I am today to his love, guidance, and the many things he shared with me—and not just his blue eyes and cheeky sense of humor."

I pause, looking out at the smiles recognizing the reference.

"He shared his love of world travel experienced through his years of service in the Royal Navy. In later years when I too sailed through the Panama Canal, lived by the Great Pyramids at Giza, and visited the Tiger Balm Gardens in Singapore, I thought of Dad being there before me, and I tried to envision seeing these sights through the eyes of a young lad from Glasgow. The fact that he had been to these places too, I felt a part of Dad was there with me.

"My dad also instilled into me a love of learning, a desire to do better in life. Dad didn't complete his formal education. He left school at fourteen to become a carpenter's apprentice but was determined that I and later my sister would get a better education than he ever had. Dad was always buying me books, atlases, always pushing me to reach my full potential, urging me to do better than he ever did. My dad was the catalyst in my many achievements, my numerous college degrees, my position as a lawyer in a top United States law firm. But the irony is, no matter what I do, I can never have a better life than he did. I will never be half the person he was because, you see, I will never be able to earn the enormous respect he earned in his quiet, unassuming way.

"Respect for Dad comes from the many lives he touched with his kindness, his sense of humor, and his nonjudgmental manner. He always gave so much of himself without hesitation, without question, and asking nothing in return. Love and respect from others are the things that give us a better life, and Dad had these in abundance."

I pause, taking a deep breath, steadying my feelings.

"I had the task of going through my dad's personal belongings, and it was with mixed emotions that I saw what he had kept over the years, his treasures, things he valued the most.

"There were thousands of photographs of mum, myself, my sister Loretta, his grandson Mark. Photos of family and friends. And on the back of many of them, Dad had taken the time to write a little note as if it was important for him to always remember that moment.

"Dad kept photos and mementos from his time onboard the Royal Yacht *Britannia*. Dad was proud of his service to Queen and country, and proud to be awarded the Royal Victorian Medal for his services to the Queen. But above all he was proud to be a part of that elite group of men, the royal yachtsmen, many of whom became lifelong friends."

I look over to where a group of royal yachtsmen and Dad's friends are sitting and smile warmly at them.

"Books were of a great value to my dad. Dad kept all of his books: books from his days as a carpenter's apprentice in the

1940s, books on science and naval engineering. And dozens of notebooks full of his meticulous notes, written in the beautiful handwriting that he had, made all the more amazing considering his limited education.

"And of course Dad had his records of Scots music. He loved playing his rousing recordings of bagpipe music, probably much to the chagrin of our Irish neighbors in Manchester Road."

A gentle laughter responds to the words. I smile.

"Probably the oddest thing he kept, and maybe because he had so little as a child he hated throwing anything away, was his false teeth, much to the dismay of my mother who opened one of Dad's drawers to find it full of teeth smiling up at her. We found more teeth in his closet, in the attic, in his coat pockets. Perhaps this was Dad's way of literally getting the last laugh on us all."

The laughter is louder. We all knew about Dad and his jokes.

"And of course there were Dad's tools, symbols of his time and effort freely given to so many of us. I cannot remember a time when Dad didn't have a long list of jobs to do for other people, those jobs always getting done—until now. It is rare to go into a home without seeing some evidence of Dad's handiwork: wallpaper hung, trim painted, shelves built, gardens landscaped, and the number of cars kept roadworthy with Dad's careful tuning and maintenance. Dad has left his mark with us all."

And as I am speaking, for a fleeting moment between words, time seems to pause, and during that briefest of moments, I stop and look out at the people filling the chapel. I see faces from Dad's childhood: his brother, his childhood companion and his wife, my mother. I see his daughter Loretta, and grandson Mark. I see his nieces and nephews, and their children. I see four generations of his family. I see his shipmates from his early years with the Royal Navy, and friends and coworkers from his later years at the factory. I see next-door neighbors, both from the present day and from years ago. I see people who had been his friends, some for decades, others he had known only in recent years. I see people he did odd jobs for, people we hadn't seen in many years but who had come to pay their respects. I see people from as far away as Scotland, and those from all over England. I see many generations of people, from young babies to elderly persons. I see people who had known Dad since his birth in 1931, and those who were close to him at his death in 2007, seventy-six years later.

I realize in that moment, as I stand looking out at these faces, that I am looking out at my dad's entire life lying before me, at the people that had made up Dad's lifetime, the people that had traveled Dad's journey with him. And only I have the privilege of seeing this because of the unique position of where I now stand. I had relinquished my time with my father, something I have regretted until I now see this tableau of Dad's entire life laid out before me.

I realize in that moment that we have choices in how to interpret our life experiences. I can choose regret, remorse, guilt, anger, and sadness at not spending more time with my father, or I can recognize that my choices to travel and become educated in life experiences were to prepare myself to be the one person to make sure Dad lives on in the memories of each one of us on this most significant of days.

As I look out at the mourners, at the faces looking back at me, I see so many tears. My heart breaks seeing my mother crying; my sister, my son, my cousins are all crying. Even the stoic faces of my uncles are belied by wetness on their cheeks. I become aware of the gentle sound of rain and see streams of moisture gliding down the windowpanes. *Heaven is crying with us,* I think. I glance over at the vicar, and am surprised to see tears are streaming down her cheeks, too. The tributes to a man the vicar never knew have touched her. So much sadness. So much grief. But this is how it is supposed to be. I want this moment to be memorial. I want them to remember this service and, above all, to remember my dad.

Tears well in my own eyes. I struggle to keep my emotions in check, managing just barely. I continue to speak.

"I have to believe the Lord said, 'Ian, you've done enough. You've spent your entire life doing things for other people. You've given as much of yourself as any man can give. It's time for you to rest.'"

I turn to look back toward Dad's photograph.

"Dad, may you rest in peace with the knowledge that everything you did for us was appreciated. To my mother you were a loving husband and companion. To Loretta and I you were a mentor and inspiration. To your grandson Mark, you were a hero, and for so many others you were a true friend. You will be forever loved and missed."

I turn back to face the chapel.

"One final thing I found in my dad's belongings that I want to share with you now is a prayer by Winifred Holtby, one that he had kept for many years. It reads:

God give me work
'til my life shall end
And life
'til my work is done.
Dad's work here is done."

A warm feeling comes over me. I feel my father's presence among us in the hush of the chapel. I have a sense of well-being, as though I have finally given something back to my father after all that he had given to me.

I look behind me at my father's photos, his cheeky grin smiling back at us all.

"I love you, Dad."

author's father, photo © Laraine Denny Burrell

EPILOGUE

J never took Loretta on the holiday of a lifetime that I promised her. Shortly after Dad passed away, her second leg was amputated. Her struggles continued on for three more years through a pancreas transplant, more blood transfusions, more medicines and treatments—all while I waited for her to get better, always thinking that "next year" we would go on holiday. Next year never came. She died in October 2011, aged forty-one. I will always be haunted by the promise to my sister that I didn't keep.

In 2014, for my mother's eightieth birthday, I took her on a trip up to Glasgow so she could visit the site of her childhood home, where she went to school, and the church where she and Dad got married. The highlight of the trip was our visit to the Royal Yacht Museum in Leith, near Edinburgh.

Following the proscribed route of the museum tour, we walk along the familiar decks, we pass the engine room once Dad's domain, and finally, we make it into the mess, where still above the bar is the sign THE VERGE INN. On the mess bulkhead are photographs, including one with my father's cheeky grin staring out from among a group of yachtsmen.

Mum asks a steward where we can find the Book of Remembrance, explaining that her husband is in the book and she would like to see it. On hearing that we are family of a royal yachtsman, the steward takes us under his wing. He escorts us through the ship to what was once the Queen's Private Apartments. Standing at the side of the anteroom is a glass cabinet. Inside the cabinet is the Book of Remembrance, a tribute to yachtsmen who have passed "over the bar."

The steward opens the cabinet and helps us find the page showing the photograph of Dad. The photograph is one I know well. It is of my father in his uniform, holding the Royal Victorian Medal he received from the Queen that day so long ago at Buckingham Palace. Next to the photograph is a verse by Rudyard Kipling chosen to memorialize my father. The steward closes the cabinet, leaving Dad's photograph as the one on display.

Mum and I stand alone by the cabinet, each of us silent, both studying Dad's image and lost in our own memories. Again I recall what an amazing life he had lead and how his ever-determined effort and hard work had given him this significant distinction. I take photographs of my mum standing next to the cabinet and Dad's photograph. I see the pride in Mum's face as she looks down at Dad, her hand resting on the cabinet glass above the image of my father. I feel enormous pride for both of them. I click the camera shutter, capturing the moment and the memory.

Toward the end of 2014, I moved from Las Vegas to Washington State to live near my son, Mark. As I wrote this book, revisited my life and adventures over the years, and evaluated my choices and accomplishments as a dancer and as a lawyer, I can confirm that Mark is still, and always will be, my greatest success.

Images of Ian Denny in Book of Remembrance in Royal Yacht Museum, photo © Laraine Denny Burrell

author's mother reviewing her husband's photo in Book of Remembrance in Royal Yacht Museum, photo © Laraine Denny Burrell

ACKNOWLEDGMENTS

Thank you to Brooke Warner and She Writes Press for giving me the vehicle to share my story. But the story could not have been published without the editorial genius of Liz Kracht, who took my eight years of writings and ramblings and tirelessly worked with me to create a coherent message of transforming a daughter's guilt over a loved one's death into a positive understanding of life. A final acknowledgement has to be given to my family, Scots, English, and the rest of you, who were my anchor in this world of drama, disappointments, all tempered with amazing achievements. Cheers all!

ABOUT THE AUTHOR

*L*araine Denny Burrell was born and raised in England and at sixteen won a full scholarship to the Royal Academy of Dancing in London, England. Burrell spent many years living and working all over the world, performing as a professional dancer, singer, and actress. Eventually, she moved to the United States to join the cast of what was then the largest stage show in the world, *Hello Hollywood Hello*, at the MGM Grand in Reno, Nevada. After retiring as a performer, she went on to obtain three academic degrees, including a law degree. Burrell currently practices as an intellectual property attorney and litigator for a well-established law firm in Washington State. She has written many law-related articles for legal, trade, and general publications. Her short story "The Perfect Crime" was published in *Woman's World Magazine*.

SELECTED TITLES FROM SHE WRITES PRESS

She Writes Press is an independent publishing company founded to serve women writers everywhere. Visit us at www.shewritespress.com.

Don't Leave Yet: How My Mother's Alzheimer's Opened My Heart by Constance Hanstedt. $16.95, 978-1-63152-952-8. The chronicle of Hanstedt's journey toward independence, self-assurance, and connectedness as she cares for her mother, who is rapidly losing her own identity to the early stage of Alzheimer's.

The Space Between: A Memoir of Mother-Daughter Love at the End of Life by Virginia A. Simpson. $16.95, 978-1-63152-049-5. When a life-threatening illness makes it necessary for Virginia Simpson's mother, Ruth, to come live with her, Simpson struggles to heal their relationship before Ruth dies.

The Butterfly Groove: A Mother's Mystery, A Daughter's Journey by Jessica Barraco. $16.95, 978-1-63152-800-2. In an attempt to solve the mystery of her deceased mother's life, Jessica Barraco retraces the older woman's steps nearly forty years earlier—and finds herself along the way.

Where Have I Been All My Life? A Journey Toward Love and Wholeness by Cheryl Rice. $16.95, 978-1-63152-917-7. Rice's universally relatable story of how her mother's sudden death launched her on a journey into the deepest parts of grief—and, ultimately, toward love and wholeness.

Scattering Ashes: A Memoir of Letting Go by Joan Rough. $16.95, 978-1-63152-095-2. A daughter's chronicle of what happens when she invites her alcoholic and emotionally abusive mother to move in with her in hopes of helping her through the final stages of life—and her dream of mending their tattered relationship fails miserably.

The Sportscaster's Daughter: A Memoir by Cindi Michael. $16.95, 978-1-63152-107-2. Despite being disowned by her father—sportscaster George Michael, said to be the man who inspired ESPN's SportsCenter—Cindi Michael manages financially and heals emotionally, ultimately finding confidence from within.